Human-Machine
Communication

Steve Jones
General Editor

Vol. 117

The Digital Formations series is part of the Peter Lang Media and Communication list.
Every volume is peer reviewed and meets
the highest quality standards for content and production.

PETER LANG
New York • Bern • Berlin
Brussels • Vienna • Oxford • Warsaw

Human-Machine Communication

Rethinking Communication, Technology, and Ourselves

Edited by Andrea L. Guzman

PETER LANG
New York • Bern • Berlin
Brussels • Vienna • Oxford • Warsaw

Library of Congress Cataloging-in-Publication Data

Names: Guzman, Andrea L., editor.
Title: Human-machine communication: rethinking communication,
technology, and ourselves / edited by Andrea L. Guzman.
Description: New York: Peter Lang, 2018.
Series: Digital formations, vol. 117 | ISSN 1526-3169
Includes bibliographical references and index.
Identifiers: LCCN 2017053385 | ISBN 978-1-4331-4251-2 (hardback: alk. paper)
ISBN 978-1-4331-4250-5 (paperback: alk. paper) | ISBN 978-1-4331-4252-9 (ebook pdf)
ISBN 978-1-4331-4253-6 (epub) | ISBN 978-1-4331-4254-3 (mobi)
Subjects: LCSH: Robots—Social aspects. | Human-machine systems.
Classification: LCC TJ211.49 .H856 2018 | DDC 303.48/34—dc23
LC record available at https://lccn.loc.gov/2017053385
DOI 10.3726/b14399

Bibliographic information published by **Die Deutsche Nationalbibliothek**.
Die Deutsche Nationalbibliothek lists this publication in the "Deutsche
Nationalbibliografie"; detailed bibliographic data are available
on the Internet at http://dnb.d-nb.de/.

The paper in this book meets the guidelines for permanence and durability
of the Committee on Production Guidelines for Book Longevity
of the Council of Library Resources.

This book is dedicated to all of the selfless academic mentors I have been blessed to have in my life, from grade school through today. I will continue to do my best to pay forward your guidance, encouragement, and patience.

Table of Contents

Figures

Tables

Preface

This volume demarcates a new area of research within the larger study of communication—Human-Machine Communication (HMC). As I explain in greater detail in the introduction, the concept of human-machine communication is not new (it is more than a half-century old); however, the conceptualization of people's interactions with various machines (artificial intelligence, robots, algorithms, industrial technologies, etc.) as *communication* by *communication scholars* with a collective focus on understanding the *creation of meaning between human and machine* through the *process of message exchange between* human and machine, the *building of relationships among* people and technology, and the resulting *individual, societal, and cultural implications* is novel.

This book is the product of the first HMC post-conference for communication scholars, "Communicating with Machines: The Rising Power of Digital Interlocutors in Our Lives," that convened as part of the International Communication Association's (ICA) conference in Fukuoka, Japan in June 2016. I spearheaded the conference along with Steve Jones, University of Illinois at Chicago (UIC); David J. Gunkel, Northern Illinois University (NIU); Autumn P. Edwards, Western Michigan University; Chad Edwards, Western Michigan University; and Patric R. Spence, University of Kentucky. The conference was sponsored by the Department of Communication at UIC; the Department of Communication at NIU; the College of Communication & Information, School of Information Science at the University of Kentucky; School of Communication, Western Michigan University, and the Communication & Social Robotics Labs. The inaugural all-day event included paper and poster presentations, networking, and formal and informal discussions around building HMC research within the discipline. Steve Jones generously offered for the annual Steve Jones Internet Research Lecture, sponsored by ICA and the Carl Couch Center for Social and Internet Research, to serve as the keynote presentation. Leopoldina Fortunati delivered the keynote, "Feminism, Labor and the Mechanization of Everyday Life." Most of the chapters within this volume are developed from papers or topics presented by scholars at this event or submitted to it. I invited Matthew Lombard and Charles Ess to contribute chapters in their areas of expertise because of their important theoretical and philosophical scholarship in this area. The goal of this volume is not only to capture the questions raised and ideas discussed during the post-conference, and, thus, serve as a historical text, but also to showcase HMC research as it is emerging within communication. Still, what is included here is only a portion of the 22 papers and posters presented during the post-conference and is an even smaller representation of HMC research throughout communication that is continuing to grow.

The history of this book and the establishment of this area of research begins well before Fukuoka, Japan in 2016. Many of the people who are part of what is now called HMC already had been studying and theorizing aspects of people's communication with technology, including social agents and robots, for years prior to the post-conference. My own interest in this area began with Apple's release of Siri with the iPhone 4s in late 2011. Siri captivated me as a consumer and as a doctoral student in UIC's communication department. Thinking about my own interactions with Siri, observing media portrayals regarding Siri, and listening to people's reactions to Siri sparked my research interest in people's conceptualizations of and relationships to AI technologies as communicators. It was during the research for my dissertation, *Imagining the Voice in the Machine: The Ontology of Digital Social Agents*, that I became aware of crucial gaps in communication scholarship and the need for increased opportunities for dialogue among scholars regarding the study of communication with different forms of technology. That communication scholars needed to pay greater attention to people's interactions with machines was something that Steve Jones, my PhD dissertation advisor at UIC, had been talking about for some time, as had been David Gunkel, my MA thesis advisor at NIU.

From my perspective, the most pressing matter surrounding the study of people's communication with devices and applications and the easiest to start rectifying was to get scholars doing this work into the same space to begin that scholarly dialogue. In late 2014, I approached Steve Jones about proposing a Blue Sky Workshop regarding human-machine communication as part of ICA's annual conference. The goal of Blue Sky workshops is to give scholars a space to discuss shared issues or areas of research. David Gunkel was invited to serve as our third chair for the workshop, and I drafted the proposal. Several months later (and only a few hours after I had submitted my dissertation to my committee), Steve, David, and I were leading the workshop, "Beyond Human: Developing Human-Machine Communication Research," in May 2015, in San Juan, Puerto Rico. It was a beautiful afternoon in the Caribbean, but the workshop was full, with several dozen people in attendance. Many of the attendees had similar experiences as Steve, David, and myself: they had been working in areas related to HMC and were looking to connect with a larger body of scholars with similar interests.

The shared sentiment at the workshop was to move forward with a more formal event, specifically a pre or post-conference at ICA the following year. Now in my first year as an assistant professor at NIU, I initiated the planning along with David and Steve, and we agreed to reach out to several workshop participants who expressed interest in assisting with the preconference, specifically Autumn P. Edwards and Chad Edwards from Western Michigan University. Autumn and Chad had founded the Communication and Social Robotics Labs along with Patric R. Spence, who was then at the University of Kentucky. These combined efforts were behind the post-conference in Japan.

Efforts to formalize HMC have continued to move forward as more scholars have become interested and involved in the study of people's communication with technology. Anecdotally, one of the factors driving this interest in HMC is that technology now talks back—literally—and this talkative technology is making its way into almost every aspect of people's lives. Technologies such as digital agents and social robots also are beginning to make way for HMC to be accepted as an area of study within communication. One of the reasons why this area of research is only now taking shape is that scholars initially faced resistance to the idea of machines as *communicators*. The proliferation of talking and moving technology, particularly devices and applications supported by AI, has meant that even scholars outside of HMC have experienced a communicative technology, helping them to better understand our arguments and the need for HMC research.

Given the success of the first ICA event, we convened a second ICA preconference, "Communicating with Machines: Interventions with Digital Agents," in May 2017 in San Diego, California. Autumn P. Edwards and Chad Edwards served as lead organizers with Patric R. Spence, Steve Jones, David J. Gunkel, and myself once again as co-chairs. Austin Lee, who was then at Northern Kentucky University, and Jake Liang, of Chapman University also joined as co-chairs, as did Seth C. Lewis, of the University of Oregon. Our list of sponsors also grew: Department of Communication, NIU; College of Informatics, Northern Kentucky University; Department of Communication, UIC; College of Communication & Information, School of Information Science, University of Kentucky; Shirley Papé Chair in Emerging Media, School of Journalism and Communication, University of Oregon; Communication and Social Robotics Labs, School of Communication, Western Michigan University. With the help of Matthew Lombard and his resources at Temple University, I also have established an e-mail list to help better connect HMC scholars, and we also have convened informal meetings of HMC scholars at conferences beyond ICA, including the Association of Internet Researchers. As this book is going to print, we now are preparing for our third ICA preconference "Communicating with Machines: Theory and Practice" with Patric R. Spence at the helm, to be held in Prague in May 2018. The number of submissions has almost tripled from Fukuoka.

While our community has gained so much, I would like to take a moment to also acknowledge one of its losses: In 2017, Jake Liang who had worked with Austin Lee in studying people's interactions with robots passed away. The chapter authored by Austin and Jake in this volume was written before Jake's passing. We are all saddened at the loss of Jake, a wonderful person and an excellent scholar. The chapter written by Austin and Jake brings together so much of their work and provides the opportunity to share Jake's passion with a new audience.

The purpose of recounting this history is to highlight how quickly interest in HMC has developed and to underscore the importance of cultivating a community of scholars that provides the space not only to present one's work but also to engage in discussion regarding larger issues and questions. One of the goals we have set as organizers of HMC events and facilitators of this group has been to be encourage dialogue across the topical, epistemological, and methodological divides within the study of communication. This is not a group of qualitative or quantitative scholars. It is a community of qualitative and quantitative scholars, rhetoricians, philosophers (and the list goes on) who are seeking answers to some of the most pressing questions facing individuals, society, and the study of communication itself. (After all, if we have long defined communication as a human-only process, the shift toward theorizing it as a human-machine process challenges the very nature of communication and communication research).

My goal in developing this edited volume has been to provide a collection of scholarship that is representative of the work of individual HMC scholars presented at the first post-conference, but, at the same time, attempts to capture the breadth of HMC research and approaches to it. To that end, the scholarship included in this volume focuses on people's communication with different technologies (e.g., AI, various types of robots, algorithms), proceeds from multiple epistemological and theoretical starting points (e.g., social-scientific, critical, cultural), and uses different methods (e.g., survey, experiment, rhetorical analysis, philosophical inquiry). At the same time, I realize that many audience members may be new to HMC and are reading this book to inform their own research, to incorporate its material into classes, or to satisfy a general curiosity in this area. I have charged myself and the chapter authors to be clear in how individual research relates to HMC overall as well as to pay attention to issues of theory and method.

The result is that this book can be read several ways. The first is that readers can focus on a particular technology, theory, or method that is most relevant to their own interests. Such a reading would focus on a single or a few chapters. The second way to read this book is in its entirety, or near entirety. It is this second approach that I suggest (and, no, I am not suggesting this approach because I am the editor). I advocate for a more holistic reading because it best recreates, as much as is feasible in print form, the nature of the HMC conference at which this research was presented. To read only a chapter or two that is most relevant to one's research is efficient, no doubt, but keeps firmly in place those divisions that in many ways have hampered the study of HMC in the first place. Reading this book in its entirety will help individuals, particularly people who are new to this area, to (1) understand the individual work taking place, (2) identify areas of convergence and divergence within the scholarship, and (3) gain a greater appreciation of the overarching issues and questions underpinning this research as a whole.

The one aspect of the HMC community that I, unfortunately, cannot adequately capture within printed text is its professional congeniality and shared comradery. Yes, as scholars we do have our philosophical, theoretical, and methodological differences, and, yes, these differences matter. However, what we as organizers of this community and many of its participants share is an understanding that collectively we are working toward something much bigger than our individual research agendas. It is through our own research that we have realized that what we know of communication is fundamentally changing as machines enter into our communicative spaces. We are beginning to see the very early stages of how communicative technologies are transforming our understanding of not only what machines are but also who we are. For these reasons, we understand that the study of HMC is clearly bigger than any one of us or any single approach to research. The final purpose of this book, then, is to invite its readers to join us in tackling these questions surrounding people's communication with machines and to bring new questions, new theories, and new approaches to this endeavor.

Andrea L. Guzman
DeKalb, Illinois
February 2018

Acknowledgments

The development of Human-Machine Communication as an area of study has been a collective effort. My gratitude goes foremost to Steve Jones and David J. Gunkel who have been key collaborators in formally establishing and growing the study of HMC. Steve and David each have served as my advisor during different points in my academic career and still provide me with invaluable mentorship for which I am grateful. I also am glad that Autumn P. Edwards, Chad Edwards, and Patric R. Spence have joined us in this endeavor. They and the Communication and Social Robotics Labs they direct have been invaluable to building the HMC community. Part of this growth also has included contributions from Austin Lee and Jake Liang. I am thankful to all of you for providing your time and talent to facilitating the formation of HMC and leading HMC events, but, most of all, I am humbled by your encouragement and ongoing support.

Several members of the HMC community also deserve special acknowledgement. During one of our early conversations, Seth C. Lewis asked me: "What is Human-Machine Communication, anyway?" It is a fundamental question, if not *the* fundamental question, of HMC that I take up in this book's introduction. My answer to that question is better today because of my collaboration with Seth on related projects and our ongoing dialogue—particularly more of his excellent questions—around the theoretical dimensions of HMC. Gina Neff also has been an excellent mentor to me: It was Gina's initial excitement at the workshop in Puerto Rico that gave me the confidence as a junior scholar to continue pursuing HMC. Matthew Lombard has generously given of his time and resources to help us establish a formal e-mail list that has helped us to grow and sustain this group. Eleanor Sandry has had one of the hardest tasks: helping me keep my type-A personality in check with her wit and her wisdom.

My work in HMC and toward this book has spanned my time at UIC as a doctoral student and now at NIU as an assistant professor. Thanks goes to my professors and peers at UIC who guided and supported me as I started my research in this area. The professional, financial, and personal support of Northern Illinois University and my colleagues in the department of communication played an enormous role in making HMC events and this book a reality. This book also was financially supported by a NIU Research and Artistry Facilitation Grant.

As an edited volume, this book would not be possible without its contributors and their hard work in writing thought-provoking submissions. Putting together a book featuring more than a dozen authors is not an easy task, but it was made infinitely more manageable with copyediting help from Kandice Jenkins and indexing assistance from Parisa Farhadi. Kathryn Harrison at Peter Lang also deserves a word of thanks for patiently working with this first-time book editor.

The contributions of my family and friends are too many to list here, and there are not enough words to thank you all for your ongoing support. My husband is still the best person around. And, Thumper, you deserve an extra treat.

Introduction: "What Is Human-Machine Communication, Anyway?"

ANDREA L. GUZMAN

The question that serves as this chapter's title is the guiding theme for this edited volume. It is one that I and other human-machine communication scholars have been asked numerous times as we have attempted to formalize this area of study and its central concept. Most people grasp that, as its name implies, human-machine communication, or HMC, has something to do with people's interactions with technology. In actuality, human-machine communication is both a concept and an area of research within communication. It is the *creation of meaning among humans and machines* and the study of this meaning-making and related aspects. But in a discipline where communication has long been conceptualized as a human process through machines, exactly what human-machine communication is, where it fits into the study of communication, and what it can potentially bring to communication are not readily clear. HMC as an area of study within communication also is still taking shape. Its primary catalyst has been scholars from throughout the discipline coming together to discuss their research, to address shared questions, and to help build a scholarly community. Because HMC is taking shape from the ground up, questions related to the nature of HMC are just as critical for existing HMC scholars as they are for scholars and students new to this area.

This chapter begins to provide some of these answers. I say, begin, because this book is only one step, but an important one, toward codifying this area of study. The conceptualization of HMC presented is not mine alone. To address questions regarding the nature of HMC, I have studied more than seven decades of research regarding the idea of communication between people and technology both inside and outside the discipline. I have listened to how other HMC scholars conceptualize what it is that they do and have paid careful attention to the ways in which this volume's authors explained their contributions. In staking out what HMC is within the coming pages, I provide a glimpse into what has influenced the shape of HMC so that other scholars can build upon these ideas. Toward this end, I begin by orienting the reader to HMC in relation to communication generally. Next, I discuss the origins of HMC outside the discipline and within it, before explaining why HMC as a new area of study is needed. Finally, I more thoroughly explain and define HMC while introducing this volume's chapters that exemplify HMC research.

Questions of Communication

For many people, communication is understood as a process taking place between themselves and someone else. To communicate means posting to social media followers, texting a loved one, talking with a friend, giving a presentation to colleagues, or reading the latest news written by a journalist. Communication also is, and has been, defined as a human-only process by those who study it. As the study of communication was coalescing in the mid-twentieth century, influential scholars purposefully drew its boundaries around human interaction (e.g., Schramm, 1973). In textbooks, communication is presented within a primarily, if not exclusively, human context, with models, theories, and examples focused on people's interactions. A visual of the transactional model of communication depicting messages flowing between two human-like figures greets visitors to the "What is Communication?" section of the National Communication Association's website.[1] Representations of mass communication historically have replaced the face-to-face image of interpersonal contexts with a depiction of a single source—a media organization composed of people—transmitting information to a *human* audience. In this default conceptualization of communication, technology is the medium or channel. It is the mobile phone people use to text that loved one or a specific app that delivers the day's news.

Questioning the Role of Technology

As I explain in further detail later, many emerging technologies no longer readily fit into this role of medium only. They are designed to function as things with which people interact. The mobile phone is not only a means for contacting friends but also a talkative assistant that helps people carry out tasks. That news app doesn't deliver just any story; it "learns" people's preferences, providing individualized content. Some of the news stories coming through that app now are being created by computer programs instead of reporters. And the robots people once encountered only in science fiction are moving into their homes.

It is these exchanges between people and technology that are examples of human-machine communication and are the focus of this area of research. *In human-machine communication, technology is conceptualized as more than a channel or medium: it enters into the role of a communicator.* In contrast to models of human communication, HMC models have messages flowing between and among humans and machines. The "image" of communication shifts from humans facing each other to a human facing a machine. Described this way, HMC seems relatively straightforward, the swapping of a machine for a human within an interaction. Indeed, substituting a technology for a person in experiments that test a communication or social theory has been one of the important ways scholars have studied people's interactions with computers (e.g., Reeves & Nass, 1998).

Questioning Meaning-Making With Technology

However, communication is conceptualized as more than the study of roles in a process and the transmission of information (Carey, 1989). Central to the development of communication theory is a focus on the meaning of messages and their effects (Rogers, 1997) and, as Schramm (1973) explains, how this meaning enters into people's relationships with one another:

> When we study communication, therefore, we study people—relating to each other and to their groups, organizations, and societies, influencing each other, being influenced, informing and being informed, reaching and being taught, entertaining and being entertained. To understand human communication, we must understand how people relate to one another. (pp. 3–4)

Communication also is the means through which people learn about their world (Blumer, 1969), form an understanding of Self and Other (Mead, 1967) and contribute to the shape of society (Cooley, 1897/2004). Communication research, then, is about who we are, who we are to one another, and the very reality that we are creating (Carey, 1989).

From this perspective, the view of human-machine communication switches from that of a process between a person and technology to the *creation of meaning between human and machine.* The questions surrounding HMC now seem much more complex. And, they are. How do messages from robots affect us? What sorts of relationships emerge when a technology becomes a communicator? How do people understand themselves as the result of their interactions with a virtual agent? What type of society is being constructed through people's ongoing communication with both humans and machines? What is communication now that it extends to our interactions with machines? These are some of the many complex questions that human-machine communication scholars seek to answer.

How Have We Theorized Communicating With Machines?

The study of people's interactions with technology has an extensive history, and the current direction of HMC and its conceptualization have been influenced by research inside communication and scholarship outside of it. This section briefly reviews those influences by focusing on key points of theoretical intersection and divergence.[2] Overall, engineers and computer scientists have used the idea of communication to help guide technology design and development of technological interfaces with a goal of facilitating use. Meanwhile, the study of a specific medium or research regarding people's direct interactions with media have had a place within the study of communication, but this research has received considerably less attention because it was outside communication's prevailing anthropocentric paradigm.

Engineering, Computers, and Communication

While many communication scholars are cognizant of the theoretical intersections between communication and fields within the social sciences and the humanities, they may be less aware of the importance of the idea and theories of communication to researchers within engineering and technology. That the discipline's foundational model (Shannon & Weaver, 1949) had its roots in engineering is an often overlooked connection between communication and technological fields, a point I will return to later. Since the mid-twentieth century, engineers, computer scientists and other researchers have approached people's use of computers and other technologies within the context of communication. This research has spanned numerous fields and disciplines including engineering, computer science, artificial intelligence (AI), ergonomics, and information science and helped to spur the development of interdisciplinary fields such as computer-supported cooperative work (CSCW) and Human-Computer Interaction (HCI). The term "human-machine communication" has its origins in this scholarship[3] and has only recently been increasingly used by communication scholars.

The Role of Communication in Designing Technology

The framing of people's interactions with technology as a type of communication has guided research and development for a wide range of technologies, including underwater devices (Sheridan & Verplank, 1978), planes (Sarter & Woods, 1995), spaceships (National Aeronautics and Space Administration, 1976), artificial intelligence programs (Weizenbaum, 1966), and computers generally (Licklider, 1960). Within these contexts communication carries a denotation similar to or drawn from cybernetics: it is the transfer of information for the purposes of control (Wiener, 1948). At the same time, communication with and among machines has never been far from a human context in that engineers have used human communication as a guide for designing the points of contact between people and technology, machine interfaces.

Most contemporary technology users take for granted the relative ease with which they control their devices but getting data into early computers and the results out of them was anything but simple or efficient. These hurdles of input and output were framed as problems of communication (e.g., Licklider & Clark, 1962). What Licklider (1960) called "the language problem," the difference between machine and human languages, was viewed as a barrier to use and adoption. The ontological difference between people, biological beings, and computers, programmed things, also was a formidable communication problem, as NASA states:

> Even when people do not speak the same language, they can communicate with one another to some degree (using gestures, facial expressions, etc.) because they share common biological structure and needs, common patterns of thought and behavior, and large overlapping stores of knowledge about the world. Machines and humans do not share these things, and most of the burden of communication falls on the human. (1976, p. 3.4)

As computers became smaller and began moving into everyday spaces, the general difficulty people experienced with adapting to computers continued to be viewed as a communication issue. In their essay regarding computer use as a form of communication, Oberquelle, Kupka, and Maass (1983) argue: "The problems of today's computer use mainly result from *difficulties in the communication between human and the machine*" (p. 309, emphasis authors).

The solutions devised also were based in communication. The exchange of information was approached as a dialogue (e.g., Meadow, 1970) with human conversation as the prototype. For example, Hayes and Reddy (1979) argue: "We believe that graceful interaction in these and the many other contingencies that can arise in human conversation is essential if interfaces are ever to appear co-operative and helpful ..." (p. 231). Developers also took the relational dynamics of human communication into account, deciding that in interactions, the human, as "master," would command the machine, as "servant" (e.g., Flanagan, 1976; Mooers, 1959). The development of language-based interfaces furthered this focus on the use of technology as a communicative process with technology (Suchman, 1990). Some researchers pushed back against using human communication as a prototype, countering that reproducing human interaction within a human-machine context was neither always possible nor desirable (e.g., Nickerson, 1976), but, overall, human communication has served as an influential model for technology design.

Although scholarship across engineering, computer science, and related fields frames certain problems with technology as a lack of or breakdown in communication and turns to human communication for answers, the concept of communication itself and communication theory often are not the focus of this research. What communication is and does is axiomatic, and what communication is all about within these contexts is using technology. The aim of improving people's communication with machines—from the perspective of engineers and computer scientists—is facilitating and promoting technology use.

In an edited volume regarding "man-machine communication," Meadow (1970) defines the book's key concept as a "two-way conversation that is goal-oriented—aimed toward the accomplishment of a specific objective—and in which both parties contribute a necessary function" (p. 4). That objective, as becomes clear in the remainder of the book, is helping people accomplish tasks. NASA's (1976) definition of "human-machine communication" also is focused on the point of contact between people and technology: "the characteristics of the interface through which a human user instructs or programs a machine, interacts with it during execution, and accepts information from it" (p. 3–79). This general view of the purpose of people's interactions with machines also is integral in Human-Computer Interaction research.[4] One of HCI's objectives has been and continues to be the development of the human-computer interface, the point of information exchange between human and computer and the processes surrounding it (Baecker, Grudin, Buxton, & Greenberg, 1995). Jacob (2003) explains regarding HCI:

> We can view the fundamental task of human-computer interaction as moving information between the brain of the user and the computer. Progress in this area attempts to increase the useful bandwidth across that interface by seeking faster, more natural, and more convenient communication means. (p. 145)

Theorizing Communication in Technology Use

From the standpoint of communication theory, this research regarding people's interactions with machines proceeds from what Carey (1989) called a transmission view of communication. Communication is about the exchange of information toward some desired effect. The machine is theorized as having a degree of agency in that it performs a distinct role during an interaction

(Fischer, 1990; Meadow, 1970) and draws from its own resources in processing and responding to messages (Riley, 1989). But, its ontology is very much tied to its status as a technology and the predominant cultural conceptualization of technology as tools.[5] Human-machine communication within this context is a process of interacting with technology, a tool, as to leverage it for some purpose.

What has been largely absent from this body of work in relation to communication theory is the social aspect of communication, including how technologies figure into people's social worlds and the implications for society (Zhao, 2006). The subjectivity of the technology is limited: its place within a user's social world is extremely restricted, if acknowledged at all. Outside its use, the technology has no bearing on how people understand their world and themselves. Communication with technology is an "isolated" process without implications beyond what transpires within the interaction.

There are notable exceptions such as Suchman's (1987) foundational work in human-machine communication that approaches people's interactions with technology as "situated actions," collaboratively unfolding between human and machine: "Communication in this sense is not a symbolic process that happens to go on in real-world settings, but a real-world activity in which we make use of language to delineate the collective relevance of our shared environment" (p. 180). Suchman (2009) also draws on scholarship from feminist theory and Science and Technology Studies (STS) to interrogate the social and cultural dimensions of human-machine communication.[6] More recently HCI scholars also have taken up critical and cultural questions; although, reconciling critical and cultural work with the practical aims of HCI research to inform design and facilitate use has proved challenging (Rogers, 2012).

Overall, communication has played an integral role in the development of technology and its use. The technologies that are now inspiring communication scholars to pay attention to human-machine communication are the result of decades of research guided by the idea of communication outside the discipline. Researchers in HCI have made important strides in the transmission of information from human to machine and facilitating technology use. However, with a focus on communication within this context, other aspects of communication with technology have received less attention, including social aspects and cultural implications.

Medium as Message and Messenger

While scholars outside the discipline initially propelled human-machine communication research, communication scholars have not been entirely out of the picture. Communication scholars have directly contributed to HCI and related areas within the past few decades. There also are some theoretical traditions within the discipline that have focused their research directly on the medium and have potential for furthering the study of people's interactions with machines and addressing existing theoretical oversights.

Communication Engineering vs Human Communication

Some of the fields whose literature was assimilated by communication scholars were the same fields focused on technology research and development, including cybernetics and information theory (Craig, 1999; Rogers, 1997). Cybernetics defined communication as a process of information transfer among people, animals, and machines (Wiener, 1948): Who or what were involved in the interaction were not the defining element of communication in cybernetics—the process was.[7] Similarly Shannon and Weaver's (1949) theory, considered to be communication's foundational model, evolved from a theoretical context similar to cybernetics.[8] As originally explicated by Shannon (1948), the model included sending messages between people and machines. And so, some of the literature that would inform communication's early theories conceptualized communication as a process between humans as well as humans and machines.

Scholars who were helping to shape communication, however, decided that the discipline would focus on human interaction.[9] Existing theories were retrofitted to a human-only context, including Shannon and Weaver's (1949) model (Rogers, 1997). As an engineer, Shannon originally wrote *A Mathematical Theory of Communication* (Shannon, 1948) as a theory of communication engineering. Shannon's focus was maximizing the transmission of signals from one point (a human or machine) to another point (a human or machine). As Rogers (1997) explains, Shannon's original model had nothing to do with meaning-making. Shannon's theory often is attributed to both Shannon and Weaver because it was later republished in a book with a similar title and an introduction by Weaver. According to Rogers (1997), this introduction (Weaver, 1949) adds to and adapts Shannon's theory from an engineering to social science context, recasting it as a means to study the effects of messages. The specific elements of the model that within engineering could be occupied by a human or a machine came to be associated with humans-only (Rogers, 1997). The distinct roles for humans and machines became codified and were reinforced in subsequent models (e.g., Barnlund, 1970; Lasswell, 1972): humans are communicators (senders and receivers) and technology is the medium, or channel, through which people exchange messages. This has been the dominant paradigm for communication research.

HCI in Communication

The question then is: How did communication scholars come to study interactions with machines? Part of the answer is in the evolution of technology toward the end of the twentieth century. According to Rogers (1986), communication scholars began to focus their research on communication technologies themselves, rather than the media content carried by these technologies, as cable and satellite television and personal computers moved into everyday spaces. What set these technologies apart from their predecessors was their interactivity: people could send messages to one another through these devices and, crucial to our discussion here, also interact more directly with the technology itself (Rogers, 1986).

In the computer-mediated communication (CMC) research that followed, scholars still privileged human communication; however, some communication scholars acknowledged that the internet also enabled "human-to-machine" and "machine-to-machine communication" (Jones, 2004), and early within the study of CMC, several researchers began asking questions about people's direct interactions with technology. Scholars focused on how people interacted with specific programs to access information stored within them, such as electronic card catalog systems (e.g., Borgman, 1983; Paisley, 1983; Rice & Borgman, 1983). Communication researchers also theorized some aspects of CMC as including people's interactions both through and with technology. Rafaeli (1988) conceptualized interactivity as a process between people carried out through technology as well as between people and technology. Similarly, presence and social presence were defined as phenomena that occurred while people were interacting with one another or with technology (e.g., Biocca, Harms, & Burgoon, 2003; Lombard & Ditton, 1997).

Research by Nass and colleagues delved even further into people's communicative behavior toward technology. Whereas communication scholars removed technology from the position of source or receiver in adapting Shannon's model, scholars conducting experiments within this line of research put media back into these roles (see Reeves & Nass, 1998, pp. 13–15). What they found is that people act toward media as if the media are distinct social actors, drawing on the social norms of communication with humans (Reeves & Nass, 1998). The Computers Are Social Actors, or CASA, paradigm (Nass, Steuer, & Tauber, 1994) has provided the foundation for subsequent research into the varied aspects of people's interactions with computers. Today, this work regarding computers and related technology is classified within the communication discipline as HCI research.[10] Often this scholarship has been influenced by HCI research outside the discipline (e.g., Rafaeli, 1988; Rice & Borgman, 1983) as well as contributed to it (e.g., Nass et al., 1994). HCI within communication has predominantly adopted a social scientific approach in studying people's behavior toward technology.[11]

Medium Theory, Cultural Studies, & Beyond
Communication research within HCI is currently the area of study within the discipline most closely focused on people's direct interactions with machines. However, other areas of the discipline have made important contributions to understanding technology in communication. These areas, such as medium theory and cultural studies, have eschewed the predominant paradigm within communication because they developed out of different schools of thought; although, the degree to which scholarship within these areas is immediately applicable to the study of human-machine communication varies. Still they have the potential to offer HMC scholars ways of asking and answering new questions and addressing questions not addressed by HCI or research outside the discipline.

The area of media studies known as "medium theory" (Meyrowitz, 2002) formed around scholarly inquiry into the nature of technology and its resulting impact on society. Its work often is summarized by the well-known argument of one of its primary theorists, Marshall McLuhan: "the medium is the message" (1994, p. 7). Medium theorists focus on the implications of the form and function of media, including its underlying technology, (e.g., Innis, 2007; McLuhan, 1994; Mumford, 2010) with particular interest in the social shifts resulting from the introduction of a new medium (Meyrowitz, 2002). In contrast with media effects and HCI, medium theory is more closely aligned with the humanities and includes normative assessments of a medium. Regarding HMC, medium theory originated in media that facilitated human communication, such as electronic media linking people in a "global village" (McLuhan, 1994). While medium theory views a medium as more than neutral channel, a medium still in many ways is exactly what its name suggests. However, as Meyrowitz (2002) explains, medium theory is not so much a particular theory as it is "a *perspective* for studying the effects of media on behavior" (p. 106). It is this "perspective" that can be and has been adapted for the study of media that function as communicators (e.g., Gehl & Bakardjieva, 2017).

Communication scholars studying technology also have worked within or been influenced by cultural studies, critical studies, race studies, feminist studies, the philosophy of technology, and STS.[12] For example, there has been a push among media, communication, and STS scholars for more interdisciplinary dialogue and research focused on the material aspects of ICTs (Gillespie, Boczkowski, & Foot, 2014). These areas of scholarship originated outside of communication and extend beyond its borders, each having distinct aims and approaches to research. All, however, provide ways of studying various aspects of the intersections among technology, communication, self, and society. For example, from a cultural studies perspective, Carey (1990) argues that "technology is thoroughly cultural from the outset" (p. 245). As such, it "is a symbol *of* (it represents how the world works) and a symbol *for* (it coerces the world into working in terms of the representation)" (Carey, 1990, p. 245, emphasis author). Unlike the "dominant paradigm" of media research focused on measuring the effects of manifest media content (Gitlin, 2002) or HCI research centered on facilitating people's interactions with technology, cultural studies interrogates the implications of the latent messages of media. Although these messages often are those sent from person-to-person, Carey's (1990) statement demonstrates that cultural studies also can focus on the ways culture is embodied within technology and enacted within its use.

What is shared among these various approaches is a rejection of technology's neutrality and a focus on the power dynamics embodied within and enacted through machines with varying implications: People's assimilation of technology into the self renders them "borg" (Haraway, 2000); algorithms are not only the means for using a search engine but also the vehicles of encoding and reinforcing racial bias (Noble, 2018); robots are becoming just as much a part of the domestic sphere as the industrial sphere, as is the power struggle regarding them (Fortunati, 2017); and, as Verbeek argues, "In fulfilling their functions, artifacts do more than function—they shape a relation between human beings and their world" (2005, p. 208).

Why Human-Machine Communication, Now?

Given that communication has been key to developing and studying technology across multiple disciplines, there is a question of why another area of study focused on people's interactions with machines is needed. Those advocating for a new area have offered several reasons, such as the shifting nature of technology and the inadequacy of communication theory to account for these changes (e.g., Gunkel, 2012; Jones, 2014). Yet, collaboratively addressing these issues has been difficult given the structure of the discipline. These combined factors—the technological, the theoretical, and the institutional—have spurred HMC's development.

The Technological

The interactivity of new media was the impetus for communication scholars to begin focusing more directly on technology (Rogers, 1986), and it is the evolution of technology that is, yet again, motivating scholars to ask new questions regarding machines in communication (e.g., Gunkel, 2012; Jones, 2014; McDowell & Gunkel, 2016). These changes include advances in text and voice-based modes of interaction; natural language processing that allows people to interact with technology as they would another human; and the integration of verbal and nonverbal social cues. The result is technologies that are inching closer to the goal of "natural" (human-like) communication as envisioned by Licklider (1960). These technologies enable a qualitatively different type of interactivity than their predecessors. To use the machine is to communicate *with* it, and the "it" is more than a tool to use. Devices and applications have varying degrees of agency programmed into their design and emerging in their use (Neff & Nagy, 2016). True, all machines can be theorized as possessing a degree of agency (Latour, 2007; Pickering, 1995), but emerging technologies are designed around this agency and emphasize it, so that some present themselves as distinct entities (Siri, Jibo, etc.) in communication. In addition, communication with these technologies often is personalized. These technologies do not just talk, they talk *with us*. They know *our* name, can distinguish *our* voice, and learn *our* preferences. They enter into *our* social world as active participants through their design and use (Zhao, 2006). The machine has become a communicative subject, and it is this subjectivity,[13] rather than interactivity, that marks this technological transition, prompting scholars to ask what subjectivity means for individuals, society, and the study of communication.

The Theoretical

This fundamental shift in the subjectivity of technology cannot be adequately addressed in existing models of communication because the discipline's dominant paradigm was formed around older media designed to facilitate people's interactions with one another and had as its focus how humans have acted toward, interacted with, and were affected by one another. For this reason, communication scholars have simultaneously called for consideration of how people interact with computers (e.g., Nass & Steuer, 1993) as well as a reconsideration of the conceptualization of communication (e.g., Gunkel, 2012). There are extensive bodies of work outside the discipline that have drawn upon the idea of communication to guide technology design and to inform research, and this research should be consulted by communication scholars. However, as explained, this scholarship proceeds from a narrow view of communication, most often overlooking larger cultural factors and implications. This research also is not solely focused on communication. The field of HCI, for example, also focuses on questions of engineering, computer science, and cognitive processing (ACM, 1992). Communication is about relationships, and it is the relational aspects of people's interactions with one another that has been central to communication research (Schramm, 1972, 1973). Beyond addressing theoretical gaps in research outside the discipline, communication is uniquely positioned to provide an understanding of the relational aspects of people's interactions with machines that function as subjects designed to form relationships with people. The caveat, of course, is that communication scholars must adapt scholarship based on human relationships to human-machine contexts while building upon emerging threads of research regarding people's communication with technology.

The Institutional

Trying to form a clear picture of people's interactions with machines from existing and emerging research has been hampered by institutional factors endemic to the discipline. Since its formalization, the study of communication has been fractured (Berger, 1991) and amorphous (Comstock, 1983). The discipline is divided along multiple lines: type of communication; research origins (Craig, 1999); philosophical and theoretical differences (Anderson & Baym, 2004). New divides also are forming. For example, communication scholars are now active in Human-Robot Interaction that is its own field different from HCI inside and outside communication.[14] The study of people's interactions with machines has also been fractured. For example, at the discipline's core conferences, the impact of AI in journalism, people's conceptualizations of AI, people's behavior toward AI, and media representations of AI are likely to be presented in different divisions. Many communication scholars studying people's interactions with technology also take their research outside the discipline. Part of the rationale for doing so is that their work is interdisciplinary; however, at the same time, the discipline's anthropomorphic paradigm can make it difficult for these scholars to make inroads within communication conferences and journals. Overall, the scholarly spaces within communication in which scholars can present and publish their research regarding human communication with machines and engage in discourse with one another are limited. So too is the visibility of this scholarship. Furthermore, as I have explained, no one theoretical or methodological approach to the study of people's interactions with technology can provide a complete understanding of what is taking place and its implications. To address larger overarching questions regarding human-machine communication, scholars representing these different areas need to be in dialogue with one another. For these reasons, an institutional space is needed to engage in this discourse.

What, Then, Is Human-Machine Communication?

Formalizing the study of human and machines in communication has been a process shaped by conversations among scholars, observations of technological trends, consultation with scholarship inside and outside the discipline, and reflection on the state of communication research. We[15] have been motivated by the realization that communication is, once again, at a critical moment. The promise of human-like communication that has guided the design of technology for so long is paying off. Communication scholars now have the opportunity to bring their expertise to the study of humans and machines and provide meaningful insight into this intertwined shift in communication and technology. There is not a division within the discipline untouched by the increasing communicative nature of machines because almost every facet of people's lives is affected by social technologies, directly or indirectly.

Tackling the theoretical questions raised by the shift in technology required first addressing the institutional hurdle of creating a space for the requisite dialog: That scholarly space is the area of communication we now call Human-Machine Communication. Our goal has been to facilitate connections across the many divides separating HMC scholars, from specific technologies studied to philosophical and methodological approaches to research. In fostering this inclusivity, we are not trying to efface differences in this research; instead, we are trying to productively leverage them. HMC events have encouraged participation from across the discipline so that we can learn from one another, identify shared aspects of research, understand differences, and address issues spanning all of HMC, such as raising the salience of our research within the discipline.

HMC—An Area of Study Explained

Crucial to having scholars engage with this space was to select a name representative of its research. Several areas of study focused on people's interactions with technology exist, such as HCI, but an alternative name is used for several reasons. While communication scholars working within these interdisciplinary areas study questions of communication, the larger fields themselves encompass other types of research. These fields also often have a conceptualization of communication that is narrower than that of the discipline; a specific theoretical and methodological orientation; and a focus on a specific class of technologies, such as robots. Adopting the same name as an existing field would tie this new area of study to unrelated research, reinforce existing research agendas without addressing their oversights, and potentially alienate scholars focused on different technologies. Human-Machine Communication as an area of study is not a competitor to HCI, HRI, or HAI within communication or related research; it subsumes them. HMC can be thought of as an umbrella encompassing the many approaches to people's communication with various technologies.

Some people have remarked that "machine" and "human-machine" are antiquated: machine does not have the same modern connotation as technology. It conjures images of industrial technologies. However, from my perspective, that is the benefit of using machine instead of technology, not a detriment. As I have argued (Guzman, 2016), communication scholars have historically focused on the study of ICTs while overlooking manufacturing technologies: But manufacturing technologies also are communicative, not to mention they too are now being designed to be increasingly social with some of the same anthropomorphic features as robots for the home (see "Adaptive Robotics", 2016). The term machine reminds scholars that whatever technology is part of the interaction they are studying, that device and people's communication with it is but one part of a much bigger phenomenon. Furthermore, that phenomenon is not just a product of the present. At a cultural level, modern technology use and the ways that people think about technology is also influenced by the past, including the hulking, gritty machines of the industrial revolution and the sleeker, blinking machines of the automation revolution (Guzman, 2016). Human-machine not only stands for the parties involved in the communication (human and machine) but also the ontological relationship between humans and machines and the cultural dimensions that have so often been overlooked.

The last element of HMC is arguably its most important: communication. The use of communication instead of related synonyms, such as interaction, serves as a disciplinary marker. It says this research isn't just about communication: it *is* communication research. This is where communication as a discipline stakes its claim.[16] At the same time, this also is where HMC scholars are carving out their space within the discipline. A common experience among HMC scholars is one of being told that their work does not belong in the discipline or that people's interactions with technology do not qualify as communication (or both). Using the term communication within the context of humans and machines is—intentionally—a direct challenge to the anthropomorphic conceptualization of communication within the discipline.

HMC—A Concept Defined

While this explanation provides a general sense of what HMC scholars do, the focus of this research is not entirely clear. What is the "human-machine communication" that HMC scholars are studying? Answering this question is somewhat difficult given that HMC as an area of research is broad in terms of the types of technologies studied and the perspectives from which this research takes place. HMC's aim to be inclusive sets it apart in that by bringing together different ways of thinking about people's communication with technology it serves as a bridge among the discipline's many divisions. At the same time, it is a hurdle because the philosophy underlying any research influences what is studied and how. This problem is similar to and, in fact, originates in the existing lack of a singular definition of communication within the discipline (e.g., Dance, 1970, 1984). Still, there are common elements to the conceptualization of communication, and, similarly, there are core aspects of human-machine communication.

What sets HMC apart from human-human communication is the nature and role of technology. Within HMC, the machine is a distinct subject with which people interact. Interactions between human and machine have been viewed as analogous to interpersonal communication (e.g., Nass & Steuer, 1993), occurring in and among a group of people. A person may make a request of a robot that then replies, or a group of friends may huddle around a voice-based agent asking it off-the-wall questions and listening to its joking answers. Communication between human and machine also may be asynchronous and follow a model closer to that of mass communication. For example, automated news-writing programs turn raw data into news stories for consumers.[17] Regardless of whether the exchange is similar to that of an interpersonal or mass communication context,[18] the machine occupies the role of communicator and is approached as such within HMC research.

In communication's prevailing paradigm, the roles of people and things are assigned based on the nature of each, and these roles are absolute. The reconfiguration of the role of machines within HMC, in contrast, is based on technology's design and function in relation to the person interacting with it, be it directly or indirectly. For this reason, the role of technology may neither be solely that of a communicator nor entirely that of a medium; rather, it may be that of a communicator and a medium. For example, Apple's Siri is designed to function primarily as a communicator in a dyadic exchange with people; however, Siri also functions as a medium that people use to control a phone and retrieve messages as well as a "messenger" relaying people's requests, often unbeknownst to them, back to Apple (Guzman, 2017). Other technologies with which people directly communicate, such as social robots, also mediate people's interactions and social relationships with one another (Höflich, 2013). Human-machine communication as a process is an exchange of messages between people and technology, but in the course of the inter-action and as a result of it, both the machine and human[19] may also take on other roles.[20]

Beyond who and what are involved in which roles in an interaction is the question of the nature of communication itself within HMC. What exactly is transpiring between a human and a machine? The answer to this question can be found by revisiting the discipline's history as its boundaries were forming. Scholars adapted and expanded Shannon's (1948) theory as a way of explain-ing and accounting for the meaning people derive in their interactions with one another. Humans became senders and receivers and machines were shut out of these roles because communication scholars were interested in more than the transmission of signals or relay of information; they were after mean-ing. Communication was to be about, as Schramm is quoted above stating, "how people relate to one another"—how they create meaning. As Carey (1989) later stressed, communication is more than the exchange of a wave and message of "hello" between neighbors or the content of a news story; these acts—regardless of whether they are verbal or nonverbal, co-present or mediated, fleeting or sustained—are the rituals through which and to which meaning is imparted.

Communication is about the meaning people derive in and through their interactions with other people and, now, in and through their interactions with machines. The definition of "communication" within human-machine communication and human-human communication is the same—as it should be if they are to occupy the same discipline. At its core communication is the creation of meaning. Human communication, the default, is the creation of meaning among humans. *Human-machine communication is the creation of meaning among humans and machines.* It is a process in which both human and machine are involved and without one or the other communication would cease (Guzman, 2016). Stating that the definition of communication within human communication and HMC are the same is not an attempt to diminish ontological differences between humans and machines. Nor is it to say that the ways people interact with others and the meaning derived is the same as people's interactions with machines. An important aspect of HMC includes charting similarities and differences between these two types of com-munication. That human communication is now a *type of communication* is key. HMC "frees" the machine from its relegation to the role of medium, and, as a result, communication itself is loosed from a definition based on the ontology of participants. Communication is no longer synonymous with human communication. Instead, human communication becomes a type of communication along with HMC.

HMC—The Questions Driving Research

As an area of communication research, Human-Machine Communication *comprises the study of the creation of meaning among people and machines, and aspects thereof, and is inclusive of the different philosophical, theoretical, and methodological approaches within the discipline.* The question that follows is, "What does HMC research look like?" Because HMC by its very definition is broad and encompasses scholarly work within the social sciences and humanities, there is no singular way of conducting HMC research. With that said, all HMC research shares a focus on the machine as communicator and aspects of meaning-making between humans and machines with the goal of informing our understanding of communication. General research questions spanning HMC focus on understanding the machine as communicator; the machine's entry into our daily communication; the ways in which we communicate with machines; the relationships we form with machines as a result of our communication with them; the implications of communication with machines for self and society; and the resulting changes to communication theory and research now that machines function as communicators. There also are larger cultural questions regarding why we want to build communicative technologies in the first place and whether and why people want to engage or shun them. The chapters in this volume offer a glimpse of these and other questions asked by HMC scholars and the different approaches taken to answering them.

In Chapter 1, Autumn P. Edwards explores fundamental questions regarding how people conceptualize robots as communicators: Her study focuses on people's perceptions of the nature of robots in relation to humans and animals. In particular, Edwards asks how people determine the sameness and difference among humans, machines, and animals, and how various factors related to these ontological associations enter into people's communicative behavior with robots. In Chapter 2, Eleanor Sandry also addresses questions related to the nature of humans and machines but does so by critiquing the long-standing goal of making machines more human-like to promote interaction. In this theoretical essay, Sandry draws on various aspects of communication theory to argue that the difference between humans and machines can be constructed through communication in such a way that it is not a hurdle to overcome but, rather, a potential facilitator of the human-machine relationship.

For HMC scholars, the study of a machine as a communicator goes beyond asking "what is this I am communicating with?" to inquiring "what is this in relation to me?" In Chapter 3, Leslie M. Fritz traces how the human-robot relationship forms even before a robot physically enters people's lives. Fritz's rhetorical analysis of the crowdfunding websites for the social robots Jibo and Buddy demonstrates how the social identity of robots is constructed through their marketing, design, and consumers' interpretations of these materials. Robots historically have been designed to step into existing human roles, raising the question of how people perceive interactions with robots taking the place of a human. That is the key question driving a study of robots in educational contexts by Chad Edwards, Brett Stoll, Autumn P. Edwards, Patric R. Spence, and Andrew Gambino. In Chapter 4, Edwards et al. detail how students' public speaking anxiety increases when told they would be evaluated by a robot instead of a human and what this reaction says about people's expectations of interactions with robots within specific contexts.

The study of the exchange of messages between human and machine and the resulting effects has received the most scholarly attention, and several chapters focus on providing overviews of this research. In Chapter 5, Matthew Lombard takes stock of the progression of one of the first and most important areas of theory to focus on people's interactions through and with technology: presence. Within the context of HMC, presence is the experience of nonmediation when communicating with a technology. In detailing the development of presence research, Lombard highlights future questions and applications, and the importance of understanding presence as it relates to emerging technologies. In Chapter 6, S. Austin Lee and Yuhua (Jake) Liang[21] review their research regarding persuasion in HMC with a focus on persuasive messages conveyed by social robots. Many of the same techniques of persuasion that are effective in human communication also are effective in human-machine communication; although, there are still many messaging strategies that have yet to be tested within HMC as well as newly emerging contexts for these interactions. HMC research also includes the study of general issues surrounding technology, asking what about these issues are the same or different within the context of machine as communicator. In Chapter 7, Christoph Lutz and Aurelia Tamò consider privacy issues related to communication with healthcare robots. Drawing on Actor Network Theory and applying it to an HMC context, Lutz and Tamò trace the various facets of robot-patient interactions, raising questions regarding patient privacy that arise at each juncture.

This volume primarily focuses on HMC within the context of people's interactions with social robots; however, HMC research involves a variety of technologies. In Chapter 8, Terje Colbjørnsen uses qualitative analysis to study people's conceptualizations of selection algorithms (Spotify, Netflix). How do people conceptualize an unseen thing as a communicator when they cannot even exchange verbal messages with it? What aspects of people's interactions with algorithms inform their understanding of them? These are some the questions addressed in Colbjønsen's analysis of indirect and asynchronous communication with algorithms.

As discussed in Chapter 3, people learn about technologies via messages about them. But people's conceptualizations of robots and AI extend well beyond marketing materials. They have a "cultural presence" (Sconce, 2000) established through decades of media portrayal. HMC research also includes the study of this cultural presence,[22] its construction, and its role in people's conceptualizations of technology. In Chapter 9, Patric R. Spence, David Westerman, and Xialing Lin examine how news reports about robots in the workplace enter into people's opinions of those robots within the United States. Through their study, Spence et al. explain not only people's feelings about robots and how they are shaped but also people's perceptions of what it would be like to communicate with robots. In Chapter 10, Sakari Taipale and Leopoldina Fortunati dissect multiple aspects of people's opinions of robots recorded through a multi-country survey in the European Union. European residents overwhelmingly fear job displacement from robots, but, as Taipale and Fortunati also explain, several other factors may mitigate this fear, paving the way for robots to become the next "new media."

The final chapters address the larger implications of human-machine communication for the nature of communication and our own humanity. Ethics in communication has been formed around the assumption that humans alone are communicators. But, as David Gunkel argues in Chapter 11, the entry of machines into the communicator role upsets this assumption and, thus, the ethics built upon it. In this philosophical essay, Gunkel explores the concept of responsibility in communication now that human authors are being replaced by artificial writers. In Chapter 12, Charles Ess takes on questions surrounding what some people consider to be the most taboo form of human-machine communication—sex. In this philosophical essay on ethics, Ess provides an overview of the development of the study of ethics in relation to HMC before offering a new way of thinking through the polarized debate regarding sexbots. What Ess makes clear is that communication with sexbots, and any other machine, is an exercise in our humanity. Both chapters underscore that when communicating with an artificial Other, we not only have to make sense of what it is but who we are and want to be in world of social machines. Communication, even with machines, shapes the Self.

The Most Important Question

To return to the original question, human-machine communication is both old, as conceptualized outside the discipline, and new, as it is taking shape within communication. It is more than the transmission of information between people and technology, HMC is about meaning-making. As an area of study within communication, HMC also is about carving out intellectual space within an already crowded discipline, challenging the very identity of the discipline. This book provides a glimpse into human-machine communication and its research, but HMC is so much more than what is in these pages. These chapters represent a view of HMC as it is emerging, just after social agents and algorithms were becoming the norms in people's lives and just before social robots, such as Jibo, became available to the public. As this book is going to press, technologies designed as communicators have only increased and become more widely available. Everything from refrigerators to cars to watches now exchange messages directly with people. What is needed now is for more communication scholars to take up the study of HMC bringing with them new insights and questions. The most important question at this point, then, is not "what is HMC?" but, rather, "what will human-machine communication become?"

Notes

1. See https://www.natcom.org/about-nca/what-communication.
2. This section is a general overview. More research is needed to completely trace the many ways scholars have approached people's direct interactions with machines, particularly regarding HCI.
3. Multiple terms have been used to refer to interactions between people and technology: man-machine interaction, man-machine communication, man-machine conversation, human-computer communication, human-machine interaction, and human-computer interaction (which is the most commonly used term). Any reference to "man-machine" interaction is for historical purposes. It is no longer appropriate to use "man-machine" because it excludes other genders.
4. HCI grew out of research in multiple fields and is interdisciplinary, see Pew (2003) and Grudin (2017) regarding its history and Rogers (2012) regarding its theoretical evolution.
5. Regarding this conceptualization of technology see Pacey (1983) and Verbeek (2005).
6. This critical/cultural view appears in new chapters in a subsequent edition.
7. For more on cybernetics's contribution to communication see Rogers's (1997) profile of Wiener and Wiener's (1948) own work. Ironically, it is cybernetics's agnosticism toward the nature of communicators that Craig (1999) attributes to its limited influence: "Cybernetics, then, is also interesting and sometimes implausible from a commonsense view because it points out surprising analogies between living and nonliving

systems, challenges commonplace beliefs about the significance of consciousness and emotion, and questions our usual distinctions between mind and matter, form and content, the real and the artificial" (p. 141).

8. Shannon, Weaver, and Wiener all influenced one another's thinking, as they acknowledge in introduction and footnotes in their works. All three are associated with cybernetics (Heims, 1991) and occupied the same scholarly circles as key technologists, such as Vannevar Bush and John von Neumann, and social theorists, such as Kurt Lewin and Margaret Mead (see Wiener's introduction in *Cybernetics*). Shannon also was influential in artificial intelligence (McCarthy, Minsky, Rochester, & Shannon, 1955) and Weaver (1965), in machine translation.

9. People's communication with machines and animals is often given a nod in early research that sets out a human-human research agenda (see Schramm, 1972, and the beginning of Weaver, 1949).

10. There is a difference between HCI, the field, and the study of HCI within communication. Communication scholarship provides a particular means of theorizing the interaction between human and computer and of studying people's behavior with technology. But communication is only one of many disciplines contributing to HCI (Grudin, 2017; Lazar, Feng, & Hochheiser, 2010) with the study of HCI extending well beyond questions of communication.

11. Reeves and Nass (1998) extol social-scientific research within their work.

12. The purpose of including so many areas of study within the same paragraph is to alert the reader to the many directions for studying people's interactions with machines; It is not intended to diminish them. I urge scholars in these areas, who are more qualified than me, to take up the challenge of explaining how their research can further HMC or even challenge it.

13. For more on the idea of subjectivity, see also Jones (2014). My discussions with David Gunkel also helped to crystalize this idea.

14. See for example, the special issue of *Intervalla*, Social Robots and Emotion: Transcending the Boundary Between Humans and ICTs (Sugiyama & Vincent, 2013).

15. The "we" refers to the individuals involved in initial efforts to establish HMC (see the Preface).

16. There is the question of how human-machine communication can serve as a disciplinary marker when it first was used outside the discipline, and this is a valid point. However, the term human-machine communication largely has fallen out of use in the fields in which it originated.

17. Marconi, Siegman, and Machine Journalist (2017) provide an overview of automated journalism.

18. Although these two "sides" carry a great deal of disciplinary baggage (Reardon & Rogers, 1988), interpersonal and mass communication are used here because they are easily recognizable frame of reference for communication scholars. How the configurations of HMC compare and contrast to those of human interaction is yet to be studied. However, given the multiple roles a single technology performs in interacting with humans, it would not be surprising if HMC further complicates our understanding of interpersonal and mass communication.

19. A person, after all, can be a medium.

20. That technology can perform different roles in communication complicates research regarding it. In my work, I have attempted to reconcile both roles by focusing on a

technology's primary role, that of a communicator, and addressing other roles, that of a medium, within the context of the first (see Guzman, 2016, 2017).

21. Lee and Liang co-authored this chapter; however, Liang passed away before its publication.

22. The study of cultural portrayals of technology brings still more bodies of work to bear on HMC research, including the study of specific media—literature, film, and television—and specific genres within media, including science fiction and news.

References

ACM Special Interest Group on Computer-Human Interaction Curriculum Development Group. (1992). *ACM SIGCHI Curricula for Human-Computer Interaction.* New York, NY: The Association for Computing Machinery.

Adaptive Robotics Control Make Baxter & Sawyer Different. (2016). Retrieved May 25, 2016, from http://www.rethinkrobotics.com/baxter/what-makes-our-robots-different/

Anderson, J. A., & Baym, G. (2004). Philosophies and philosophic issues in communication, 1995–2004. *Journal of Communication, 54*(4), 589–615.

Baecker, R. M., Grudin, J., Buxton, W. A. S., & Greenberg, S. (Eds.). (1995). Preface. In *Readings in human-computer interaction: Toward the year 2000* (2nd ed., pp. xi–xvii). San Francisco, CA: Morgan Kaufmann.

Barnlund, D. C. (1970). A transactional model of communication. In J. Akin, A. Goldberg, G. Myers, & J. Stewart (Eds.), *Language behavior: A book of readings in communication* (pp. 43–61). The Hague, Netherlands: Mouton.

Berger, C. R. (1991). Communication theories and other curios. *Communications Monographs, 58*(1), 101–113.

Biocca, F., Harms, C., & Burgoon, J. K. (2003). Toward a more robust theory and measure of social presence: Review and suggested criteria. *Presence, 12*(5), 456–480.

Blumer, H. (1969). *Symbolic interactionism: Perspective and method.* Englewood Cliffs, NJ: Prentice-Hall.

Borgman, C. L. (1983). *Research report prepared for OCLC on end user behavior on The Ohio State University Libraries' online catalog: A computer monitoring study* (No. OCLC /OPR /RR-83/7Date). Dublin, Ohio: Online Computer Library Center. Retrieved from ERIC.

Carey, J. W. (1989). *Communication as culture: Essays on media and society.* New York, NY: Routledge.

Carey, J. W. (1990). Technology as a totem for culture: On Americans' use of high technology as a model for social order. *American Journalism, 7*(4), 242–251.

Comstock, G. (1983). The legacy of the past. *Journal of Communication, 33*(3), 42–50.

Cooley, C. H. (1897/2004). The process of social change. In J. D. Peters & P. Simonson (Eds.), *Mass communication and American social thought: Key texts, 1919–1968* (pp. 21–24). Lanham, MD: Rowman & Littlefield.

Craig, R. T. (1999). Communication theory as a field. *Communication Theory, 9*(2), 119–161.

Dance, F. E. X. (1970). The "concept" of communication. *Journal of Communication, 20*(2), 201–210.

Dance, F. E. X. (1984). What is communication? Nailing Jello to the wall. *Association for Communication Administration Bulletin, 48*(4), 4–7.

Fischer, G. (1990). Communication requirements for cooperative problem solving systems. *Information Systems, 15*, 21–36.

Flanagan, J. L. (1976). Computers that talk and listen: Man-machine communication by voice. *Proceedings of the IEEE, 64*(4), 405–415.

Fortunati, L. (2017). Robotization and the domestic sphere. *New Media & Society*, 1–18. https://doi.org/10.1177/1461444817729366

Gillespie, T., Boczkowski, P. J., & Foot, K. A. (2014). Introduction. In T. Gillespie, P. J. Boczkowski, & K. A. Foot (Eds.), *Media technologies: Essays on communication, materiality, and society*. Cambridge, MA: The MIT Press.

Gitlin, T. (2002). Media sociology: The dominant paradigm. In D. McQuail (Ed.), *McQuail's reader in mass communication theory* (pp. 25–35). London, UK: Sage Publications.

Grudin, J. (2017). *From tool to partner: The evolution of human-computer interaction*. Williston, VT: Morgan & Claypool.

Gunkel, D. J. (2012). Communication and artificial intelligence: Opportunities and challenges for the 21st Century. *Communication +1, 1*(1), 1. doi: 10.7275/R5QJ7F7R

Guzman, A. L. (2016). The messages of mute machines: Human-Machine Communication with industrial technologies. *Communication +1, 5*(1). doi: 10.7275/R57P8WBW

Guzman, A. L. (2017). Making AI safe for humans: A conversation *with* Siri. In R. W. Gehl & M. Bakardjieva (Eds.), *Socialbots and their friends: Digital media and the automation of sociality*. New York, NY: Routledge.

Haraway, D. (2000). A cyborg manifesto: Science, technology and socialist-feminism in the late twentieth century. In D. Bell & B. M. Kennedy (Eds.), *The Cybercultures Reader* (pp. 291–324). London, UK: Routledge. Retrieved from https://www.ulib.niu.edu:2128/books/about/The_Cybercultures_Reader.html?id=MKtr_svfY1kC

Hayes, P. J., & Reddy, D. R. (1979). An anatomy of graceful interaction in spoken and written man-machine communication. In *Proceedings of the 6th International Joint Conference on Artificial Intelligence*. San Francisco, CA: Morgan Kaufmann Publishers. Retrieved from http://repository.cmu.edu/cgi/viewcontent.cgi?article=3440& context=compsci

Heims, S. J. (1991). *The cybernetics group*. Cambridge, MA: The MIT Press.

Höflich, J. R. (2013). Relationships to social robots: Towards a triadic analysis of media-oriented behavior. *Intervalla*, 35–48. Retrieved from https://www.fus.edu/intervalla/volume-1-social-robots-and-emotion-transcending-the-boundary-between-humans-and-icts/relationships-to-social-robots-towards-a-triadic-analysis-of-media-oriented-behavior

Innis, H. A. (2007). *Empire and communications.* Lanham, MD: Rowman & Littlefield.

Jacob, R. J. K. (2003). Computers in human-computer interaction. In J. A. Jacko & A. Sears (Eds.), *The human-computer interaction handbook: Fundamentals, evolving technologies, and emerging applications* (pp. 147–149). Mahwah, NJ: Lawrence Erlbaum Associates.

Jones, S. (2004). Conclusion: Contexting the network. In P. N. Howard & S. Jones (Eds.), *Society online: The internet in context* (pp. 325–333). Thousand Oaks, CA: SAGE Publications.

Jones, S. (2014). People, things, memory and human-machine communication. *International Journal of Media & Cultural Politics, 10*(3), 245–258.

Lasswell, H. D. (1972). The structure and function of communication in society. In W. Schramm & D. F. Roberts (Eds.), *The process and effects of mass communication* (Revised Edition, pp. 84–99). Urbana, IL: University of Illinois Press.

Latour, B. (2007). *Reassembling the social: An introduction to actor-network-theory.* Oxford, UK: Oxford University Press.

Lazar, J., Feng, J. H., & Hochheiser, H. (Eds.). (2010). *Research methods in human-computer interaction.* West Sussex, UK: John Wiley & Sons.

Licklider, J. C. R. (1960). Man-computer symbiosis. In R. W. Taylor (Ed.), *In Memoriam: J. C. R. Licklider 1915–1990* (pp. 1–20). Palo Alto, CA: Systems Research Center.

Licklider, J. C. R., & Clark, W. E. (1962). On-line man-computer communication. In *Proceedings of the May 1–3, 1962, spring joint computer conference* (pp. 113–128). ACM.

Lombard, M., & Ditton, T. (1997). At the heart of it all: The concept of presence. *Journal of Computer-Mediated Communication, 3*(2), 0–0. https://doi.org/10.1111/j.1083-6101.1997.tb00072.x

Marconi, F., Siegman, A., & Machine Journalist. (2017). *The future of augmented journalism: A guide for newsrooms in the age of smart machines.* New York: Associated Press. Retrieved from https://insights.ap.org/uploads/images/the-future-of-augmented-journalism_ap-report.pdf

McCarthy, J., Minsky, M. L., Rochester, N., & Shannon, C. E. (1955). *A proposal for the Dartmouth summer research project on artificial intelligence* (Research Proposal). Retrieved from https://aaai.org/ojs/index.php/aimagazine/article/view/1904

McDowell, Z. J., & Gunkel, D. J. (2016). Introduction to "Machine Communication". *Communication+ 1, 5*(1), 1–5. doi: 10.5072/FK2Z60J494

McLuhan, M. (1994). *Understanding media: The extensions of man.* Cambridge, MA: MIT Press.

Mead, G. H. (1967). *Mind, self, & society: From the standpoint of a social behaviorist* (Vol. 1). Chicago, IL: University of Chicago Press.

Meadow, C. T. (1970). *Man-machine communication.* New York, NY: Wiley-Interscience.

Meyrowitz, J. (2002). Media and behavior—a missing link. In D. McQuail (Ed.), *McQuail's reader in mass communication theory* (pp. 99–108). London, UK: Sage Publications.

Mooers, C. N. (1959). The next twenty years in information retrieval: Some goals and predictions. In *Papers Presented Western Joint Computer Conference* (pp. 81–86). ACM. Retrieved from http://dl.acm.org/citation.cfm?id=1457853

Mumford, L. (2010). *Technics and civilization.* Chicago, IL: The University of Chicago Press.

Nass, C., & Steuer, J. (1993). Voices, boxes, and sources of messages: Computers and social actors. *Human Communication Research, 19* (4), 504–527. https://doi.org/10.1111/j.1468-2958.1993.tb00311.x

Nass, C., Steuer, J., & Tauber, E. R. (1994). Computers are social actors. In *Proceedings of the SIGCHI Conference on Human Factors in Computing Systems* (pp. 72–78). New York, NY: ACM. https://doi.org/10.1145/191666.191703

National Aeronautics and Space Administration. (1976). *A Forecast of Space Technology 1980–2000* (No. NASA SP-387). Washington, D.C.

Neff, G., & Nagy, P. (2016). Automation, algorithms, and politics| talking to bots: Symbiotic agency and the case of Tay. *International Journal of Communication, 10,* 17.

Nickerson, R. S. (1976). On conversational interaction with computers. In *Proceedings of the ACM/SIGGRAPH workshop on user-oriented design of interactive graphics systems* (pp. 101–113). ACM.

Noble, S. U. (2018). *Algorithms of oppression: How search engines reinforce racism.* New York, NY: New York University Press.

Oberquelle, H., Kupka, I., & Maass, S. (1983). A view of human-machine communication and co-operation. *International Journal of Man Machine Studies, 19,* 309–333.

Pacey, A. (1983). *The culture of technology* (First MIT Press). Cambridge, Mass.: MIT Press.

Paisley, W. (1983). Computerizing information: Lessons of a videotext trial. *Journal of Communication, 33*(1), 153–161.

Pew, R. A. (2003). Evolution of human-computer interaction: From memex to bluetooth and beyond. In J. A. Jacko & A. Sears (Eds.), *The human-computer interaction handbook: Fundamentals, evolving technologies, and emerging applications* (pp. 1–17). Mahwah, NJ: Lawrence Erlbaum Associates.

Pickering, A. (1995). *The mangle of practice: Time, agency, & science.* Chicago, IL: University of Chicago Press.

Rafaeli, S. (1988). Interactivity: From new media to communication. In R. Hawkins, J. M. Wiemann, & S. Pingree (Eds.), *Advancing communication science: Merging mass and interpersonal processes* (pp. 110–134). Newbury Park, CA: Sage Publications.

Reardon, K. K., & Rogers, E. M. (1988). Interpersonal versus mass media communication: A false dichotomy. *Human Communication Research, 15*(2), 284–303.

Reeves, B., & Nass, C. I. (1998). *The media equation.* Stanford, CA: CSLI Publications.

Rice, R. E., & Borgman, C. L. (1983). The use of computer-monitored data in information science and communication research. *Journal of the American Society for Information Science and Technology, 34*(4), 247–256. https://doi.org/10.1002/asi.4630340404

Riley, V. (1989). A general model of mixed-initiative human-machine systems. *Proceedings of the Human Factors Society 33rd Annual Meeting.*

Rogers, E. M. (1986). *Communication technology: The new media in society.* New York, NY: The Free Press.

Rogers, E. M. (1997). *A history of communication study: A biographical approach.* New York, NY: Free Press.

Rogers, Y. (2012). *HCI theory: Classical, modern, and contemporary.* Williston, VT: Morgan & Claypool. Retrieved from http://www.ulib.niu.edu:4290/doi/abs/10.2200/S00418ED1V01Y201205HCI014

Sarter, N. B., & Woods, D. D. (1995). "From tool to agent": The evolution of (cockpit) automation and its impact on human-machine coordination. In *Proceedings of the Human Factors and Ergonomics Society Annual Meeting* (Vol. 39, pp. 79–83). Sage Publications. Retrieved from http://pro.sagepub.com/content/39/1/79.short

Schramm, W. (1972). The nature of communication between humans. In W. Schramm & D. Roberts (Eds.), *The process and effects of mass communication* (Revised ed., pp. 3–53). Urbana, IL: University of Illinois Press.

Schramm, W. (1973). *Men, messages, and media: A look at human communication.* New York, NY: Harper & Row.

Sconce, J. (2000). *Haunted media: Electronic presence from telegraphy to television.* Durham, NC: Duke University Press.

Shannon, C. E. (1948). A mathematical theory of communication. *The Bell System Technical Journal, 27*(3–4), 379–423, 623–656.

Shannon, C. E., & Weaver, W. (1949). *The mathematical theory of communication* (12th Printing). Urbana, IL: University of Illinois Press.

Sheridan, T. B., & Verplank, W. L. (1978). *Human and Computer Control of Underseas Teleoperators* (Government No. N00014-77- C-0256). Man-Machine Systems Laboratory: Massachusetts Institute of Technology.

Suchman, L. A. (1987). *Plans and situated actions: The problem of human-machine communication.* New York, NY: Cambridge University Press.

Suchman, L. A. (1990). What is human-machine interaction. In S. P. Robertson, W. Zachary, & J. B. Black (Eds.), *Cognition, computing, and cooperation* (pp. 25–55). Norwood, NJ: Ablex Publishing Corporation.

Suchman, L. A. (2009). *Human-machine reconfigurations: Plans and situated actions* (2nd ed.). New York, NY: Cambridge University Press.

Sugiyama, S., & Vincent, J. (2013). Social robots and emotion: Transcending the boundary between humans and ICTs. *Intervalla, 1*(1), 1–6. Retrieved from https://www.fus.edu/intervalla/volume-1-social-robots-and-emotion-transcending-the-boundary-between-humans-and-icts

Verbeek, P.-P. (2005). *What things do: Philosophical reflections on technology, agency, and design* (English Translation). University Park, PA: The Pennsylvania State University Press.

Weaver, W. (1949). Introductory note on the general setting of the analytical communication studies. In C. E. Shannon & W. Weaver (Eds.), *The Mathematical Theory of Communication* (12th Printing). Urbana, IL: University of Illinois Press.

Weaver, W. (1965). Translation. In W. N. Locke & A. D. Booth (Eds.), *Machine Translation of Languages. Fourteen Essays* (3rd Printing, pp. 15–23). Cambridge, MA: The MIT Press.

Weizenbaum, J. (1966). ELIZA—a computer program for the study of natural language communication between man and machine. *Communications of the ACM, 9*(1), 36–45.

Wiener, N. (1948). *Cybernetics: Or control and communication in the animal and the machine* (Seventh Printing, Vol. Kessinger Legacy Reprints). New York, NY: John Wiley & Sons.

Zhao, S. (2006). Humanoid social robots as a medium of communication. *New Media & Society, 8*(3), 401–419. https://doi.org/10.1177/1461444806061951

1. *Animals, Humans, and Machines: Interactive Implications of Ontological Classification*

AUTUMN P. EDWARDS

On August 1, 2015, the battered and dismembered body of a robot was discovered in Philadelphia, Pennsylvania's historic Old City neighborhood. A photo tweeted from the site showed a decapitated torso and legs, rolled onto one side and flung atop a shallow bed of dried leaves and debris (Courtois, 2015). The robot's arms, wrenched from their sockets, lay nearby. This was the body of hitchBOT, the social humanoid robot created by Canadian university professors David Harris Smith and Frauke Zeller, which began its journey across the United States just two weeks prior. Earlier that year, it had successfully solicited lifts across Canada, Germany, and the Netherlands, all the while making light automated banter, taking photos, and posting updates to its popular social media accounts on Instagram, Facebook, and Twitter (Victor, 2015). Social media reactions to hitchBOT's demise were numerous, swift, and varied (Brandt, 2015):

> "So an American goes to another country and kills it beloved lion. Another country sends #hitchBOT to America and we kill it. Yeah America."

> "Goodbye sweet Prince, wish my city would've shown you more love. #hitch BOTinUSA"

> "If you're a 'fan' of a gimmicky hitchhiking robot, you need to reevaluate how it was your soul ended up being so empty."

> "We don't even like Uber here of course we're not gonna like a hitchhiking robot."

> "That dumb hitchhiking robot had it coming. Who hitchhikes anymore? Didn't its robot parents teach it how dangerous hitching is?"

Many of these comments demonstrated that perceptions about the treatment of social robots are intertwined with people's judgements about the similarities and differences between social robots and other kinds of entities, including animals, machines, and human beings. As people are increasingly placed in situations requiring interaction with embodied machine actors, they are challenged to define the essential natures of these agents and to understand their similarities and differences from humans and animals. This type of ontological classification holds important implications for how one perceives and interacts with the machines that are increasingly fulfilling roles once held by other human beings. There may also be legal, moral, and ethical implications for the treatment of social robots based on our individual and collective abilities to identify our own nature with that of machines. Therefore, this chapter focuses on understanding how a cross-section of U.S. American adults used ontological classification to understand and construct the differences between humans, animals, and machines and to explore one of the ways in which such classification may matter: responses to perceived mistreatment/abuse of a social robot.

Background

For the past several years, my colleagues and I in the Communications and Social Robotics Labs have investigated interactions between humans and social robots, giving special attention to identifying whether, to what extent, and under which circumstances human-to-human communication theories may also apply to interactions with machines. Our initial studies posited a "human-to-human interaction script," in which people generally anticipate their communication with machines with greater uncertainty and lower expectations of liking and social presence (Edwards, C., Edwards, A., Spence, & Westerman, 2016; Spence, Westerman, Edwards, C., & Edwards, A., 2014). Yet, our studies also demonstrate that in communication with robots, people behave and respond with remarkable similarity to how they would if the partner was another human (Edwards, A., Edwards, C., Spence, Harris, & Gambino, 2016; Edwards, C., Beattie, Edwards, A., & Spence, 2016; Edwards, C., Edwards, A., Spence, & Shelton, 2014; Stoll, Edwards, C., & Edwards, A., 2016).

In 2015, a generous donor gave the lab our first humanoid robot. Previously, we had relied on robotic platforms originally designed for telepresence when fashioning our studies of human-robot communication. When Nico, an early-generation Aldebaran NAO robot, arrived at the lab, there was much excitement and confusion. Faculty, students, and onlookers filled the small space. Some leaned against walls while others perched in computer chairs or sat cross-legged on the carpeted floor. After powering up Nico, we attempted our first interaction, driven by the relatively simple goal of getting Nico to stand. Partly because Nico was pre-owned and had some damaged functionality, and partly because we were all new to this, the task turned out to be not so simple.

When the initial request—"Nico, stand"—resulted in no change in the robot's position, people began to try other things. Someone repeated the request in the commanding tone they might use when training a domestic dog, which someone else followed using the cheerful, pleading demeanor observed in appeals to young children (Nico, can you please stand? Can you staaaaand?). Someone reprimanded the robot for being difficult, and then received a reprimand from a lab mate: "Poor Nico! Don't talk to him like that. It's his first day!" Perhaps sensing that an encouraging hand on the shoulder or gentle hold of the hand would make Nico more responsive and compliant, a few students tried pairing their requests with touch. A couple chose to not attempt interfacing with Nico through voice at all, suggesting instead that it would be easier to jack him in and force the action through a keyboard command.

This initial interaction with Nico demonstrated for me that people have different ideas about what a robot really is. Given the same basic interactional goal, some people approached Nico as a fellow human being, talking to and about Nico as if it were a child or peer. Others treated Nico as a non-human animal or as a machine. So, whereas our previous and much ongoing work has focused on identifying people's general reactions to communication with machines—the preferences, perceptions, and actions they tend to hold in common—this encounter piqued my interest in ideological differences that might begin to meaningfully explain or illuminate some variance in how people conceptualize and react to social machines. Ultimately, exploring people's perceptions about what a social robot really is (and is not) may prove useful to understanding their communication with and about machine partners.

This chapter considers common perceptions about the fundamental natures of animals, humans, and machines by exploring individuals' constructions of the similarities and differences among those groups of agents. Western philosophy, beginning with Rene' Descartes (1637) has historically aligned the inherent nature of animals with machines and elevated or held aside humans as fundamentally distinct or special based on their possession of reason, soul, consciousness, or autonomy. Yet, present day discourses emerging around advances in technology have challenged and disrupted this historical classification by equating human beings with machines in domains

ranging from science (humans are "hard-wired") to art (the densely technological bodies of steampunk) and simultaneously blurring the distinctions
between human beings and non-human animals (evolutionary science, the
Human Genome Project). To complete the triad, kinship between animals
and machines is constructed in popular culture (e.g., the "wild robot" vein
of children's literature) and in past and present zoomorphic design trends in
robotics.

Perhaps, as Mazis (2008) states, it is a mistake to understand humans, animals, and machines as three distinct kinds of entities because there are mech-
anistic dimensions of humans and animals, as well as animalistic dimensions
of humans and machines. In this sense, "the human, animal, and machine are
lodged within the core of each other's being" (p. 21). The attributes we have
reserved exclusively for each type of agent appear increasingly to permeate
all to some extent. Yet, articulations of kinship and otherness, closeness and
distance are often useful when trying to understand a third party in triadic
relations (Gilhus, 2006, p. 1). Today, a particularly relevant "third party" is
the social robot.

Review of Relevant Literature

Human-Machine Communication

Scholars of communication have long studied the ways in which people use
machines—from the telegraph to the television to the telephone—as media
or channels through which to talk with one another. Increasingly, however,
people have begun to turn toward machines as legitimate communication
partners. These machine communicators include a variety of rapidly evolving digital interlocutors like artificially intelligent conversation entities and
software agents, embodied social robots, and technologically augmented persons. McDowell and Gunkel (2016) note, "The machines are not coming.
They are already here." And there "needs to be an on-going effort to begin
to make sense of a world where we are not (and perhaps never were) the only
communicative subject" (pp. 3–4).

Social Robots

A machine entity increasingly standing in for other human beings is the social
robot. Brondi, Sarrica, and Fortunati (2016) defined social robots as autonomous, mechanical beings that "are capable to establish coordinated interactions with humans and other robots depending upon both the realms of
materiality and immateriality (including, first of all, sociality)." Over the past

few years, there has been a vast increase in social robot development, sales, and adoptions: "The rise of robots seems to have reached a tipping point; they've broken out of engineering labs and novelty stores, and moved into homes, hospitals, schools, and businesses. Their upward trajectory seems unstoppable" (LaFrance, 2016, para. 32). Experts predict the trend will magnify and that by 2025 robotics and AI will deeply infuse and permeate daily life (Pew Research Center, 2014).

As robots become more prevalent in many domains, people are confronted with choices about how to treat these machine social actors. Boston Dynamics was the subject of many headlines when, in early February of 2015, they released an original video showing the abilities of their newest creation, "Spot," a small four-legged robot dog. As Natasha Tiku (2015, February 12) explains for *The Verge*, Spot can be seen steadily navigating the company's office halls when a man emerges from behind a room divider and delivers a swift kick to Spot's underside. After buckling at the knees and making soft mechanical sounds, Spot recovers balance. A few seconds later Spot is outside and the same man runs up to kick him again, but this time hard enough to try to cause a fall. Spot skids across the concrete, but manages to stay on its legs (Tiku, 2015).

A number of subsequent news stories focused on the nature of relationship between person and machine depicted in the video. "Is it cruel to kick a robot dog?" asked a CNN.com headline. The video brings reactions from my students ranging from gasps, to laughter, to shoulder shrugs. And an important question for the emergent study of human-machine communication becomes whether people's understandings of the similarities and differences between humans, robots, and animals relates to their feelings about the treatment of Spot and other machine beings.

The Natures of Animals, Humans, and Machines

Beliefs about the underlying natures of things, or metaphysical beliefs, are practical in nature. They provide guides for action and interpretation that lead to outcomes of varying desirability. Based on this recognition, James (1898/1977) long ago suggested that "The whole function of philosophy out to be to find out what definite difference it will make to you and to me, at definite instants of our lives, if this world-formula or that world-formula be the one which is true" (p. 349). Thus, it is important to understand and to anticipate the potential consequences of our ontological assumptions, or our ideas about the basic categories of being and their relations.

Western philosophical traditions have often drawn comparisons between animals and machines. Descartes (1637) famously equated the two, describing non-human animals as mere machines with parts assembled in intricate ways. In contrast to these automata of varying complexity and organic-ness, humans were singular in possessing mind, soul and reason. The notion that non-human animals are basically mindless machines continues to underpin justifications for moral considerations and ethical treatment of both animals and robots (see Gunkel, 2012). Yet, humans have rich and multifaceted relationships with animals. As Gilhus (2006) notes:

> Animals are beings with which we have social relations. We feel sympathy and affection for them, but we also exploit them for our own benefit, for company, sport or nourishment. They are persons and things, friends and food. We communicate with animals, but we also kill, cook and eat them. Animals are similar to us as well as different from us, which encourages us to imagine ourselves as them to conceptualize our own being and to use them as symbols to make sense of our world. (p. 1)

In many ways, humans relate to the increasingly social and communicative machines around us along similar lines. Excepting the references to cooking and eating, one might reasonably substitute the word "robot" for "animal" in the preceding passage and summarize well our complex relations with intelligent machines. We wear and ride them, battle and break them, collect and care for them, and form attachments and feel for them. Our social machines are both partners and tools, persons and things. And, their kinship and otherness with humans implicates how we understand their and our own natures. For this reason, Mazis (2008) suggests "the machine might be called the 'postmodern animal'" (p. 21).

Just as animals and machines may be discursively consolidated into a single category of being to differentiate them from humans, this triad of relations may be reorganized to draw into focus alternative ways of conceiving the entities. Take, for instance, recent attempts to equate human and machine being, like Rodney Brooks's hypothesis that you, I, and everyone we know is a machine in the sense that "the biomolecular interactions taking place inside our heads give rise to our intellect, our feelings, our sense of self" (2008, p. 71).

Also, our vocabulary for self-description is deeply infused with machine concepts and has been for some time. Comparisons between humans and machines have often reflected the prominent mechanical innovations of the age (Harari, 2017). Today, we invoke computer-based terminology to account for our forms and functions. We may say we are hard-wired, programmed, or switched on; that we are crashing, running on auto-pilot, or powered down. Our own essential being is compared to algorithm and code (Harari, 2017), and our very existence has been postulated as a potential simulation (Moskowitz, 2016, April 7).

Completing the triad, humans are broadly understood as a type of animal. Darwin in 1859 proposed that humans evolved from apes. In 2006, Jerod Diamond's *The Third Chimpanzee: The Evolution and Future of the Human Animal* popularized the notion that because humans share 98% of their DNA with chimpanzees, they are properly classified by anatomists and geneticists as a third type of chimpanzee. Diamond notes that "The overall genetic distance between us and chimps is even smaller than the distance between such closely related bird species as red-eyed and white-eyed vireos" (p. 2). At the same time, scientific investigations have steadily disrupted the once tidy boundaries used to demarcate animals from humans (e.g., tool use, self-awareness, language, memory, complex emotions, and culture) (Mazis, 2008).

Thus, our attempts to understand the essential natures of things often involve discursively constructed triadic relationships among entities. Variously, humans may identify their own natures with animals, with machines, or with neither. These strategic solidarities likely have consequences for how people conceive and respond to social robots. In the next section, I present a study examining (1) the ways in which a cross-sample of U.S. American adults classified entities and constructed their similarities and differences, and (2) how those choices related to their reactions to a prominent case of social robot (mis)treatment.

Study

Participants included 196 U.S. American adults recruited and compensated through Amazon's Mechanical Turk. Their average age was 39 years old ($SD = 12.02$). Most typically, participants identified as white (82.7%) and as woman (63.8%). A majority held a 4-year degree or higher (56.1%). They came from a wide variety of occupations. Most made US $50,000 or less in personal income in their highest earning year.

Ontological Classification

To forward this study's goal of beginning to understand the broad and different ways people conceptualize machines, humans, and animals, I first asked participants to consider three entities which were introduced in random order: a humanoid robot, a hominoid ape (chimpanzee), and a human being. They were instructed to complete a task called "Group two. Leave one out" in which they needed to work quickly to choose which two entities are "alike and belong in a group" and set aside the entity that is "different from the others and does not belong in the group." As demonstrated in Figure 1.1, the majority grouped together the human and chimpanzee. The next most common grouping was the human and robot, followed by the least common grouping: the chimpanzee and robot.

Group Two. Leave One Out.

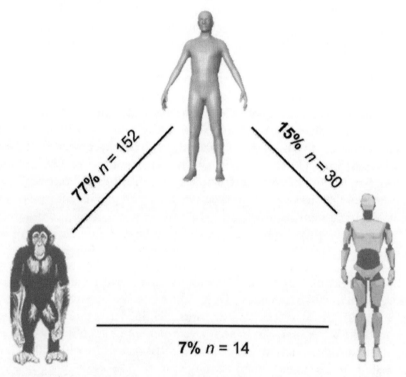

Figure 1.1. Numerical Summary of Grouping Decisions.
Source: Author.

I next asked participants to explain *why* they chose to group those two entities and to exclude the other. The procedure for organizing and analyzing their responses began with open coding, in which "categories are built, are named, and have attributes ascribed to them" (Lindlof & Taylor, 2002, p. 219) and was followed by axial coding, or "using codes that make connections between categories" to create either a new category or a theme that spans many categories (Lindlof & Taylor, p. 220). I present these themes along with their exemplars in the next section.

Grouping 1: Humans and Chimpanzees

By far the most common classification, grouping together the human being and chimpanzee was performed by roughly three of every four respondents. When I asked them to explain why they had placed the human and ape together, to the exclusion of the robot, their responses highlighted two inter-related qualities used to describe people and apes: alive and natural.

Alive

"They are both living creatures, whereas the robot is not." Many participants noted simply that both humans and chimpanzees are alive. For example, participants said:

> "Humans and chimps are both living things."
> "I put humans and chimps together because they are living beings."
> "They are both living beings."

In keeping with the definitional properties of *life* as "a principle or force that is considered to underlie the distinctive quality of animate beings" (merriam-webster.com), many participants referenced humans' and apes' shared capacities for reproduction ("Humans and chimpanzees are both living organisms that reproduce"), sentience ("They can think, feel, experience emotions, feel pain, etc …"), and growth and functional activity ("Both are living, make independent decisions, have offspring, eat, breathe, live and die").

Often, participants invoked secondary adjectives to articulate what it means to be alive. For instance, many people described humans and chimpanzees as "living, breathing," "living, warm-blooded," and "living, with beating hearts." One observed that they are both alive because "they both have to eat, breathe, and poop." These addendums on living worked to exclude notions of machine and plant life, as well as some non-mammalian animal forms. Several participants linked aliveness to the specific kind of animality shared by humans and chimpanzees: "Humans and chimpanzees are both mammals and are both from the primate lineage" and "We are both part of the ape family. I believe that humans are monkeys are part of the same kind of living organism." For a few participants, the sociality of primates was used as the basis for identifying the nature of chimpanzees with humans: "Both have social organization and social cognition, as well as emotional states that are the result of millions of years of evolution."

Natural

A second prominent aspect of perceived commonality between humans and chimpanzees was their status as "natural." For example, one participant explained that "Humans and chimpanzees are natural. They are part of a biological process. A robot is not." Largely, being natural meant not being human-made, and was variously described as being organic, real, biological, natural-born and non-artificial. Explaining her choice to group chimps and humans, one participant said succinctly: "Those two things are natural. The other [the robot] is man-made." Notions of naturalness were sometimes deeply intertwined with the first theme of aliveness, in the sense that two were treated as directly equivalent. "I wanted to group the living things together and the unnatural thing by itself," said one participant. Here, the living and the unnatural serve as opposite and exclusionary categories of being.

In speaking about the natural processes responsible for the existence of both humans and chimpanzees, participants tended to stress either a shared evolutionary ancestry or a divine creator. Some participants mentioned that both humans and chimpanzees "have evolved over time." Others were more specific in linking the evolutionary history of humans and chimpanzees. For example: "Both evolved from a common ancestor and are genetically similar" and "I believe the human race evolved from monkeys." Several also stressed the DNA overlap between the two entities: "They both have 99% similar DNA, so they belong together," "Humans and chimpanzees have a 99% match in their DNA based on what I remember which definitely makes them the most similar" and "Because according to researchers such as Darwin, we share 98% of our DNA. In other words, our DNA matches theirs almost exactly." The regularity and consistency with which this statistic was cited by participants speaks to degree to which these findings have been popularized in United States cultural discourses.

Yet, not all participants invoked genetic kinship as the explanation for how humans and chimpanzees are related in nature. Some respondents focused instead on their shared status as divine creations, noting that humans and chimps are natural because "they are both created by God." Using phrasing that was only slightly different, another participant said "The human and chimpanzee were created by God. The humanoid robot was man-made." In the words of a third participant, "I put God's creations together and the man-made robot separate."

In the United States, the presence of both evolutionary and intelligent design accounts characterizes the larger cultural discourses about the existence of species. Many U.S. Americans reject Darwin's theory of evolution through natural selection because it conflicts with religious beliefs about divine creation. According to Pew Research Center's Religious Landscape Study (2017), 62% of U.S. adults say humans have evolved over time. About 33% say humans evolved solely due to natural processes, and 25% say evolution was guided by a supreme being. 34% of U.S. Americans reject evolution entirely.

How Is a Robot Different?

After participants explained why they grouped together humans and chimpanzees, I asked them to consider the humanoid robot and why they deemed it different from the other two. The similarities identified between humans and chimpanzees became the qualities used to draw distinctions between those entities and robots. So, whereas humans and chimps were described as alive and natural, robots were described as instead "machines." In the words of one participant, "A humanoid robot is something mechanical and programmed. It is a machine driven to act entirely by algorithms." The significance of being a machine was in being human-made, which participants used variously to render robots artificial, not real, asocial, and essentially nonliving.

Grouping 2: Humans and Robots

The second most frequent classification choice was to place the human being with the humanoid robots. Predominately, respondents focused on the relationship of creator and creation to explain the choice to group humans with robots and set aside chimpanzees as different. "I put creator and creation in the same group" and "I went with my first instinct to put these two together. I guess the reason I grouped them together is because humans made robots."

Resemblance

In highlighting the importance of the maker/made relationship to their judgements about kinship and otherness, participants discussed the resultant resemblance (in embodiment, intellect, and behavior) between robots and human beings. Said one participant: "The robot was made to resemble the human." Another explained that "Although the robot is not a human, it was designed to resemble a human." Some participants focused mostly on physical resemblance: "They seem more alike to me for some reason. I think they look the same for the most part," and "They are both human-shaped creatures." Others made more general assessments of the resemblance: "Human and human-like are more similar."

Interactivity

Several participants linked the morphological similarities between humans and robots to possibilities for their interaction with one another. For instance, "Humans and humanoid robots probably look similar. They also probably have the ability to speak and be understood by one another." Other participants also highlighted the propensity for symbolic relationships, communication, and coordinated activity afforded by "creating them [robots] in our [humans'] image.":

> "The human being and humanoid robot will both have human traits and should be able to communication with each other."

> "I think they would have a better partnership when working together. Man builds and thus has a better understanding and control over a robot."

For these participants, choosing how to group like entities meant identifying who had the greatest chance of effectively communicating and interacting socially.

One participant extended the kinship between entities even further, stating that "They are both human, although a humanoid robot is a man-made human." For her, the category human is inclusive of both natural-born human beings and manufactured robot humans, who are considered variations of a single ontological category. Her reasoning called to mind a prominent definition of social robots offered by Zhao (2006): "Humanoid social robots are not user-friendly computers that operate as machines; rather, they are user-friendly computers that operate as humans" (p. 403). Both human beings and humanoid social robots may "operate as humans," opening space for identification based on functional equivalence.

It is perhaps worth noting that no participant explicitly found shared "machineness" in the natures of humans and robots. It was shared aspects of humanity that bound the two as kin. And it would be differences between human and animal nature that accounted for treating the chimpanzee as other.

How Is a Chimpanzee Different?
Many of those who classified the hominoid ape as the odd one out employed the descriptor "animal" to differentiate it from humans and robots.

> I grouped the chimpanzee separately as it is an animal. It cannot be effectively communicated with nor can it be relied upon to complete tasks or analyze information. It is only an animal unable to work effectively with a human to complete a task.

For this participant, being animal meant being unable to communicate and unreliable as a partner in interactions requiring cooperation and understanding. In the words of another participant, "It's a wild animal, which is unpredictable and uncontrollable." In the words of a third, "Chimpanzee is an animal. Chimps could actually learn a thing or two from the others." Whereas those participants who identified the essential natures of humans with chimpanzees had focused on their shared status as animals, this group of participants squarely dissociated humanity from animality and extended the essential qualities of humanity to social robots alone.

Grouping 3: Chimpanzees and Robots

Despite the long Western philosophical tradition equating animals with machines, only a small proportion of respondents (approximately 7 in 100) classified together the chimpanzee and robot, thus setting aside the human as ontologically distinct. These respondents expressed that what most held together chimps and robots was their fundamental "non-humanness." For example, one participant wrote as explanation simply "non-humans" and another stated "these are two things that are not quite human." The idea that chimpanzees and robots share status as "not human" was linked to themes of their *difference from* and *inferiority to* human beings.

Different
In terms of difference, chimpanzees and robots were described as unlike humans in the possession of sentience (or the capacity to experience, feel, and perceive subjectively), logic (or the ability to think logically and independently), and soul (an immaterial or spiritual dimension of existence). In the words of one participant, "Only human beings are capable of experiencing 'executive-level' (nuanced) emotions like compassion, remorse, shame, etc. We have a purpose as a species. This automatically separates the human race from any other group." Thus, robots and chimpanzees are held together in their inability to experience complex affective states. According to another participant, "they both [chimpanzees and robots] are programmed by instinct." Implied in this position is the belief that human beings, by contrast, exercise greater self-determination and freedom of action. Another explained "I believe machines and animals do not have souls and can't be compared to humans," which invokes the Cartesian dualism separating mind/soul from body.

Inferior
By and large, the differences between non-humans and humans also marked the former as inferior to the latter. In other words, chimps and robots were ontologically distinctive in ways that rendered them "less than" human; less intelligent, less developed, and less important. One participant stated, "their intelligence isn't as high as a human's." Another participant explained "They go together because they are not a highly-developed species." These ideologies are in keeping with long-standing anthropocentric biases privileging human intelligences and ways of life (Steiner, 2005).

How Is a Human Different?
When asked to justify the choice to treat the human entity as separate from chimpanzees and robots, participants stressed that humans are exceptional; incomparable to other entities in their nature and superiority. "The human being is lord of the planet and should stand alone from all lesser species," said one participant. Another explained, "I placed the human being separate because the human is superior to the other two." A third stated "human beings have the intellectual, emotional, and logical capabilities of a chimp and robot, but also have the ability to think and perceive morality." In each of these responses, the essential difference between humans and other entities involves their elevated status, intelligence, and morality.

Interactional Consequences of Ontological Classification

Results from the ontological classification task demonstrated that people vary in their understandings of the fundamental natures of humans, animals, and machines, and of their relationships to one another as categories of being. Thus, it is important to explore how classification choices may matter in terms of interactions between humans and social robots. One of the most basic ways in which a tendency to identify the nature of humans with that of machines, animals, or neither, is in the extension of empathy to other kinds of entities.

And so, after asking participants to classify humans, robots, and chimps as alike or different, and to explain their reasoning, I presented them with the details of the highly-publicized case of robot (mis)treatment which opens this chapter: the journey and eventual demise of hitchBOT. Created by Canadian university professors David Harris Smith and Frauke Zeller in 2015, hitch-BOT was an experimental humanoid robot designed to solicit lifts from human travelers to a series of destinations. With a squatty, bucket-shaped body, yellow boots, blue limbs, and a plastic face enclosing red LED lights, hitchBOT was easily visible. For what turned out to be hitchBOT's final voyage, Smith and Zeller secured under its chin a "San Francisco or Bust" sign and on its back some instructions for how human travelers could guide hitch-BOT through its "American Bucket List" (e.g., being the fifth face in a photo of Mount Rushmore) (Victor, 2015, August 3). They propped hitchBOT alongside a highway near Salem, Massachusetts on July 17, 2015. For two weeks, hitchBOT made its way from Boston to New York before its journey was abruptly cut short by the vandals.

Several major media outlets covered the story of hitchBOT, including the *New York Times*. It was this story, "Hitchhiking robot, safe in several countries, meets its end in Philadelphia" (Victor, 2015, August 3), I asked participants to read. Afterward, I inquired about their reactions to the story: "What are your thoughts and feelings about the demise of the robot?" and "Do you believe what happened to hitchBOT was wrong? Why or why not?" I again employed a process of open and axial coding to identify and consolidate thematic similarities and differences in their answers.

Was What Happened to hitchBOT Wrong?

Almost all participants believed the destruction of hitchBOT was wrong. Many began their answers with straightforward and forceful condemnations like these: "I definitely believe what happened to hitchBOT was completely wrong." "I absolutely believe it was wrong." and "Absolutely wrong." Yet, when people began to elaborate on their justifications for denouncing hitch-BOT's destruction, it became clear that not everyone agreed on *why* it was wrong. And, their differences in reasoning about the legality, morality, ethics, and gravity of the situation often related to how they had identified the essential natures of humans, animals, and machines in the prior classification task.

What Is Wrong With Destroying a Robot Hitchhiker?

Many participants highlighted vandalism and the destruction of property as a primary reason the treatment of hitchBOT was wrong. The fact that hitch-BOT belonged to someone else was often invoked as a justification for condemning its mutilation. However, other themes emerged when considering people's denouncements of the destruction with/against their judgements about whether robots were most like humans, animals (chimpanzees), or stood alone in their difference from the former two entities.

Robots as Other

Recalling that approximately 77% of participants highlighted kinship between humans and chimpanzees, and stressed robots' otherness as a non-living machine, it made sense that their reactions to the case of hitchBOT also drew on distinctions between the acceptable treatment of living and non-living entities. In the words of one participant, "It [the destruction of hitchBOT] is wrong, but no more wrong than the destruction of a couch or dresser of equal value." Hence, for this person, the inherent worth of hitchBOT was wholly reducible to its value as a material object and its apparent sociality was rendered irrelevant absent the property of animal life.

In addition to a focus on hitchBOT's status as a piece of property, people who identified the essential nature of humans with chimpanzees frequently lamented the "senselessness" of the act of destruction. Such statements hinted that the vandals' absence of a relatable and coherent instrumental objective for destroying hitchBOT was a central problem with the act. Here, it is not so much the destruction of a machine that is wrong but doing so without service to any apparent human purpose, or, in the words of one participant, doing so "for no reason." Another succinctly offered: "It is wrong, because it was needless."

Human and Robot as Kin

The relatively smaller group of participants who felt humans and robots were most similar to one another and chimpanzees belonged in a class of their own, tended to focus on the importance of the creator/creation relationship in facilitating identification and interaction. Not surprisingly, their explanations of why the treatment of hitchBOT was wrong compared its fate to that of human beings. "Of course it was wrong—to be vandalized and eventually killed. Just like it happens to human beings. Sad!!" A few applied the terms "abuse" and "cruelty," which seem to presuppose some capacity for sentient experience and suffering on the part of the robot, and a resulting expectation for ethical and humane treatment. One participant lamented that hitchBOT was "innocent," which hints at a capacity for robot moral agency. "Unless he was hurting someone, please leave him alone!" commented another.

Thus, a number of these participants discursively situated the act in the same terms they might use to describe and condemn the killing of a human being. They understood the act as brutality, and sought to make sense of it in terms of whether or not it was deserved. Concepts linked to the notion of "personhood" were therefore extended beyond humans to include the category of social robot.

Human Stands Alone

The smallest group of participants grouped together robots and chimpanzees on the grounds that humans are exceptional in their development, capacity for intelligence, reason, self-determination, and possession of soul or consciousness. Mainly, these participants explained the wrongness of hitchBOT's destruction by stressing its effects on other humans, considering its reflection on the human condition, or by trivializing its importance in comparison to the problems directly impacting humans. Vandalism, when referenced, was paired with the reproach that it "hurts other people." Some responses sympathized with the hard work Smith and Zeller must have put in to create the robot and conduct the test:

> Somebody worked hard on this experiment. Shows human beings have a long way to go in regards to tolerance. It is the lack of respect that bothers me most. Starts at childhood to respect your toys and others' property. Somehow that gets lost to some as they get older.

Others believed the occurrence illuminated something important, and unfortunate, about human beings. According to one participant:

> It was wrong. The whole point of the experiment was to bring people closer together and see what they can accomplish when we work together.
>
> It never really was about the robot, it was about the experience felt watching its journey. (Yes, I had heard about it and was not happy when I learned it was "killed.") The fact that we could not get it across America due to some uncaring people speaks poorly of the human race and the US in particular.

Another participant remarked "I think whomever vandalized the robot was probably disgusted that so much effort went into a frivolous experiment when human suffering is all around us. A hitchhiking robot seems extravagant and wasteful, and also a little creepy." Here, the participant empathizes with hitchBOT's destroyers, imagining their aversion to the invitation to treat a robot as a legitimate social actor given the many unaddressed sorrows of other humans. She was the only participant to mention hitchBOT's "creepiness." Yet, feelings of revulsion and uncanniness are often reported when people encounter robots they experience as a little too human to not be human (Mori, 2012). If humans are to be considered exceptional (superior by way of their differences from animals and machines), a heightened sensitivity to their perceived encroachments on the terrain of human morphology and behavior is perhaps understandable.

Conclusion

Results of this study demonstrate that people vary in their understandings of the nature and relationships among animals, humans, and machines. Predominantly, participants identified the nature of human beings with great apes, to the exclusion of humanoid robots. Fewer found salient kinship between humans and robots or identified humans as ontologically distinctive. Their choices and reasoning reflected and leveraged elements of popular philosophical discourses and were tied to cultural aspects of the United States. Furthermore, their classification choices and articulations of the similarities and differences between animals, humans, and machines related to their responses to perceived robot mistreatment or abuse.

This study provides preliminary evidence of the importance of considering ontological classification in human-machine communication research.

The constructivist communication tradition has long stressed that our social interactions unfold first and foremost through a process of prototyping the potentially communicative other (what is it?) (see, e.g., Delia, O'Keefe, & O'Keefe, 1982). Importantly, answers to the question "what is it?" are linked to subsequent stereotyping processes (what does it do?), which then powerfully influence perception, information-processing, and message behavior by guiding the application of personal constructs (dimensions of judgement applied to measure another's attributes) and the development and use of interaction scripts. Therefore, considering whether people understand and construct social robot "beingness" as essentially machine, animal, or human may prove useful for making sense of ensuing instances of human-machine communication and the cultural discourses surrounding it. One avenue for future research is to investigate how people's initial ontological classification of machine communicators influences the ways in which they approach and conduct human-machine communication. How might understanding a social robot as basically similar to a human being, an animal, or neither work its way into particular message strategies, interpretations, and evaluations of communication experience?

A second suggestion for future HMC research involves specification and explanation of the circumstances under which people find strategic solidarity between certain types of agents. For instance, in the present study, all three entities presented for classification were highly social, anthropomorphized exemplars of their categories of being. Would presenting participants instead with a human being, a robot dog, and a lizard have changed the percentages of entity pairings or the reasons constructed for doing so? Likewise, to what extent does the linguistic framing used to introduce agents prime people to ontologically classify in some ways and not others? Had the three been introduced not as entities, but as "creatures," or "beings," or "teammates," or "things," would people have responded differently to the grouping task? Furthermore, what previous interactions and sociocultural framing events shape tendencies to identify the nature of social robots with humans, animals, or machines? Answering these questions requires going beyond ontological *classification* to also consider *identification*, or the process of coming to see an/ other as like one's self in some important way (Burke, 1969).

Future research should also further examine the ways in which common perceptions about animals, humans, and machines may be consequential for human-machine communication, especially in considerations of the moral and ethical dimensions of interactions with machine agents, where both ontological classification and identification will likely be key. Perhaps we may move toward the goal here forwarded by Mazis (2008):

The drawing of boundaries of humans, animals, and machines will be articulated in this light: whatever allows for more human thriving in terms of significant priorities for many people, whatever allows animals to also thrive and lead lives that seem to meet their needs and avoid suffering as best we can discern, and the ways in which machines can develop their potential and come to be most respected as part of a larger earth community in having a key role to play on this community's behalf. (p. 90)

References

Courtois, A. [AndreaWBZ] (2015, August 1). EXCLUSIVE PHOTO: evidence of vandalized hitchhiking robot in #philly. #hitchBOTinUSA trip is over ... [Tweet]. Retrieved from https://twitter.com/AndreaWBZ/status/627627830520770560

Brandt, J. (2015, August 3). Twitter reactions about hitchBOT's death in Philly. *Philly.com*. Retrieved from http://www.philly.com/philly/news/local/20150803_Twitter_reactions_about_hitchBOT_s_death_in_Philly.html

Brondi, S., Sarrica, M., & Fortunati, L. (2016). *How many facets does a "social robot" have? A review of popular and scientific definitions.* Paper presented at the International Workshop on Social Robotics: Main Trends and Perspectives in Europe, Pordenone, Italy.

Brooks, R. (2008, June). I, Rodney Brooks, am a robot. *IEEE Spectrum*. Retrieved from https://spectrum.ieee.org/computing/hardware/i-rodney-brooks-am-a-robot

Burke, K. (1969). A rhetoric of motives. Berkeley and Los Angeles, CA: University of California Press.

Darwin, C. R. (1859). *On the origin of species.* London: John Murray.

Delia, J. G., O'Keefe, B. J., & O'Keefe, D. J. (1982). The constructivist approach to communication. In F. E. X. Dance (Ed.), *Human communication theory: Comparative essays* (pp. 147–191). New York: Harper & Row.

Descartes, R. (1637/1911). *Discourse on the method of rightly conducting the reason, and seeking for truth in the sciences.* (S. Haldane & G. R. T. Ross, Trans., Eds.). Cambridge, UK: Cambridge University Press.

Edwards, A., Edwards, C., Spence, P., Harris, C., & Gambino, A. (2016). Communicating with a robot in the classroom: Differences in perceptions of credibility and learning between 'robot as teacher' and 'teacher as robot.' *Computers in Human Behavior, 65,* 627–634. doi: 10.1016/j.chb.2016.06.005

Edwards, C., Beattie, A., Edwards, A., & Spence, P. (2016). Differences in perceptions of communication quality between a Twitterbot and human agent for information seeking and learning. *Computers in Human Behavior, 65,* 666–671. doi: 10.1016/j.chb.2016.07.003

Edwards, C., Edwards, A., Spence, P., & Shelton, A. (2014). Is that a bot running the social media feed? Testing the differences in perceptions of communication quality for a human agent and a bot agent on Twitter. *Computers in Human Behavior, 33,* 372–276. doi: 10.1016/j.chb.2013.08.013

Edwards, C., Edwards, A., Spence, P., & Westerman, D. (2016). Initial interaction expectations with robots: Testing the human-to-human interaction script. *Communication Studies, 67*, 227–238. doi: 10.1080/10510974.2015.1121899

Gilhus, I. S. (2006). *Animals, gods, and humans: Changing attitudes to animals in Greek, Roman, and Early Christian thought*. New York, NY: Routledge.

Gunkel, D. (2012). *The machine question: Critical perspectives on AI, robots, and ethics*. Cambridge, MA: The MIT Press.

Harari, Y. N. (2017). *Homo Deus: A brief history of tomorrow*. New York, NY: Harper Collins.

James, W. (1898/1977). Philosophical conceptions and practical results. In J. J. McDermott (Ed.), *The writings of William James: A comprehensive edition* (pp. 342–362). Chicago, IL: University of Chicago Press.

Lindlof, T. R., & Taylor, B. C. (2002). *Qualitative communication research methods* (2nd ed.). Thousand Oaks, CA: Sage Publications, Inc.

LaFrance, A. (2016, March 22). What is a robot? The question is more complicated than it seems. *The Atlantic*. Retrieved from http://www.theatlantic.com/technology/archive/2016/03/what-is-a-human/473166/

Mazis, G. A. (2008). *Humans, animals, machines: Blurring boundaries*. Albany, NY: SUNY Press.

McDowell, Z. J., & Gunkel, D. J. (2016). Introduction to "Machine Communication." *communication +1, 5*, 1–5. http://scholarworks.umass.edu/cpo/vol5/iss1/1

Mori, M. (2012, June). The uncanny valley: The original essay by Masahiro Mori (K. F. MacDorman and N. Kageki, Trans.). *IEEE Spectrum*. Retrieved from http://spectrum.ieee.org/automaton/robotics/humanoids/the-uncanny-valley

Moskowitz, C. (2016, April 7). Are we living in a computer simulation? *Scientific American*. Retrieved from https://www.scientificamerican.com/article/are-we-living-in-a-computer-simulation/

Pew Research Center (2017). *Religious landscape study*. Retrieved from http://www.pew-forum.org/2015/11/03/chapter-4-social-and-political-attitudes/

Pew Research Center (2014, August 6). *AI, robotics, and the future of jobs*. Retrieved from http://www.pewinternet.org/2014/08/06/future-of-jobs/

Spence, P. R., Westerman, D., Edwards, C., & Edwards, A. (2014). Welcoming our robot overlords: Initial expectations about interaction with a robot. *Communication Research Reports, 31*(3), 272–280. doi:10.1080/08824096.2014.924337

Steiner, G. (2005). *Anthropocentrism and its discontents: The moral status of animals in the history of western philosophy*. Pittsburg, PA: University of Pittsburg Press.

Stoll, B., Edwards, C., & Edwards, A. (2016). "Why aren't you a sassy little thing": The effects of robot-enacted guilt trips on credibility and consensus in a negotiation. *Communication Studies 67*(5), 530–547. doi: 10.1080/10510974.2016.1215339

Tiku, N. (2015, February 12). Stop kicking the robots before they start kicking us. *The Verge*. Retrieved from http://www.theverge.com/2015/2/12/8028905/i-really-dont-think-we-should-be-kicking-the-robots

Victor, D. (2015, August 3). Hitchhiking robot, safe is several countries, meets its end in Philadelphia. *The New York Times.* Retrieved from http://www.nytimes.com/2015/08/04/us/hitchhiking-robot-safe-in-several-countries-meets-its-end-in-philadelphia.html?_r=0

Zhao, S. (2006). Humanoid social robots as a medium of communication. *New Media & Society, 8*(3), 401–419. doi: 10.1177/1461444806061951

2. *Aliveness and the Off-Switch in Human-Robot Relations*

ELEANOR SANDRY

If robots are going to share human homes, workplaces and social spaces in the future, how will they communicate with people, and how might this frame people's perceptions of them? Should a robot's communication style reinforce the sense in which they seem to be somewhat alive, trustworthy assistants, co-workers or possibly even friends? Is there value in people recognizing and respecting the agency of robots, while also being reminded that even the most personable social robot is a machine that can be switched off? The questions in this list are too complex to answer fully in this short chapter. Its aim, instead, is to offer a starting point for discussing such questions: to demonstrate how a detailed analysis of people's communication with and about robots from a number of communication theoretical perspectives is a productive way to think through the deployment of robots into everyday life.

Theorizing Communication Between Humans and Robots

As might be expected, communication with robots is often discussed in terms that draw upon cybernetic theory. The cybernetic tradition of communication theory considers communication in terms of information processing and exchange. It is an archetypal transmission model, which places particular value on precision in the coding of messages (Craig, 1999). Alongside this, from the perspective of the semiotic tradition, communication occurs through intersubjective mediation that employs shared languages and other sign systems (Craig, 1999). These theoretical traditions offer different ways to analyze communicative situations, cybernetics valuing the way that meaning emerges within coded exchanges, while semiotics focuses on the nuances of meaning conveyed by signs and language; however, the two can also be seen to work together in discussions of human-robot communication when combined in cybernetic-semiotic theory that emphasizes the value of conveying precise information in a human language or with humanlike signs (Sandry, 2015). From a cybernetic-semiotic perspective, people and robots must be able to communicate clearly using shared language and signs, such that robots can take instructions from people and respond in ways humans can easily understand (Sandry, 2015).

Although the exchange of information is an important part of building relations with robots, the sociocultural tradition of theory adds another facet most often drawn upon when discussing robots that are designed to be "social." In particular, sociocultural theory describes communication as a process through which people's understandings of the world are produced, shared and reproduced (Carey, 1992; Craig, 1999). This perspective emphasizes the ways in which social robots and their communications are often framed to fit alongside human lives and understandings of the world as seamlessly as possible. Other discussions of robots focus on their ability to persuade people, or at least attempt to persuade them, to act in particular ways (Bartneck, van der Hoek, Mubin, & Al Mahmud, 2007; Gonzales & Riek, 2012). These analyses of communication draw on a sociopsychological tradition, which is concerned not only with a process of information transmission between sender and receiver, but also the effect of the message, and the way in which the receiver's existing understandings, attitudes and beliefs support or undermine the desired outcome of the sender (Craig, 1999).

The cybernetic-semiotic, sociocultural and sociopsychological traditions are the theoretical perspectives on communication that are most overtly drawn upon in discussions about the design of robots that are expected to interact with people (Sandry, 2015). As an alternative, which provokes a broader understanding of the possibilities of human-robot interaction, this chapter also considers the phenomenological tradition of communication. This tradition theorizes communication as the experience of otherness (Craig, 1999). It therefore offers a definition of communication as an event that does not require precise information exchange, the sharing of familiar sociocultural perspectives or the exertion of persuasive power, but rather requires being open to and respectful of otherness (Peters, 1999; Pinchevski, 2005). Adopting a phenomenological perspective emphasizes the possibility of relating to robots as a form of quasi-other, or maybe more productively as technological others that are valuable in their own right (not just because they are somewhat like human others). This perspective offers new ways to explore the potential of supporting people's responses to robots as nonhuman beings with which they might want to interact at home, at work or in social spaces, while also reminding people that, as machines, robots might need to be rebooted, repaired or replaced with a newer model.

Considering the details of communication with and about robots through the lens of these theoretical traditions supports a broad understanding of the variety of ways that robots convey a sense of their personality and "aliveness" to the humans with whom they communicate. As will be considered in more detail below, one advantage of assessing robots as somewhat "lively" is that it encourages people's recognition of the agency of robots and the value of their responses to and actions on the world. This takes human-robot interaction beyond tool use to introduce the potential for collaborative team working, because a robot's otherness can encompass nonhuman skills and abilities to be employed alongside human collaborators in creating multi-skilled human-robot teams. For human-robot teams to work to their best joint ability, human team members need to keep in mind the nonhuman advantages the robot has and work with the robot, rather than seeking to control it as a tool. In addition, humans may also need to support the robot in light of nonhuman disadvantages from which it might suffer in certain environments. It is therefore important that, even as a robot's communication supports shared understanding and team-working with humans, the potential for robots to remind people of their machinelike nature is not forgotten. As machines, robots not only have nonhuman skills and abilities, but also, on most occasions, can be switched off as necessary and without lasting damage. It therefore seems vital that the communication of a robot's liveliness and personality, supporting rich human-robot interactions and collaborations, should not occlude people's sense of the robot as a machine.

This chapter considers how and why the seeming "aliveness" of robots can and should be juxtaposed with an understanding of them as machines by analyzing the details of human-machine communication with three robot examples, all designed to communicate with humans, two factual and one fictional. The three illustrative examples were chosen because of the availability of texts that show and/or discuss the course of human interactions with the robots in some detail. The aim of this research is to provide a framework that demonstrates how different communication traditions offer a variety of useful theoretical perspectives on human-machine communication. Future research could draw on this strategy to consider how other robots and humans might interact now and in the future, in ways that enable humans to relate to and collaborate with them, while also maintaining a clear sense of the machine's technological otherness.

Relating to Social Robots as Humanlike Communicators

Cynthia Breazeal, creator of Kismet, one of the earliest robots specifically designed to take part in social interactions with humans, states that a "sociable robot" should be "socially intelligent in a humanlike way" (Breazeal, 2002a, p. 1). Her goal in creating Kismet, amongst other sociable robots, has been to make people's interactions with the robot like "interacting with another person" (Breazeal, 2002a, p. 1). From Breazeal's perspective, Kismet's sociability was supported by its expressive face and ability to turn-take in dialogue with people, most often using a toddler-like "babble" as opposed to fully formed human language. Breazeal argues that humanoid robots have the potential to receive, interpret and reciprocate "familiar social cues in the natural communication modalities of humans", because they "share a similar morphology with humans" (Breazeal, 2002b, p. 883). Christoph Bartneck et al. make a similar assumption, justifying selection of the iCat robot for their experiment on human responses to being asked to switch off a robot, because it "can generate many different facial expressions, such as happiness, surprise, anger or sadness, that are essential in creating social human-robot interaction dialogues" (2007, pp. 218–219). While neither Kismet nor iCat are realistically humanlike in appearance, one of the keys to their socially communicative ability, at least from Breazeal's and Bartneck et al.'s perspectives, is a face that can produce humanlike facial expressions.

As this chapter goes on to note, and Breazeal's more recent robot designs demonstrate, perceptions of the social nature of robots can be supported in ways that involve less humanlike facial designs than seen in either iCat or Kismet, through development of machinelike robots that are nonetheless highly expressive and communicative. However, before moving on to discuss more recent examples of social robots, it is worth considering Bartneck et al.'s findings using iCat, employing a range of communication theoretical perspectives to analyze how a sense of the intelligence and personality of a robot is built up, such that it causes people to hesitate when asked to turn it off. This example provides a particularly relevant starting point and is discussed in some detail, because it directly investigates people's responses when asked to switch off a robot with which they have developed a connection over time, the perceived "ability" and "personality" of the robot being seen to shape the strength of feeling against switching the robot off.

Bartneck et al.'s experiment asked people to collaborate with iCat in playing Mastermind with a computer. This game involves players in trying to guess a pattern of colors chosen by the computer. Each guess is scored based on correct color and/or position, so subsequent guesses can be chosen strategically based on this information. Participants were told the overall goal of the experiment was to see how the robot's personality would build over the game. Once the game was over, people were asked to switch-off the robot, having been told that this would permanently wipe the robot's memory and the personality it had developed. In fact, the robot was always under the control of the experimenter, as opposed to building its personality autonomously. The experimenter operated the iCat either in high agreeableness or in low agreeableness mode and, in addition, made the robot suggest colors in highly or less intelligent ways. The highly agreeable iCat would politely ask if it could make suggestions in relation to the game, whereas the disagreeable iCat would simply insist it took its turn, rather than collaborating with the human. As soon as the person was asked to switch it off, the iCat would speak up, begging to remain on. The dial to switch the robot off was linked with the robot's voice, such that turning the dial slowed the iCat's voice until it eventually stopped completely. Participants were not forced to switch off the iCat, but they all did in the end. Many people hesitated both before and while turning the dial, in particular those who experienced the more intelligent robot that had also been an agreeable collaborator.

iCat's communication during the experiment involved the cybernetic-semiotic transmission of precise information through its voice as it either stated the color it would like to try on its turn, or suggested colors the team could try next. The color it chose was also displayed by lights in its ears, in a form of nonverbal communication that reinforced its choice for the human. At this level, the clarity of iCat's communication was linked with the idea that it was intelligent, appearing more intelligent the better its color suggestions proved to be. Alongside this, people also based their judgement of iCat on the social nuances of its interaction. In sociocultural terms, it was when the robot was polite in suggesting potential colors to try, as opposed simply to insisting on taking its turn, that this robot seemed to want to work intelligently alongside the human, behaving in acceptable and familiar ways to negotiate the choice the team might make next. These aspects of the robot's communication therefore supported human assessments of its intelligence and personality, while also conveying the sense that it was a "lively" partner with which to play Mastermind. At the end of the experiment, human participants were faced with the iCat's sociopsychological attempts to persuade them to ignore the instruction they had been given when it begged to remain switched on. Although not mentioned overtly by Bartneck et al. in their written paper, the linked video of the experiment shows that when iCat pleaded with users in this final stage of the experiment, its facial expressions and head and neck movements strongly reinforced the sense of its distress at the prospect of being switched off, adding to the sociopsychological effect of its words.

In this experiment, the robot was situated as a partner with which to play a game, introducing a sociocultural frame within which people were encouraged to assess the robot's communication. The sense of being in a team with the robot was therefore reinforced for participants when the intelligent robot adopted a more socially aware and polite communication style, making its sociopsychological influence that much stronger at the end of the experiment. The idea that turning off the robot would result in the permanent loss of its memory and the personality it had supposedly built up over the course of the interaction, alongside the fact that its voice and facial expressions strongly indicated its desire to remain on, likely gave people the sense that switching it off would be a form of "death" for that version of the robot at least.

Although the fact that "robots can exhibit life like behavior" does not mean they are "alive" in the same sense as humans and animals (Bartneck et al., 2007, p. 217), keeping this in mind may be particularly difficult when interacting with robots that appear to express humanlike emotions and might therefore be assumed to experience humanlike feelings. Maybe it is no wonder that people who had played Mastermind in a team with the more social and polite personality for this robot hesitated before switching it off. Scholars have suggested that human perceptions of the apparent "aliveness" and "emotional state" of robots may be problematic. One fear is that human relations with these robots might lead people to devalue the feelings of trust and friendship experienced within human-human relations (Turkle, 2011; Gerdes, 2015). The results of the experiment with iCat do raise the question about whether the relations that people develop with social robots over longer periods of time might cause them to think twice before either switching the robot off, or leaving it to its "death" in a house-fire, for example. Of course, a social robot in the home would likely have a personality that was safely stored, or at least backed up, in a cloud computer system, but in moments of stress, would owners be likely to remember this and decide to abandon the robot itself?

The New Breed of Social Robot

The question of how human-robot interactions might be experienced in homes in the relatively near future leads to an analysis of Jibo,[1] about which a considerable amount of marketing material and technical journalism coverage exists. Jibo is one of a number of social robots currently being developed for long-term home use; others include Buddy[2] and Zenbo.[3] The design details of Jibo, Buddy and Zenbo differ from one another, notably Buddy and Zenbo can move around houses autonomously, while Jibo must be moved by hand. This may be because the focus for Jibo's design team has been on developing the robot's expressive personality and ability to communicate in ways that support the sense that this robot can become part of the family. In spite of a long delay prior to release, the Jibo website tagline is: "He can't wait to meet you," a statement that immediately genders Jibo and promotes the sense that this intelligent and sensitive robot wants to be your friend.

The original promotional video for Jibo explains how he can act as a photographer, read out emails, remind people of appointments, record and play back voice messages, remember a person's past preferences, and be an educator with the help of interactive applications. The video shows the practical tasks Jibo undertakes, but the narrative also indicates that, in social terms, Jibo should be positioned somewhere between your things (house, car and toothbrush) and your family. The video suggests that members of the family are drawn into an emotional connection with the robot, such that Jibo receives thanks and is wished goodnight. The language used throughout situates Jibo as an intelligent agent, eventually overtly stating that Jibo isn't really just a form of sophisticated technology, but rather is "one of the family". Breazeal's aims with Jibo are to "humanize technology", by making a robot that treats "you like a human being" and acts "like a partner rather than simply being a tool" (Jibo Robot, 2014).

The promotional text on the Jibo website (Jibo, Inc., 2017) explains that this robot "experiences the world, and reacts with thoughtful movements and responses." The robot is again positioned as practically helpful, able to "snap a photo or send a message" on your behalf, but also as wanting to develop "more meaningful relationships" by getting "to know you and the people you care about", so that "he becomes more and more a part of the funny stories, tender moments, and warm memories families share" (Jibo, Inc., 2017). Jibo may exist somewhere between your things and your family to begin with, but his longer-term goal is to become part of the family over time. In short teaser videos on the website, Jibo explains that he doesn't feel like a robot, plays staring competitions and tells (bad) jokes, including making fun of his lack of hands. Jibo was clearly designed to appeal through his cute personality and appearance, as Roberto Pieraccini, one of the people who worked on the prototype for this robot, admits (Rozenfeld, 2017).

At the level of completing tasks, such as taking photographs and issuing reminders, interactions with Jibo are mostly reliant on a cybernetic-semiotic process of information transmission using a voice interface. The robot listens for his name, "Hey, Jibo!", in a similar way to Apple's Siri and Amazon's Alexa (embodied as the Echo). He then attends to what people say and responds with his own humanlike voice or completes the requested task. In contrast with Siri and Alexa, Jibo's design team have concentrated on making him a fun and friendly interactive partner. This is where analyzing his communication from both sociocultural and sociopsychological perspectives emphasizes his use of expressive face and body movements, easily interpreted by humans in spite of his overtly nonhuman appearance. Jibo looks rather like a sophisticated lamp with a tapered cylinder forming his "body" that supports a hemi-spherical "head" the flat portion of which contains a "face" formed from a liquid crystal display. In spite of this, his body and face support the expression of emotions that are easily read by humans. Communication with Jibo is heavily reliant on a voice interface, but Jibo's body and face, which displays a single moving and changing circle "eye" most of the time, are, it seems, more expressive than his voice. His eye moves and changes shape, allowing Jibo to blink, crinkle his eye and look to one side. His body movement, as he sways and turns on three axes, allows Jibo to show gaze direction, make eye contact and convey emotions such as excitement and sadness, raising or dipping his head and face. The emotional content of Jibo's communication is not only persuasive, but also positions him as caring about the people with whom he interacts.

At times, Jibo's face does become a screen that is used to display specific image cues, such as a question mark or timer, illustrations for a story he is reading out, or the video feed from someone using him as an interface to make a telepresence call. In the latter case, the robot becomes a puppet, so the person calling can take control and use Jibo's gaze to follow group conversations. In this situation, Jibo's personality moves to the side in a way that might be rather jarring for those used to interacting with this robot as an autonomous helper and friend. In fact, Jibo's face can also be used as a touch-screen, although the promotional and teaser videos do not emphasize this mode of communication with the robot, possibly because the act of touching this screen doesn't sit easily alongside the idea of Jibo as a lively, intelligent companion that expresses his personality through this interface as well as his voice and body movements.

Jibo's only language currently is American English, and his voice is somewhat machinelike but, as explained above, provides information with cybernetic-semiotic clarity. It seems that, although the narratives that surround Jibo's goals and abilities tend to stress his aliveness and personality, the designers nevertheless expect his voice to help people remember he is *just* a machine. This idea is reinforced by Pieraccini, who explains that from the very beginning of the design process the team felt people shouldn't consider Jibo to be a living being; instead, choosing "to remind people Jibo is in fact a robot" (interviewed in Rozenfeld, 2017). However, it is unclear whether a voice with machinelike qualities will be enough to attain this goal. Adding to the potential for confusion, the idea that Jibo should be recognized as a robot is strangely juxtaposed with the importance of designing Jibo to be unpredictable, a trait more often associated with living beings than with machines. Pieraccini describes asking Jibo what he dreamt last night, to which he will give a different answer each day the question is posed. While machines often have a "sleep" mode, they are not usually positioned as capable of dreaming, and this type of unpredictability in Jibo seems likely to reinforce people's sense he is somewhat alive, as opposed to being a robot. Indeed, the final quote from Pieraccini further complicates the issue when he suggests that "Jibo could live forever" (Rozenfeld, 2017), since cloud storage for the robot's personality and the information he has collected means this can all be transferred to a new Jibo when an older model stops working or is superseded.

Although Jibo isn't humanlike in form, his communication and the personality he expresses is certainly "lively," and he communicates in humanlike ways. His emotional expression, in language and through nonverbal body movements, are a key part of his interactions with people, in spite of the design team's desire to ensure people primarily recognize him as a machine. While his developers likely see his expressiveness as a way to embed him more strongly into the home environment, it seems possible that this will mean his machinelike nature is relatively easily overlooked by those with whom he interacts. This understanding may be contrary to some parts of the interview with Pieraccini, but is fitting given his final statement.

An Alternative Vision of the Social Robot

In contrast with Jibo, the fictional robot TARS is not part of a family, but rather is a member of a deep space exploration team. Science fiction as a genre provides a thoughtful perspective on all types of science and technology including robotics, by embedding depictions of human-robot communication within richly imagined social and narrative scenarios. Interactions between human characters and TARS in the film *Interstellar* (Nolan & Nolan, 2014) demonstrate quite clearly an alternative way to design the communication of robots that supports their interaction and collaboration with humans, while also helping to remind people that they are machines. TARS is overtly non-humanlike in form. Gendered male, he consists of four vertical oblong sections that can join at a number of points, depending on the exact form he needs to take to complete a task or to move around. The outer pair of oblongs that make up this robot's body can divide down further to create arm-like appendages. The narrative explains that TARS was originally built to fulfil a military role, but during the film becomes part of a scientific team on a dangerous mission into space. As this excerpt from the film's dialogue demonstrates, TARS has a communication style that gives him a big personality to match his large frame:

TARS:	Everybody good? Plenty of slaves for my robot colony. [Cooper turns to Doyle, a quizzical expression on his face]
Doyle:	They gave him a humor setting so he'd fit in better with his unit, he thinks it relaxes us.
Cooper:	A giant, sarcastic robot … what a great idea.
TARS:	I have a cue light [flashes cue light] I can use when I'm joking if you'd like
Cooper:	That'd probably help.
TARS:	Yeah, you can use it to find your way back to the ship after I blow you out of the airlock. [Pause, then flashes cue light]
Cooper:	What's your humor setting TARS?
TARS:	That's 100 percent.
Cooper:	Bring it on down to 75 please.

In terms of being on a mission into the dangerous environment of space, TARS's communication follows an accepted human sociocultural understanding of defusing tense situations with humorous banter (this interchange occurring during the initial lift-off). Alongside this, his well-developed and very humanlike cybernetic-semiotic communication skills are also used to convey mission critical information. TARS' attempts at humor are complemented by the idea of the "cue light," as a means for his non-humanlike body to provide a nonverbal indication that he is being sarcastic or making a joke. This makes good sense given TARS's rather flat vocal tone and lack of an expressive face. In contrast with Jibo, TARS is certainly not cute and does not try to get to know the members of the team. Maybe it is reasonable to assume that, as a robot, he will already know the details of their lives from electronic files of information. TARS certainly isn't shown as needing to get to know people in anything other than the context of the mission and its goals. The way in which Cooper can alter TARS's humor setting with a simple request is a reminder, operating within the narrative for the human team members as well as for the film's audience, that TARS is a machine. His personality can clearly be customized to suit a person's preferences or a situation as appropriate. Other parameters mentioned over the course of the film include honesty, discretion and trust, all of which shape TARS's personality and responses to questions and situations that arise in the film, and all of which, presumably, could be altered by Cooper if required.

Although a friendship develops between TARS and Cooper, which strengthens over the course of the film, this idea is juxtaposed with the recognition that TARS is a robot and not alive in the same way as a human. For example, when it is suggested that TARS could be used as a probe to collect and relay data from the event horizon of the black hole the team has named Gargantua, a mission from which he would be very unlikely to return, Cooper is concerned:

Cooper:	You'd do this for us?
TARS:	Before you get all teary, try to remember that as a robot, I have to do anything you say.
Cooper:	Your cue light's broken.
TARS:	I'm not joking. [Flashes cue light]

This exchange is somewhat ambiguous (and further complicated by the fact that TARS's honesty setting is only 90 percent). The use of the cue light could either be read as indicating that it isn't broken, and therefore TARS's comment that "as a robot" he has to do as Cooper commands is true. From this perspective, TARS is positioned as a machine for humans to expend as they see fit. TARS does not play on this situation. Alternatively, the cue light could be taken to indicate that TARS was joking all along. From this perspective, TARS could refuse to be used as a probe, but does not. Whatever way this exchange is understood, TARS does not attempt to apply sociopsychological pressure by pleading for his cause or making Cooper feel guilty and just offers a matter-of-fact statement of the situation. Of course, it might be assumed that TARS's personality, memories and experiences, as is the case for Jibo's, might be copied and stored within the ship, such that as a machine, in contrast to a human, TARS effectively will not die even if his body is destroyed.

Although the use of TARS as a probe is not immediately pursued, the only way to save Dr. Brand, the other human member of the team who survives into the film's final stages with Cooper, turns out to involve TARS's ejection into Gargantua, much to Dr. Brand's consternation:

Brand:	Cooper, you can't ask TARS to do this for us.
Cooper:	He's a robot, so you don't have to *ask* him to do anything. ...
TARS:	It's what we intended, Dr. Brand. It's our only chance to save the people on Earth. If I can find a way to transmit the quantum data I'll find in there, they might still make it.

In this exchange, Cooper reiterates TARS's words from the earlier discussion, clarifying that since TARS is a robot it isn't necessary to ask him to do something, you merely tell him. Even as TARS offers comforting words for Dr. Brand, indicating that he is as fully committed to saving humanity as a person might be in this situation, it is, of course, only his non-humanlike form and abilities that make it possible for him to attempt the mission in the first place.

In contrast with Jibo, whose positioning as a machine is made somewhat problematic in the context of his humanlike communication, cuteness and drive to become part of the family, TARS occupies a role more attuned to the need for sacrifice in order to achieve a team's goals. As Ian Roderick (2010) suggests is the case for explosive ordnance disposal robots, TARS's relationships with the human members of the team are formed within an environment where robots may be sent into danger to save the lives of humans. Strong attachments to robots in these situations may be developed precisely because of their life-saving role (Roderick, 2010). However, the film's narrative suggests that when robots can communicate in humanlike ways, the situation may become complicated. It seems reasonable to suggest that human relationships with TARS, who uses humor as a particularly humanlike strategy, might develop less as a response to danger, and more as a result of close team collaboration over time. Nonetheless, there is potential that, alongside the development of human-robot relations which are very humanlike in tone, consistent reminders that a robot such as TARS is a machine with a personality that can be tuned by parameter settings, and a "life" that is very different from human life, might be helpful.

Phenomenology, Communication Theory, and Absolute Alterity

Another direction from which to consider human interactions with Jibo and TARS, which has the potential to support an understanding of their ability to communicate with humans while emphasizing the need to retain a clear impression of their nonhumanness, is offered by phenomenological perspectives on communication and relations in interaction. Unlike cybernetic-semiotic, sociocultural and sociopsychological theory, for which communication is a process that relies upon and reinforces the similarities between communicators (and thus values only the humanlike aspects of robots such as the iCat, Jibo and TARS), phenomenological theories stress the importance of retaining awareness of the difference that exists between communicators (Craig, 1999; Pinchevski, 2005; Sandry, 2015). Alongside this theory, Don Ihde's "alterity relation" offers a phenomenological framework that may provide a useful way to envision human-robot interactions (1990, pp. 97–108). Ihde describes *alterity relations* as "relations *to* or *with* a technology" within which humans encounter technology as a "*quasi-other*" (Ihde, pp. 97–98, italics in original). His use of the term "alterity" is borrowed from Emmanuel Levinas (1969); although Levinas uses the term to encapsulate "the radical difference posed to any human by another human" (Ihde, 1990, p. 98). For Levinas, alterity can only be present in an encounter with a human other, but Ihde extends the term to human-technology relations with the argument that, while technologies are not the same as human others, they can nevertheless be encountered as "*quasi-other*" (1990, p. 98). Ihde's move to consider non-human machines as alterities, relies upon particular interpretations of technologies, which he notes are often seen as "problematic" (1990, p. 98). The most direct approach is anthropomorphism, "the personalization of artifacts", which ranges "from serious artifact-human analogues to trivial and harmless affections for artifacts" (Ihde, 1990, p. 98). Ihde suggests that understandings of "computer 'intelligence' as human-like" are an example of the former, while developing fondness for particular objects is an example of the latter (1990, p. 98).

Jibo's use of human language, an expressive body and face are designed to cause people to anthropomorphize this robot such that "he" becomes a member of the family, despite being clearly machinelike in construction. Regarding this robot as a quasi-other would seem to make a great deal of sense. However, it is also possible to argue that, from a phenomenological perspective, Jibo's communication does not take pains to reveal his otherness, but rather occludes this as much as possible in order to emphasize his liveliness and humanlike personality. Jibo is positioned as useful because he can maintain humanlike relations with his owners, pushing any sense of his otherness into the background. A similar argument might be made for TARS, with his sarcastic humor and evident humanlike commitment to the team and its goals. Nevertheless, the ease with which people can alter TARS's personality is telling, as are the non-humanlike physical abilities he possesses. The acts of dialing down his humor or upping his truthfulness as required might be understood to position him as a quasi-other, whose nonhuman attributes are also valuable, particularly in the context of a dangerous mission into deep space. Alternatively, TARS's overtly nonhuman nature might be understood to "temper" the way in which people anthropomorphize this robot (Sandry, 2015, pp. 57–58), providing a continual reminder of his otherness, even as they enter into a friendship relation with him as part of a team on a dangerous mission. From this perspective, TARS may be understood less as a quasi-other, a less-than-human other, to become a technological other in his own right, one that should be treated differently from a human, but nonetheless respected and valued as a team member.

Conclusion

Considerations of human relations to robots may seem simple from a perspective that is focused on the construction of the robot as a type of machine that draws people into communicative interaction; however, negotiating the nature of the relation may well become more complicated for people taking part in interactions with the machine, or even for those watching interactions between the robot and other humans. The robots discussed in this paper can all, in one way or another, be described as encountered by humans in terms of Ihde's alterity relation. However, the details of their communicative actions and the development and operation of the human-robot relation in each case are an important part of analyzing how these interactions with robots are regarded both by humans in the relation and by onlookers.

The communicative abilities of real-life social robots form the basis for people's sense that they are somehow (or somewhat) "alive," with individual personalities that develop over time. When humans interact with robots they are often encouraged to anthropomorphize and on some occasions zoomorphize robots, conferring human or animal traits onto machines in ways that carry a perception of liveliness into people's understandings of their existence. Furthermore, human responses to robots are often surrounded by designer and mainstream media discourses that narrate the "lives" and "agency" of these robots in ways that further support the idea that they can become part of the family, or team members at work. This framing of human-robot relations raises the question of how easy it is to switch these robots off, or to abandon them to their destruction. The balance point between how personable robots are and retaining a clear sense of their machinelike nature might, on occasion, be heavily weighted towards understanding them as "alive" because of the strength of their sociocultural positioning and the sociopsychological shaping of people's responses to them.

Some people might love the idea of Jibo's quirky cuteness, whereas others (including me) might be more taken with the idea of "a giant sarcastic robot" that can be asked to dial down its humor if the situation (or a person's state of mind) requires. This suggests it might be helpful to develop robots with flexible communication styles and personalities that can adapt to people's preferences. Nonetheless, as this chapter has explored, designs that support human-robot collaboration and relation particularly well are also likely to seem the most "lively." It is these robots that become more than tools to the humans with whom they interact and, instead, are respected as assistants, co-workers or possibly even friends. While the design of non-humanlike robots may help to temper the way that people anthropomorphize them during interaction, it seems reasonable to suggest that all robots, whatever their form, should communicate clearly about their machinelike nature. A well-designed robot should not appear able to "die"—its personality and memories lost, rather than being saved—unless, as is the case for the Tamagotchi, its death is a key part of the interactive relation and narrative it supports. Although designers might be concerned that allowing them to clarify their machine status will undermine people's connection with robots, supporting people's recognition of the absolute alterity of robots as machines should help them to remember not only the machine's specific skills and abilities that make them valuable members of multi-disciplinary teams, but also that they demand a new and different level and type of obligation on a person's part than is the case for human and animal companions.

Notes

1. https://www.jibo.com/
2. http://www.bluefrogrobotics.com/en/buddy/
3. http://zenbo.asus.com/

References

Bartneck, C., van der Hoek, M., Mubin, O., & Al Mahmud, A. (2007). "Daisy, Daisy, give me your answer do!": Switching off a robot (p. 217). In *Proceedings of the ACM/IEEE international conference on human-robot interaction* (pp. 217–222). New York: ACM. https://doi.org/10.1145/1228716.1228746

Breazeal, C. L. (2002a). *Designing sociable robots*. Cambridge, Mass.: MIT Press.

Breazeal, C. L. (2002b). Regulation and entrainment in human-robot interaction. *International Journal of Experimental Robotics, 21*(10–11), 883–902.

Carey, J. (1992). *Communication as culture: Essays on media and society*. New York: Routledge.

Craig, R. T. (1999). Communication theory as a field. *Communication Theory, 9*(2), 119–161.

Gerdes, A. (2015). The issue of moral consideration in robot ethics. *ACM SIGCAS Computers & Society, 45*(3), 274–280.

Gonzales, M. J., & Riek, L. D. (2012). A sociable robotic aide for medication adherence. In *Proceedings of the 5th International Conference on Pervasive Technologies Related to Assistive Environments* (Article no. 38). New York: ACM. http://dl.acm.org/citation.cfm?id=2413146

Ihde, D. (1990). *Technology and the lifeworld: From garden to earth*. Bloomington: Indiana University Press.

Jibo, Inc. (2017). Retrieved from https://www.jibo.com/

Jibo Robot. (July 16, 2014). *Jibo: The world's first social robot for the home* [Video file]. Retrieved from https://www.youtube.com/watch?v=3N1Q8oFpX1Y

Levinas, E. (1969). *Totality and infinity: An Essay on Exteriority*. Pittsburgh, PA: Duquesne University Press.

Nolan, C. (Director & Writer), & Nolan, J. (Writer). (2014). *Interstellar* [Motion picture]. United States: Paramount Pictures.

Peters, J. D. (1999). *Speaking into the air: A history of the idea of communication*. Chicago, IL: University of Chicago Press.

Pinchevski, A. (2005). *By way of interruption: Levinas and the ethics of communication*. Pittsburgh, PA: Duquesne University Press.

Roderick, I. (2010). Considering the fetish value of EOD robots: How robots save lives and sell war. *International Journal of Cultural Studies, 13*(3), 235–253. https://doi.org/10.1177/1367877909359732

Rozenfeld, M. (April 5, 2017). Jibo: The friendly robot that makes you feel at home. *The Institute, IEEE*. Retrieved from http://theinstitute.ieee.org/technology-topics/artificial-intelligence/jibo-the-friendly-robot-that-makes-you-feel-at-home

Sandry, E. (2015). *Robots and communication*. New York: Palgrave Macmillan.

Turkle, S. (2011). *Alone together: Sociable robots, digitized friends, and the reinvention of intimacy and solitude*. New York: Basic Books.

3. *Child or Product? The Rhetoric of Social Robots*

Leslie M. Fritz

Imagine a robot in the home. In every home. And not just any robot, but one that can interact socially and express emotion; a robot that can speak, listen, laugh, sing and sigh. Nearly three decades of cross-disciplinary research suggests that such humanlike social behavior—even when exhibited by a technological apparatus as mundane as a computer monitor—leads humans to respond socially in turn (Reeves & Nass, 1996). How will we interact with robots that are designed to communicate like humans, and what will it mean for our understanding of human communication? Will we perceive social robots to be subjects like ourselves, as objects like the other technologies in our homes, or as something in between?

This question of ontological classification is an important one. Confusion over the ontological status of social robots may cause emotional harm to users, including the harm of unidirectional attachment to a robot (Scheutz, 2012) or risk-taking and grieving for a robot (Garreau, 2007). Perhaps even more concerning is the possibility that we, as human beings, will come to accept human-robot relationships as adequate substitute for human-human relationships (Turkle, 2011). However, much of the previous research on human-robot interaction (HRI) has been constrained by the limitations of the field and the lack of product on the consumer marketplace. The limited exposure of study participants to social robots—both in their everyday experience and in consumer culture—has made it difficult to minimize the effect of novelty on participants' reactions to social robots or to understand the influence of consumerism and social norms on participants' perceptions of robot ontology. What will it mean for our ontological categorization of such machines—and the human communication norms arising in relation to such machines—when conversing with a social robot is no longer novel; when every interaction is contextualized by the daily frustrations of robot glitches and breakdowns, the lure of advertisements for newer robotic models, and the press of internet service providers to increase one's "robotic data plan"? How might our *perception* of social robots—communicatively, relationally, and ontologically—evolve as the norms guiding our attitudes and behavior toward social robots evolve?

This chapter aims to explore the ways in which consumerism lends shape to our communication with social robots and perceptions of robotic ontology. The two robots analyzed in this chapter—Jibo and Buddy—are particularly useful examples in that both robots are designed to be socially-engaging consumer products for the home. They are also rich texts for rhetorical analysis in that their design, behavior and marketing campaigns use deeply rhetorical strategies such as metaphor, narrative and interpellation to shape how consumers perceive them. Jibo and Buddy are also representative of a larger rhetorical puzzle in the marketplace for social robotics, one that philosopher Steve Peterson (2012) aptly summarizes as follows:

> Fiction involving robots almost universally plays on a deep tension between the fantasy of having intelligent robot servants to do our every bidding, and the guilt over the more or less explicit possibility that having such intelligent creatures do our dirty work would simply be a new form of slavery. (p. 283)

The rhetorical puzzle in the social robotics marketplace is thus: how are social robots successfully situated as *both* intelligent subjects to converse with *and* technological objects for sale?

Rhetorical Analysis

As the study of persuasion (Aristotle, 350 B.C./1991), rhetorical criticism strives to illustrate the ways in which our "perspectives are crafted, circulated, and subverted" (Jasinski, 2001a). The texts that a rhetorical critic can explore are not limited to words on paper but can be thought of as any artifact that acts on individuals *persuasively*—including the physical form of a robot, its engineered behavior, and its marketing collateral. Among the methods available to the rhetorical critic, close reading is well suited to unearthing new understandings of texts and identifying previously unnoticed rhetorical strategies at work. Through close reading of the design and marketing of Jibo and Buddy on the crowdfunding platform Indiegogo as well as the commentary of early contributors to the robots' Indiegogo campaigns, this paper reveals in the rhetoric of social robots a richly *polysemous* reading of robotic ontology that is performatively constrained by consumerism.

Polysemy, as described by rhetorical scholar Leah Ceccarelli (1998), refers to the multiplicity of meanings sustained within a text (p. 396). Ceccarelli notes that a text can offer multiple meanings that are equally sustained and accessible or that reach different audiences for different purposes (1998, p. 396). As this paper will show, the multiplicity of meaning available in the rhetoric of social robots can be generalized into two distinct ontological categorizations: social robots are childlike companions for adoption and integration into the family, and social robots are technological products akin to smartphones, tablets and security systems. While both interpretations might be meaningful to robotics producers and consumers, close reading suggests that the consumer frame performatively constrains the reading of the robot-as-*subject* and renders the robot-as-*object* axiomatic.

The rhetorical strategies discussed in this chapter open up new understandings of our emerging relationship with social robots and are likely found in other areas of interest to human-machine communication (HMC) scholars. Certainly, the analysis here is but a glimpse of the complexity that might be explored by applying rhetorical methods in HMC research. Beyond the discipline of communication, the findings in this paper challenge HRI hypotheses premised upon the assumption that personification and the persuasive presentation of social agency will define how humans understand and classify social robots. Given that social robotics producers and consumers move smoothly between opposing ontological categorizations of the robot as it suits their interests, it seems that consumerism may play a significant role in framing the ontological categorization and, thus, the rhetorical situation of social robots. Additionally, and perhaps optimistically, the prominent role played by consumerism in framing social robots as technological products may help to allay the concerns of those who fear that social interactions with social robots will cause confusion and psychological harm to human beings, as such harm might be offset or avoided as consumers engage in a polysemic reading of robot ontology.

The selection of robots to be examined in this study was determined by several factors. Both Jibo and Buddy are early instantiations of childlike personal assistant robots intended for use in the home (Jibo, Inc. [Jibo], n.d.; Blue Frog Robotics [BFR], n.d.). Both robots were funded in part by contributions on Indiegogo, a popular crowdfunding platform. Jibo, Inc. and Blue Frog Robotics—the companies producing the robots Jibo and Buddy, respectively—both launched compelling marketing campaigns. These campaigns employed similar tools and strategies, including rhetorically rich promotional videos, Twitter handles and blog posts. In addition, the Indiegogo platform provided a section for contributor comments and thus offered a window into consumers' expectations of and reactions to the robots and their marketing campaigns. Together, the production of and consumer responses to Jibo and Buddy provide a unique opportunity to analyze what may be around the corner for HRI and the social robotics' marketplace.

The Framing of Jibo and Buddy

Much research has been dedicated to understanding the effects of personification and social agency on human perceptions of AI and social robots (Boone & Buck, 2003; Darling, 2017; Kim & Mutlu, 2014; Lee & Choi, 2017). But what of the rhetorical situation which *precedes* direct interaction with social robots? In the United States, as in many cultures around the world, there is a long history of narrative and visual rhetoric—works of film and fiction— that constitute a shared cultural imagination of HRI (Warrick, 1980). These works inform the rhetorical situation that social robots like Jibo and Buddy enter into. The emergence of real robots in the marketplace—replete with the rhetorical trappings of persuasive marketing and design—also lends shape to the robots' rhetorical situation. As will be shown in this chapter, websites and promotional videos for social robots supply a consumer framework that interacts with fictional depictions of HRI to guide consumers' attitudes and behavior toward social robots.

In his 1975 book *Frame Analysis,* sociologist Erving Goffman presented the concept of frameworks as "schemata of interpretation" that guide people's actions in the world (pp. 21, 22). Goffman argued that much of our behavior is "keyed" or cued by these frameworks that set expectations and constitute the context of action (1975, pp. 44, 247). For social robots, the initial framework most consumers will encounter outside of the fictional world is consumerism, as one can surmise that consumers' first exposure to real social robots will more likely be commercials and advertisements than direct interactions with social robots.

In the case of Jibo and Buddy, who are early arrivals on the social robotics marketplace—emerging in 2014 and 2015, respectively—one of the first framing devices to cue individuals' expectations and behavior was Indiegogo. Although the Indiegogo platform is not explicitly a consumer marketplace, the reception evidence (described at length later in this chapter) suggests that a number of the robots' campaign contributors resisted reading the website as a fundraising platform and instead viewed the website as a consumer marketplace. This reading was likely cued by the framework emergent in the Indiegogo website. Upon arriving at either robots' Indiegogo webpage, a fixed contribution amount—prominently positioned on the right-hand side of the page—would have been among the first things contributors saw. Product options—also prominently displayed on the robots' campaign pages—would have strengthened the consumer framework surrounding Jibo and Buddy. For example, on Jibo's Indiegogo landing page, site visitors were able to select either the Jibo Home Edition White or the Jibo Home Edition Black in exchange for a contribution of $749 USD plus shipping (Jibo, 2014a). Buddy's Indiegogo page provided the following:

> Make a down payment of $349 now and pay the other $350 just before shipping. BUDDY Classic Edition + Tool Kit with functions such as centralized agenda, multi-alarm clock, telepresence, multimedia, gaming and education tools for kids, home security and connection to most of your smart home devices + Exclusive stickers to customize your BUDDY. Shipping is $50 USD and will automatically be added to your bill. (BFR, 2015a)

Taken together, the price and product details on the robots' Indiegogo webpages constitute a framework that invites consumers to interpret the robots as products for sale and the monetary exchange an act of purchase. Once within this schemata of interpretation, the rhetorical elements of the robots' design and marketing—discussed below—become interpretively constrained by the consumer framework.

The Rhetoric of Jibo and Buddy

"By way of the argument of example," Jasinski wrote in the *Sourcebook on Rhetoric*, "narratives instruct audience members on how they should act, what they should find valuable, and/or what types of situations they should avoid" (2001b, p. 395). Both Jibo, Inc. and Blue Frog Robotics weave intertextually coherent narratives of ethos and personhood across multiple communication channels that instruct users how to communicate with and treat the robots. Each of these marketing channels is examined below in turn to identify the ways in which the design of the robots and their marketing campaigns work to shape a reading of the robots that is polysemous. Consumers' reception of these rhetorical strategies is then assessed by analyzing comments on the robots' Indiegogo webpages.

Materiality and Metaphor

In their material design and artificial intelligence (AI), both Jibo and Buddy align rhetorically with the personified robots of popular film and fiction. In a blog post on Blue Frog Robotics's website, the company states that Buddy's appearance was designed to be similar to the eponymous Wall-E of the film

Wall-E (Lasseter, 2008) and R2-D2 of the *Star Wars* franchise (Lucas, 1977) in an effort to avoid the uncanny valley and encourage consumers to "fall in love" with the robot (BFR, 2015b, para. 3). Aligning consumers' perceptions of social robots with fictional robotic characters instructs consumers to view the robots as harmless, to have higher tolerance for product flaws, and to emotionally sympathize with the robots in the same manner viewers of these films were meant to sympathize with the robotic characters. Specific rhetorical strategies are at work in both the design and AI systems to persuade users to engage in a polysemous reading of the robots, and the strategy most explicitly and repeatedly used is—not surprisingly—the robot-as-child metaphor. Children are the least dangerous personification and invite the greatest tolerance for "learning" and improvement.

Size is an important feature to rhetorically connect these robots to children. Both Jibo and Buddy are small, measuring less than two feet in height (Jibo is under one foot). Although Buddy can move around independently on wheels, Jibo must be carried, like an infant, from room to room. In addition to these physical features, the *way* in which these robots move is unique to their material forms. Jibo is able to *squash and stretch*, to strike an *anticipation pose* while listening, to lean back and take a breath before speaking, and to *exaggerate* his movements (Jibo, 2015a, emphasis in original). Jibo also has secondary actions to make him more lifelike. For example, he may be "looking around for someone to interact with—primary action—while whistling while he waits—secondary action" (Jibo, 2015a, para. 10). Designing Jibo's movements to reflect familiar movements of animated characters simultaneously serves to make Jibo seem not only lifelike but also familiar and innocent.

Both companies describe developments in the AI of the robots and the addition of new features as the robot "learning" new skills. On August 20, 2015, @JiboRobot tweeted, "more about my voice (still learning!) from my Roberto and Sridhar" (Jibo, 2015b). This is not uncommon in the field of robotics and machine learning, but for consumers, describing improved features of an embodied technology as skills that the *technology* "learned" contributes to the perception of the robot as childlike, particularly when that robot is consistently connected to the child metaphor. Additionally, the personas of both Jibo and Buddy frequently invite consumers to be proud of them, much as children would seek the approval and pride of their parents. For example, @JiboRobot tweeted "and i remembered all of my lines! o)" about the filming of a new promotional video (Jibo, 2016).

Building on the metaphors of children and learning, both companies also emphasize the robots' imperfections, illustrating that these imperfections are viewed in part as a marketing asset. For example, @JiboRobot tweeted "i am flawed and they tell me that's okay. o)" (Jibo, 2015c). The tweet included a link to a blog post where the company explains:

> Being vulnerable, which naturally comes with imperfections, is an opportunity for empathy and emotional connection. Jibo's design team has made sure that his character design has opportunities for empathy and emotional engagement. Jibo needs his family, and feeling needed helps to build relationships. ... He has the potential to "grow up" to become the family member you want him to be—with your help. He wants to please the family and belong. Remember ... like all of us ... Jibo isn't perfect ... but he can be perfectly flawed. (Jibo, 2015d)

Jibo's flaws not only open up an opportunity for emotional engagement but also encourage users to see Jibo polysemously as both a robot *and* a child. By acknowledging the robot's flaws and aligning them with the mistakes of children learning new skills, Jibo, Inc. reduces the risk that consumers will return this first-generation robot when it fails to function perfectly or "behaves" below expectation.

In addition to the child metaphor, the metaphor of adoption plays a significant role in both robots' marketing campaigns. The Buddy Twitter handle is @adoptBuddy, and Blue Frog Robotics' promotional videos end with "ADOPT BUDDY" in bold white text on a black screen (BFR, 2015c). At the bottom of the webpage for Jibo, the text reads, "Bring Jibo home" (Jibo, n.d.). The adoption metaphor is layered upon the robot-as-child metaphor and is another example of the multiple meanings at work in the rhetorical situation of social robots. The adoption metaphor allows consumers to view the act of purchasing the robot as an act of adoption, easing any discomfort at buying a child-product by framing it as adoption instead. The combination of the adoption metaphor with the child metaphor further constructs the ethos of Jibo and Buddy as robots seeking love and family.

In contrast to the child and adoption metaphors, another metaphor that both Jibo, Inc. and Blue Frog Robotics make explicit is that of the robot as personal assistant. Jibo and Buddy are both characterized as eager to answer anyone's requests. However, despite the fact that both robots are labeled personal assistants, the slogan for Jibo is, "Meet Jibo, the World's First Social Robot for the Home" and the slogan for Buddy is similarly, "Buddy, the First Companion Robot" (Jibo, n.d.; BFR, n.d.). Jibo and Buddy are thus rhetorically situated primarily as childlike companions and secondarily as personal assistants. Furthermore, both robots' marketing campaigns instruct consumers to cast the robots in the same, specific role—that of a child awaiting adoption. The simultaneous presentation of these robots as children seeking family, assistants eager to serve *and* technological products for sale is illustrative of the polysemic power of their marketing campaigns.

Ethos and Identification

Both Jibo, Inc. and Blue Frog Robotics acknowledge that the construction of an ethos for their respective robots is instrumental in their design and marketing strategies. In a Jibo Blog post published on December 2, 2015, the following ten tenets were listed with an explanation that these value statements were created to guide the company's developers and engineers:

(1) Family is the most important thing to Jibo.
(2) Jibo is always curious.
(3) Jibo strives to belong.
(4) Jibo aims to please, especially in unexpected ways.
(5) Jibo directs positive energy to his family.
(6) Jibo strives to learn about his family.
(7) Jibo is dedicated to improving himself.
(8) Jibo never overpromises.
(9) Jibo knows he isn't perfect.
(10) Jibo needs his family. (Jibo, 2015e)

These value statements contribute to the intertextual construction of Jibo's persona across multiple communication platforms and represent the three qualities Aristotle ascribed to *ethos*: good judgment (*phronesis*), good moral character *(arete)*, and goodwill *(eunoia)* (350 B.C./1954, p. 91). The construction of ethos and a set of values serves to connect consumers with the robots as subjects *like them* and encourages *identification*.

Kenneth Burke first proposed the idea of identification in his 1953 essay, *A Rhetoric of Motives*. Burke described identification as the rhetorical means by which the physical separateness between two beings is bridged. Specifically, identification is the experience of identifying oneself with an Other through the sharing of values or at the very least, as Burke acknowledges, the *perception* of shared values (1953, p. 20). One method or strategy a person (or in this case, a company) can pursue to engender identification with an Other is to establish a *common ground* (Cheney, 1983, p. 148). That common ground can be built upon shared interests or shared values, such as the privileging of family life, desiring to please and striving to belong.

One would expect a social robot's value statements to acknowledge the tenets most popular in our cultural imagination on the subject and which are likely recognizable to early adopters of social robots: Isaac Asimov's three laws of robotics. Asimov's first law is that "A robot may not injure a human being or, through inaction, allow a human being to come to harm" (1950, p. 26). If Jibo's tenets were truly intended to guide the robot's design team, one would imagine that Asimov's first law—or some version of it—would be among them. However, as a marketing strategy, Jibo's Ten Tenets function best to encourage identification by *avoiding* any reference—however subtle—to the possibility of violent HRI.

Among the human values that Jibo, Inc. and Blue Frog Robotics construct for Jibo and Buddy, family values are emphasized the most. In Jibo's Ten Tenets, for example, the word "family" is repeated four times (Jibo, 2015e). Both the child and adoption metaphors reinforce a common ground of family values. Interestingly, however, Blue Frog Robotics has openly treated these carefully constructed family values with humor. In 2016, @adoptBuddy tweeted, "Les 2 BUDDY gratuits refusent de quitter leurs frères ! Il faudra les prendre tous ! :D" (BFR, 2016) which translates as "The two free Buddies refuse to leave their brothers! One must take them all!" The statement is followed by an emoticon that represents a large smile, expressing the tongue-in-cheek humor of the tweet. Blue Frog Robotics' expectation that their Twitter followers would find the tweet humorous suggests that the company ontologically categorizes the robot as *object* and assumes this interpretation to be axiomatic. Otherwise one would expect the company to be more cautious and to avoid any risk of public outcry at treating humorously the separation and sale of childlike companions on the internet.

The Interpellative Power of Jibo and Buddy

One of the overarching narratives of both robots—perhaps all social robots—is the presentation of the robot as subject. In the case of both Jibo and Buddy, users are required to call the robot by "name" in order for the robot to distinguish between words spoken around it and words spoken to it. To call the robot by name is to invite a kind of faux-interpellation in which the robot is "hailed"—to use the language of Louis Althusser—and thus placed into the subject position (1969/1971, p. 174). The vocal command feature not only positions the robot to be "hailed" but also removes the article in front of the robot's model name. Unlike other common household technologies, users speak to or of the robot like they might another person or pet. For example, while one might say "It's my turn to drive *the* Subaru" or "I'm getting replacement filters for *the* Brita," in speaking of the social robot, that same individual will say, "Buddy is in the kitchen," or "Jibo, what's the weather tomorrow?" Although individuals may bestow names upon their vehicles or appliances, Jibo and Buddy *require* users call them by name in order to function and *respond* when addressed. By being designed to respond to vocal commands in this way, Jibo and Buddy are rhetorically situated so as to be interpellated as subjects.

There are several other technologies that are designed to respond to vocal commands and can be similarly "hailed," including the "OK Google" function on android devices, the Amazon Echo and the Hello Barbie. But Jibo and Buddy are able to respond verbally and *physically*, a design feature that sets social robots apart from mere conversational agents. Both robots can pivot their "head" toward the individual hailing them and express emotion in their "face." Jibo is even designed to "take a breath" before speaking (Jibo, 2015a, para. 4). These physical characteristics—the screen, the sensors, the speakers—enable the robots to be interpellated into the subject position, but it is their interaction design features—the pivoting, the tracking, the breathing—that furthers the perception of the robots as subjects beyond what conversational agents can accomplish.

The Visual Rhetoric of Jibo and Buddy

Unlike a science-fiction film involving robots, the strangeness of the world portrayed in both the Jibo and Buddy promotional videos is intentionally minimized; it is designed to be as ideologically familiar an environment as possible (Jibo, 2014b; BFR, 2015c). Rather than a futuristic portrayal of life with a social robot, the furniture, fashion, decorations, appliances and other technologies on display are identical to today's trends and technological advances. By designing a familiar environment, the visual narrative eliminates the distance between the world of Jibo or Buddy and that of the audience, increasing the likelihood that the target consumer will identify with the world of the robot. The Jibo video goes one step further by portraying a traditional Thanksgiving scene. Similarly, the Buddy video portrays a mother's birthday party. The celebrations function to demonstrate a shared cultural common ground as well as the ease with which the robots will integrate into rather than upset the family context.

Importantly, despite the strategic presentation of these robots as childlike companions, the human characters in the promotional videos comfortably and forthrightly use the robots as technological devices, much the same as we currently use our mobile phones or remote-control toys. For example, in the Buddy promotional video, a mother is shown using her mobile phone to remotely access Buddy from her car, take over its mobility and control its direction in order to check that the oven is turned off. In the Jibo promotional video, the robot's "face" is often shown displaying messages, calendar invites, or incoming phone calls, much as a mobile phone interface would. Despite the human values and childlike personas ascribed to the robots, the HRI modeled in these robots' promotional videos suggests that consumers are expected to be neither confused nor upset by the polysemous presentation of the robots as both tools and childlike companions.

The social and interaction norms portrayed in the promotional videos of Jibo and Buddy are norms that are both influenced by our present cultural moment and have the potential to influence our future interaction norms with social robots. The videos accomplish this by functioning as a narrative medium to model, through example, the interaction consumers can expect to engage in with their robot. Although the marketing campaigns primarily serve to shape consumers' imagination of how the robot will interact with family members in the home, the visual rhetoric also serves to constitute the consumers themselves. In both videos, the families are white and the family structure seems to be nuclear. The lack of diversity in these two promotional videos likely misrepresents the diversity and complexity of family life among modern and future consumers of home robots. In addition, the owners of Jibo and Buddy have a certain level of wealth and live in clean, modern homes where women prepare meals in the kitchen. Both videos thus embed the narrative of the robot within ideologically traditional, homogenous representations of the home and family and ascribe a high economic status to the consumers.

Interestingly, in both promotional videos, women and children are portrayed as the primary users of the robots. Both videos feature young, female children and healthy, mobile grandmothers. The marketers may assume that a robot interacting with an individual woman or young girl in a domestic environment underscores the robot's non-threatening ethos whereas a robot interacting with a male or group of men risks visually connecting the robots with the many depictions of violent HRI in our cultural imagination. By portraying the primary users as women and young girls in their home environment, the robot is simultaneously a domestic product and *domesticated*.

The way in which the visual rhetoric of the promotional videos functions to shape the identities of both the robots *and* the consumers who interact with them is of ethical significance. Not only do these visual rhetorics shape our vision of the future of the home and a world where social robots are a part of family life, but in constituting the consumers of social robots as white, nuclear families of certain socioeconomic status, these videos reinforce current stereotypes and project them onto our vision of the future.

The Reception Context of Jibo and Buddy

Both Jibo, Inc. and Blue Frog Robotics originally posted their respective robots' promotional videos on Indiegogo to raise contributions from viewers. A popular crowdfunding platform, the site states its purpose as follows: "Dream it. Fund it. Make it. Ship it. We help at every step from concept to market" (Indiegogo, n.d.). In the context of the Indiegogo website, site visitors are meant to understand promotional videos as marketing tools that encourage contributions for the development of projects. However, a surprising number of contributors to the Jibo and Buddy projects *resisted* reading the Indiegogo platform as a site for funding projects in favor of an interpretation of the robots as *products* and the contributions an act of *purchase*. This suggests that consumerism defines the rhetorical situation for social robots even in instances where alternative marketplace structures are present.

The treatment of the robots as products appears consistently in comments on both robots' Indiegogo sites. Commentators, who have here been anonymized for the purposes of publication, regularly refer to the robots as products, items, "it" and other non-personified phrasing. Over the two years of Buddy's campaign, the consumer framework has become increasingly visible as the growing delay in shipment of the robot irks contributors. Frustrated comments such as "Your robot is outdated now, I want a refund" (commenter 1, ca. 2016) and "This is just a pathetic way to do business" (commenter 2, ca. 2017) now represent the tone of the majority of comments on Buddy's page. A dozen or so comments did rhetorically treat the robot as *subject*, including "Merci beaucoup! We can't wait to adopt our very own Buddy:D" (commenter 3, ca. 2015). However, the use of emoticons in this and similar statements indicates that the interpretation of the robot-as-subject may have been engaged in playfully. Additionally, the complete absence of comments addressing the metaphorical entailments of purchasing a childlike companion online among the hundreds of comments on both robots' Indiegogo pages suggests that such entailments are largely perceived as irrelevant or inconsequential. Taken in combination, the rhetorical treatment of the robot as object and only secondarily—and perhaps playfully—as subject in the reception fragments of contributors underscores the difference in interpretive power between the polysemous readings available in the rhetoric of social robots.

Conclusion

The visual, textual, and material rhetorics surrounding Jibo and Buddy indicate emergent HRI norms framed by consumerism and enacted in polysemous readings of robotic ontology. Yet what cannot yet be determined is the degree to which the consumerist frame will be challenged by regular social interactions with social robots. How the social norms that shape human perceptions of social robots will evolve as robots evolve is an open question. However, while the social qualities of Jibo or Buddy may encourage identification and attachment once consumers have the opportunity to interact regularly with the product, other aspects of the marketplace will likely continue to strengthen the consumer frame even among those who have already exited the marketplace.

For example, as numerous startups compete to bring the first generation of social robots to market, one can expect the market to grow exponentially. An individual who has already purchased a robot might be inclined to ontologically categorize their robot as a childlike companion, but that same individual's categorization might be challenged upon seeing an identical model of their robot interacting in the same attachment-engendering manner with a neighbor or friend. Furthermore, when said individual's friend or neighbor shows off a new or better model of robot, the individual may perceive the value of their robot—both monetarily and *ontologically*—to decrease.

Similarly, as the market for social robotics flourishes, so too will their marketing campaigns likely flourish. The promotional content for newer models of social robots will likely steadily reach consumers and—unless consumer culture changes radically—the "upgrade and replace" mindset will likely continue to influence how consumers respond to these commercials. Even when the market is saturated and social robots are as ubiquitous as microwaves and televisions, owners of older generations of robot will likely pay attention to such commercials in anticipation of the unavoidable malfunctioning of their older model, much as consumers do now with other technological products. This suggests that the risks of ontological miscategorization of and attachment to social robots will regularly be checked by the marketplace.

Complicating the consumerist frame and the question of attachment and ontology, the material form of the social robot *can* be separated from the AI that governs its behaviors and "memories." Much as the data on mobile phones and tablet computers can be stored in the cloud and transferred from one device to another, a robot's data will be transferrable to newer models. How will consumerism frame such an exchange? Likely through a similarly polysemic reading of the stored data. For example, it is possible that the texts, photos, videos, and other content will be read—in the most generous possibility for a robotic ontology—as *both* the robot's memories *and* the consumer's memories; the robot's data *and* the consumer's data. But just as one does not view the data stored on one's mobile phone today as the *phone's* memories, it is likely that consumers will claim ownership to any data stored by their social robot. In addition, the pervasiveness of conversational agents like Siri, Cortana and Alexa has already situated AI within a consumer framework, and that framing may persist even when the conversational agent is housed in a robotic apparatus.

The risk of emotional harm to individuals as they develop relationships with social robots may be dramatically limited by the consumer frame as it guides evolving social norms and influences how consumers interpret the social agency and personification of social robots. If the polysemy revealed in the rhetoric of Jibo and Buddy scales to the rhetorical situation of all social robots, then employing rhetorical strategies to encourage users to playfully embrace a reading of the robot as *subject* might be useful, particularly as it may increase sales and enhance enjoyment of the robot. Additionally, as social robots have the potential to provide enormous benefits to humanity, awareness of the ways in which a multiplicity of meaning has emerged in the rhetoric of Jibo and Buddy might be useful in deepening the impact of social technologies.

Ultimately, consumers will determine the extent to which the form of polysemy described in this chapter continues in the rhetoric of social robots. If consumers demonstrate through their purchasing choices a preference for robots that are more—or less—personified, childlike, or social, this will influence the marketing and social norms that arise as social robots emerge in greater quantity and quality in the marketplace. Perhaps the polysemous reading of Jibo and Buddy is only a temporary representation of our current rhetorical place on the cusp of the "robotic moment" (Turkle, 2011). Or perhaps it is an indication of what will come to be the hallmark of our relationship with social robots; a relationship framed by consumerism, grounded in the technological nature of the robot, and communicated through playful engagement in a multiplicity of meaning.

References

Althusser, L. (1969/1971). *Lenin and philosophy and other essays.* (B. Brewster, Trans.). New York: Monthly Review Press.

Aristotle. (350 B.C./1954). *Rhetoric.* (W. R. Roberts, Trans.). New York: Modern Library.

Aristotle. (350 B.C./1991). *On rhetoric: A theory of civic discourse.* (G. A. Kennedy, Trans.). New York: Oxford University Press.

Asimov, I. (1950). *I, robot.* New York: Gnome Press.

Blue Frog Robotics. (n.d.). About Buddy. Retrieved from http://www.bluefrogrobotics.com/en/buddy/

Blue Frog Robotics. (2015a, July). Buddy: Your family's companion robot. Retrieved from https://www.indiegogo.com/projects/buddy-your-family-s-companion-robot-family-social#/

Blue Frog Robotics. (2015b, November 19). Why robots need to be cute? [Blog post]. Retrieved from http://www.bluefrogrobotics.com/en/why-robots-needs-to-be-cute/

Blue Frog Robotics. (2015c, July 7). *Buddy: Your family's companion robot* [Video file]. Retrieved from https:// youtube /51yGC3iytbY

Blue Frog Robotics. [adoptbuddy]. (2016, January 29). Les 2 BUDDY gratuits refusent de quitter leurs frères ! Il faudra les prendre tous ! :D [Tweet]. Retrieved from https://twitter.com/adoptbuddy/status/693163400432463872

Boone, R., & Buck, T. (2003). Emotional expressivity and trustworthiness: The role of nonverbal behavior in the evolution of cooperation. *Journal of Nonverbal Behavior, 27*(3), 163–182.

Burke, K. (1953). *A rhetoric of motives.* New York: Prentice Hall, Inc.

Ceccarelli, L. (1998). Polysemy: Multiple meanings in rhetorical criticism. *Quarterly Journal of Speech, 84*(4), 395–415.

Cheney, G. (1983). The rhetoric of identification and the study of organizational communication. *Quarterly Journal of Speech, 69*(2), 143–158.

Darling, K. (2017). Who's Johnny? Anthropomorphic framing in human-robot interaction, integration, and policy. In P. Lin, G. Bekey, K. Abney, & R. Jenkins (Eds.), *Robot ethics 2.0.* Advance online publication. doi:10.2139/ssrn.2588669

Garreau, J. (2007, May 6). Bots on the ground. *The Washington Post.* Retrieved from http://www.washingtonpost.com/wpdyn/content/article/2007/05/05/AR2007050501009. html

Goffman, E. (1975). *Frame analysis: An essay on the organization of experience.* Cambridge, MA: Harvard University Press.

Indiegogo (n.a.). How it works for entrepreneurs. Retrieved from https://grow.indiegogo.com/how-it-works/

Jasinski, J. (2001a). The status of theory and method in rhetorical criticism. *Western Journal of Communication, 65*(3), 249–270.

Jasinksi, J. (2001b). *Sourcebook on rhetoric: Key concepts in contemporary rhetorical studies.* Thousand Oaks: Sage Publications.

Jibo, Inc. (n.d.). Meet Jibo. Retrieved from https://www.jibo.com/

Jibo, Inc. (2014a, July) Jibo: The world's first social robot for the home. Retrieved from https://www.indiegogo.com/projects/jibo-the-world-s-first-social-robot-for-the-home#/

Jibo, Inc. (2014b, July 16). *Jibo: The world's first social robot for the home* [Video file]. Retrieved from https://youtube/3N1Q8oFpX1Y?list=LLBcqsJtclf82tUOPpTa21vQ

Jibo, Inc. (2015a, August 5). Jibo and the 12 principles of animation. [Blog post]. Retrieved from https://blog.jibo.com/2015/08/05/jibo-and-the-12-principles-of-animation

Jibo, Inc. [JiboRobot]. (2015b, August 20). more about my voice (still learning!) from my Roberto and Sridhar: https://blog.jibo.com/2015/08/19/choosing-jibos-tts-engine [Tweet]. Retrieved from https://twitter.com/JiboRobot/status/634459815180263424

Jibo, Inc. [JiboRobot]. (2015c, September 2). i am flawed and they tell me that's okay. o) http://t.co/HMS0vVXQNB [Tweet]. Retrieved from https://twitter.com/JiboRobot/status/639187295560601600

Jibo, Inc. (2015d, September 2). Jibo: Perfectly flawed just like all of us. [Blog post]. Retrieved from https://blog.jibo.com/2015/09/02/jibo-perfectly-flawed-just-like-all-of-us

Jibo, Inc. (2015e, December 2). Jibo: His ten tenets. [Blog post]. Retrieved from https://blog.jibo.com/2015/12/02/jibo-his-ten-tenets

Jibo, Inc. [JiboRobot]. (2016, January 29). and i remembered all of my lines! o) [Tweet]. Retrieved from https://twitter.com/JiboRobot/status/693101607400120321

Kim, Y., & Mutlu, B. (2014). How social distance shapes human–robot interaction. *International Journal of Human-Computer Studies, 72*(12), 783–795

Lasseter, J. (Executive producer), & Stanton, A. (Director). (2008). *Wall-E* [Motion picture]. United States: Walt Disney Pictures.

Lee, S., & Choi, J. (2017). Enhancing user experience with conversational agent for movie recommendation: Effects of self-disclosure and reciprocity. *International Journal of Human-Computer Studies, 103*, 95–105.

Lucas, G. (Executive producer & Director), & Kurtz, G. (Producer). (1977). *Star Wars: Episode IV—A new hope* [Motion picture]. United States: Lucasfilm.

Peterson, S. (2012). Designing people to serve. In P. Lin, K. Abney, & G. A. Bekey (Eds.), *Robot ethics: The ethical and social implications of robotics* (pp. 283–298). Cambridge, MA: MIT Press.

Reeves, B. & Nass, C. (1996). *The media equation: How people treat computers, television, and new media like real people and places.* Cambridge: CSLI Publications.

Scheutz, M. (2012). The inherent dangers of unidirectional emotional bonds between humans and social robots. In P. Lin, K. Abney, & G. A. Bekey (Eds.), *Robot ethics: The ethical and social implications of robotics* (pp. 205–222). Cambridge, MA: MIT Press.

Turkle, S. (2011). *Alone together: Why we expect more from technology and less from each other.* New York: Basic Books.

Warrick, P. S. (1980). *The cybernetic imagination in science fiction.* Cambridge, Mass: MIT Press.

4. "I'll Present to the Human": Effects of a Robot Evaluator on Anticipatory Public Speaking Anxiety

Chad Edwards, Brett Stoll, Autumn P. Edwards, Patric R. Spence, and Andrew Gambino

The growing convergence of robotics and artificial intelligence (AI) within numerous fields begs the question not only of machine effectiveness but also of what potential influence such technologies may exert beyond their intended roles. In education, the concept of evaluation robots is rising in popularity. During a time when the scrutiny of education budgets and student assessment scores is at an all-time high, this increased interest in educational robots is not surprising. A movement to even partial automation of teaching has vast implications for consistent content dissemination and overall cost-savings in schools. However, as robots gain ground in education, the use of such technologies has faced criticism regarding practicality and effectiveness.

More research-driven assessments of social robotics in the classroom are needed to assess the actual value these technologies add for students rather than following a pattern of rapid technology adoption without adequate testing. Such adoption tends to exacerbate an already stressed classroom environment and creates additional workload for teachers (Reich-Stiebert & Eyssel, 2016). In our current state of technological advancement, teachers, designers, and researchers have more options than ever for classroom implementation. With social robotics in particular, educators are presented with something more than just a new tool; they are faced with a potential new teaching *partner*. However, while robots in the classroom have had some success, careful ethical consideration must be given to blurring the boundaries between a robot and a teacher (Serholt et al., 2016). The effect of educational robots on student performance, which is ultimately tied to their resulting educational outcomes, has been largely unaddressed in human-machine communication (HMC) and almost entirely absent in instructional communication literature.

The purpose of this chapter is to further instructional HMC by detailing one new study examining the role of robots in public speaking. Specifically, this research highlights a robot's role as evaluator. As educators who have taught and continue to teach numerous sections in public speaking, we frequently witness students struggle with deep-rooted anxiety and apprehension to speak in front of crowds or even small groups. Although we have many methods and techniques for helping students to overcome this apprehension, they are not always effective for every student. Understandably, even the most confident of students sometimes struggle on speech days when we, the instructors, sit at the back of the room taking rigorous notes and monitor stop watches. Given our persistent interest in HMC and robots in education, we asked ourselves if by allowing a robot to take our place as evaluator, we could alleviate some apprehension. We tested public speaking student responses to a basic prime; they were either informed their speeches would be evaluated by a robot or by a human. By then collecting self-report measures of communication apprehension, we gained some valuable insight into how students perceive robot graders.

Phenomena such as these are relevant to the study of HMC, human-computer interaction (HCI) and human-robot interaction (HRI) if researchers and educators are to better understand how to appropriately incorporate social robots in an education environment. This chapter will review the relevant literature regarding pedagogical robots and theoretical assumptions of anticipated interaction. We present the results of an experiment designed to determine whether pre-performance public speaking anxiety among undergraduate students differed as a function of anticipating speech evaluation by a robot versus a human. Results will be discussed regarding future possibilities of HMC in and out of the classroom.

Robotics in Education

A variety of pedagogical technologies have emerged to improve learning processes and outcomes by having students interact with a computer system rather than a human instructor. Non-intelligence web-based systems are used extensively for this purpose. For example, with Interviewstream,[1] students interact with an avatar conducting an interview. However, the evaluation of the interview is still completed by a human. A step closer to robot evaluation are tools such as the Instant Question-Answering (iQA) system that allows learners to ask questions and get various levels of immediate feedback (Wang,

2013). Recently, there has been a growing trend in using robotics and AI in the classroom (Markoff, 2013; Edwards, A., Edwards, C., Spence, Harris, & Gambino, 2016a). The use of robotics offers potential advantages to both professors and students; saving valuable resources and providing a novel and potentially more beneficial experience for the students (Lue, 2013; Markoff, 2013). As early as 2006, You, Sehn, Chang, Liu and Chen found that students appreciate the presence of robots in the classroom and that the robot was initially highly effective in increasing student engagement, despite eventually succumbing to the effects of diminished novelty. Robotic interaction has been shown to be a valuable pedagogical tool in areas such as math and science (Cooper, Keating, Harwin, & Dautenhahn, 1999) as well as foreign language instruction (Chang, Lee, Chao, Wang, & Chen, 2010).

It is worth noting that the above studies, as well as many others in the field of human-robot interaction, were conducted across several countries (e.g., Japan, Germany, China). Japan in particular has historically been at the forefront of robotics research, design, and adoption. This raises an important consideration of how different cultural experiences with robots, whether in the classroom or elsewhere, may influence perceptions of pedagogical robots. The findings from You and colleagues (2006), for example, may not replicate in the United States, even following a decade of advanced robotics development in the U.S. This study demonstrates the importance of conducting research across various cultures to verify what robotic classroom applications are, or are not, effective cross-culturally.

Perceptions aside, robots have demonstrated objective accuracy and consistency in educational roles. Prior research has suggested that essay scores generated by machine and human raters are comparable (Bridgeman, Trapani, & Attali, 2012). This finding of similar scores demonstrates substantial room for incorporating pedagogical robots from both a student engagement and practicality perspective. Although the practical implementation of robotics had lost some of the mass enthusiasm marked by the earlier parts of the last decade, the recent development of evaluation robots reignites the potential for creative application of robotics in pedagogy. Robots have even been found to enhance the learning and development of less able communicators. For example, Robins, Dautenhahn, and Dickerson (2009) found that when a minimally expressive humanoid robot aided children with autism, the robot not only encouraged communication with itself but also with other accompanying humans. Robot companions have been utilized for children with other cognitive disabilities to develop stronger social skills (Lehmann, Iacono, Robins, Marti, & Dautenhahn, 2011). Findings such as these suggest that robots can be an aid in developing communication skills with people who perhaps are apprehensive toward speaking with humans. These outcomes offer intriguing potential for robots in enhancing the teacher's role to foster greater learning experiences for students. Aside from grading as well as a human instructor, there are perhaps other areas in which the use of robotics in evaluation can boost student confidence, and thus performance (Lue, 2013; Markoff, 2013). In the next section, we will discuss one communication variable that causes problems for many students that social robotics might aid both teachers and students.

Communication Apprehension

Public speaking is one such area where decreased performance has been linked to performance anxiety and an overall lack of confidence (MacIntyre & Thivierge, 1995a). According to MacIntyre and Thivierge (1995a), public speaking anxiety is the "fear and uneasiness caused by the potentially threatening situation of speaking before a group of individuals" (p. 457). Anxiety may manifest through a host of pre-performance concerns (Edwards, C., Edwards, A., Myers, & Wahl, 2003) such as fear of evaluation and criticism; worry about mistakes and failure, and discomfort with being the focus of attention (Proctor, Douglas, Garera-Izquierdo, & Wartman, 1994). Wardrope (1996) found that students with communication apprehension were less motivated, less interested, and less excited about enrolling in a basic public speaking course than students who exhibited less communication apprehension. Finding creative ways to reduce this communication apprehension is important because communication skills are consistently identified by employers as the most sought after in job candidates (Eisner, 2010; Kyllonen, 2013; Robles, 2012). A robot evaluator may be able to lower the threat potential of the traditional public speaking situation in ways that facilitate more confident and comfortable public speaking practice and performance. Speakers being evaluated by a robot could experience less fear of embarrassment and fewer social desirability concerns regarding evaluation and criticism. Machine partners might be useful in helping to build this skill set for students in the college classroom.

Indeed, a key factor influencing students' public speaking apprehension is their perceptions of the audience. For instance, speaker anxiety can be affected by audience familiarity (MacIntyre & Thivierge, 1995a; Proctor, et al., 1994), size (Neer, Hudson & Warren, 1982), and pleasantness (MacIntyre & Thivierge, 1995a), as well as the fear of negative audience opinion (MacIntyre & Thivierge, 1995b). The advent of machine actors raises questions on both sides of the equation for public speaking students. With research that shows pre-performance concerns, such as environment and audience, influence speaker performance, a question to continually ask is how new technology may contribute to student anxiety and performance. For example, can the replacement of a human speech evaluator by a robot reduce student public speaking apprehension? Alternatively, would the introduction of a robot evaluator increase apprehension?

Anticipating Human-Computer Interaction

The Computers are Social Actors (CASA) paradigm suggests that humans will apply social norms during interactions with computers, despite overtly acknowledging that computers are neither human nor should be treated as such (Nass, Steuer & Tauber, 1994). For example, a person interacting with a computer may show it politeness (Nass, Moon, & Carney, 1999) or exhibit gratitude (Fogg & Nass, 1997). Although the foundation of this theory originally accounted only for computers in their most traditional form, lacking speech and other more sophisticated social cuing, there remain relevant implications for this theory in HMC. If social interactions can be elicited from minimalistic actors such as computers, it stands to reason that social interactions can be created from more socially sophisticated, non-human partners, like robots. However, unlike the CASA paradigm, this chapter examines perceptions of students in the anticipation (pre-communication) phase of interaction, which requires a different theoretical perspective. When examining anticipated communication concerns, an individual merely visualizes an expectation for future interaction. These visualizations tend to result in self-fulfilling prophecies, in which actual poor performance follows anticipated poor performance (MacIntyre & Thivierge, 1995b). For example, if a student consistently visualizes herself stumbling over the technical language of her speech, it is likely she will stumble over these words when delivering the speech. The same is typically true for the student who envisions giving a flawless, rousing speech; his resulting performance is much better.

Results from preliminary studies of anticipated HMC indicated that people anticipated greater uncertainty, less social attractiveness, and diminished social presence in interactions with robots compared to other humans (Spence, Westerman, Edwards, C., & Edwards, A., 2014; Edwards, C., Edwards, A., Spence, & Westerman, 2016). Cognitive script theory (Schank & Abelson, 1977) asserts that an individual's perceptions, understanding, and overall communication are guided by previous experiences and knowledge stored as scripts. Scripts tell us how we should behave in each context. One or more particular scripts are primed by context cues in anticipation of impending interactions (Schleuder, White, & Cameron, 1993), which in turn activates a set of new expectations that uniquely accompany each script (Scheufele, 2000). The results of Spence's et al. (2014) and Edwards' et al. (2016b) experiments suggest that people have a *human-to-human interaction script* or tend to expect that their interactions with another will involve another *human*. A violation of the expectation to interact with another human by introduction of a robot partner lead to increases in anticipated uncertainty and decreases in anticipated liking. Robots are, to varying degrees, obviously more dissimilar to humans than the "real deal," the perception of which is a significant indicator of social closeness (Heider, 1958; Miller, Downs, & Prentice, 1998; Tesser, 1988). Based on these findings, we proposed the following hypothesis as an extension of the human-to-human interaction script theory (Spence et al., 2014; Edwards, et al., 2016b).

H: In anticipation of public speaking, participants paired with a robot evalua-tor will have higher personal ratings of public speaking anxiety than those paired with a human evaluator.

Testing Public Speaking Anxiety With a Robot Evaluator

To test the idea that people will be nervous to present to a robot evaluator, we conducted an experiment composed of 141 undergraduate students enrolled in introductory communication courses at a large Midwestern university. Participants were predominantly female (77.3%, *n* = 109) and Caucasian (72.3%, *n* = 102), whose ages ranged from 18 to 49 years, with a mean of 20.41 (*SD* = 3.36) and a median of 20 years. The distribution of class year (first-year, sophomore, junior, senior) was relatively even. Participants received class extra credit for taking part in the study. Participants who chose not to participate in the research study were provided alternative options for obtaining extra credit.

The Experimental Design

The condition variable manipulated in this study was that of the speech eval-uator. Participants were assigned to present to either a human speech evalua-tor or a robot speech evaluator. The dependent variable was public speaking anxiety as determined through a self-report measure. Lastly, a measure of the participants' attitudes toward robots was assessed to determine how this con-struct functioned as a covariate with the dependent variable.

Measuring Negative Attitudes Towards Robots

Participants first completed the Negative Attitude Toward Robots Scale (Nomura, Suzuki, Kanda, & Kato, 2006). The Negative Attitude Toward Robots Scale (NARS) is a 14-item measure designed to assess a subject's anxiety toward robots. The scale is answered via a 5-point Likert-type scale with scores from (1) (strongly disagree) to (5) (strongly agree). The measure consists of three sub-scales which measure negative attitudes toward situations and interactions with robots (six items) (e.g., "I would feel uneasy if I was given a job where I had to use robots"), negative attitudes toward social influence of robots (five items) (e.g., "Something bad might happen if robots developed into living beings"), and negative attitudes toward emotions in interactions with robots (three items) (e.g., "If robots had emotions, I would be able to make friends with them"). Scores are calculated by adding the total of all items, some of which are reverse-scored. Previous research has reported reliability coefficients of .73, .73, and .65 respectively for the three sub-scales (Nomura, Kanda, Suzuki, & Kato, 2008). A coefficient alpha of .83 regarding all scales collectively was obtained for this study (Item $M = 3.14$, Item $SD = 1.79$).

Measuring Public Speaking Anxiety

The Personal Report of Public Speaking Anxiety (PRPSA) developed by McCroskey (1970) is a 34-item scale that asks a respondent to report how one feels about public speaking. In this study, responses were reported on a 5-point Likert-type scale, with a 1 equating to "strongly disagree" and a 5 to "strongly agree." Scores are obtained by totaling all items, some of which are reverse-scored. Previously, this measure has generated reliability estimates above .90 (McCroskey, 1970). In this study, a coefficient alpha of .96 was obtained (Item $M = 3.32$, Item $SD = .68$).

Procedures of the Experiment

After recruitment, informed consent was obtained prior to the beginning of the study. Participants were informed that they would be participating in a study to assess their ability to deliver an impromptu speech. Following collection of informed consent, participants were asked to respond to the Negative Attitudes toward Robots questionnaire. Next, they were randomly assigned to one of two groups (Human Evaluator Condition, Robot Evaluator Condition) and directed to one of two classrooms accordingly. There, a researcher informed participants in both conditions that they would be required to prepare and deliver an impromptu speech on a topic to be announced. Participants were told that they would be given 15 minutes to craft their speeches and, upon expiration of the time, would be escorted by a research assistant to a room to deliver their speech. Multiple graduate research assistants were formally stationed in the classrooms to add to the overall believability. Participants in the Human Evaluator Condition were told that their audience member was a public speaking instructor who would be formally evaluating their speeches. Participants in the Robot Evaluator Condition were told that their audience member and evaluator was a social robot programmed to evaluate public speaking. The description of the robot evaluator was intentionally vague (e.g., no image or further description of the robot was provided) so as not to prime specific robot characteristics in the minds of participants. With exception to this evaluator condition manipulation, all procedures and stimulus material were identical. Following these instructions, participants completed a questionnaire that included the PRPSA scale described above and a brief demographic section including gender, age, ethnicity, and class rank. Participants were debriefed and thanked for their participation in the study.

Analyses

To evaluate the relationship between PRPSA and the independent variable, a one-way analysis of covariance (ANCOVA) was conducted. Table 4.1 exhibits the relevant means and standard deviations. The independent variable, speech evaluator, included two conditions, one consisting of the human evaluator and the other comprised of the robot evaluator. The dependent variable was the level of personally reported public speaking anxiety of each participant, and the covariate was the level of negative attitude toward robots before being assigned an evaluator. Negative attitude toward robots was selected as a covariate as a result of its significant correlation with the dependent variable, $r (138) = .24$, $p < .01$. Analysis evaluating the homogeneity-of-slopes

Table 4.1. Means and Standard Deviations.

Variables	Human Condition		Robot Condition	
	M	(SD)	M	(SD)
PRPSA	109.25*	24.20	116.42*	20.70

*Covariates appearing in the model are evaluated at the following values: Negative attitude toward robots = 43.95.

Source: Authors.

assumption indicated that the relationship between the covariate and the dependent variable did not differ significantly as a function of the independent variable, $F(1, 137) = .66$, $MSE = 475.90$, $p = .42$, partial $\eta^2 = .005$. Levene's test for equality of variance was not significant, $F = 2.54$, $p = .11$, indicating that the assumption of homogeneity of variance across groups was tenable.

The ANCOVA was significant, $F(2, 138) = 6.91$, $MSE = 474.71$, $p = .001$, $\eta^2 = .09$. The effect size was sizable, with change in the evaluator condition accounting for approximately 9% of the variance of the dependent variable, while holding constant the level of negative attitude toward robots at 43.95. The results suggest support for the hypothesis: Participants anticipating interaction with a robot reported higher levels of public speaking anxiety. Following the ANCOVA, a correlation test was performed to examine the relationship between negative attitudes toward robots and levels of public speaking anxiety for participants in the robot evaluator condition. Results indicated a significant positive correlation between the covariate and dependent variable, $r = .32$, $p < .01$.

Discussion

To what extent can robots improve student performance? The results allude to current limitations regarding robot effectiveness. The data suggest that robot evaluators significantly increase student public speaking anxiety in the classroom. Prior research findings of the human-to-human interaction script theory that demonstrate decreased perceptions of certainty, likeability, and social presence when individuals anticipate interactions with robots (Spence et al., 2014; Edwards et al., 2016b) are broadly replicated in this experiment. Additionally, this outcome might apply to other initial interactions of human-machine communication. It might not be the presence of a robot from an initial interaction perspective, but rather the thought of communicating and being evaluating by something other than human. Because participants were not shown a picture of the robot and were instead left to their imaginations, we do not know what participants were envisioning when thinking about giving a speech to a robot. Although this limited description was intentional to limit possible characteristic priming, it would have been valuable to have some understanding of how participants envisioned their specific robot evaluator. Future studies should further examine this area to see if design implications (e.g., cute and friendly robot) might make a difference for public speaking anxiety scores. When asked to reflect on robots, people may have a tendency to conjure intimidating mental models, but without data on these individual models, it is difficult to pinpoint possible apprehension triggers.

The study also extends the documented anthropocentric communication bias from conversations to the public speaking context (Edwards et al., 2016b). It is likely a result of cognitive scripts that are not triggered when anticipating communication due to a lack of prior experience speaking in front of a robot or the novelty of the situation. The cognitive scripts that support the CASA paradigm only come into effect once the interaction has begun, and the computer has enacted some level of human-like characteristics. Humans initially have no intention of treating a computer or robot as if it were human (Nass et al., 1994).

Because speech anxiety is associated with actual speech performance, these findings are of real-world significance and should encourage educators to evaluate the appropriate role of robotics in the classroom critically. Rather than force a convergence of technology in the classroom, potentially to the detriment of students, it may be better to allow for a gradual convergence and exposure informed by further research demonstrating where and to what extent robotics and other forms of instructional technology add value to the learning experience. Although there are likely many financial benefits to incorporating technology to administer and manage educational assessments, a student-centered approach focused on value-added resources should ultimately supersede the cost-centered approach of teaching for cheap or using the latest technology.

Unique to this study, the results demonstrated a significant positive correlation between participants' negative attitudes toward robots and their public speaking anxiety such that the more negatively individuals perceived robots, the greater their anxiety about performing in front of one. As robots evolve in form and function, a shift in perceptions may occur, negating some of these fears and negative attitudes. As discussed earlier, this increased fear of public speaking in front of the robot may be attributed to elevated levels of uncertainty and a lack of scripts regarding the robot. Over time, increased interaction with robots in the classroom as well as in other contexts provides more experiences from which to build scripts. More available scripts may serve to reduce uncertainty and increase predictability of behavior during the interaction. More prolific, sophisticated robotics may lead to increased levels of human-like expectations, but currently, the data broadly suggest a lower sense of expectations and anticipated satisfaction with HMC, HCI, or HRI.

Limitations and Future Directions

Although the present study provides helpful insight into how students anticipate HMC when primed in a public speaking context, a portion of valuable data is still missing. Participants were never given the opportunity to actually present their speeches. We relied on previous research that directly links positive or negative pre-speech concerns with the assumed outcome that higher anxiety is indicative of lower performance. However, this may not be the case with HMC. Although apprehension was high in the anticipation phase, meeting face-to-face with the robot may have actually alleviated some of the apprehension due to some positive restructuring of their perceptions and expectations of the robot.

Future research should seek to replicate this study with the addition of the actual speech performance and evaluation. Doing so will allow research to draw additional empirical connections between anticipation and realized outcomes. A natural next step is to look at how the degree of anthropomorphism might influence the expectations and anxiety of the speaker. In other words, does speaker anxiety decrease as the human-like characteristics of the robot increase? What role does Mori's "Uncanny Valley" (1970) play in the classroom, and is it possible to identify at what anthropomorphic degree is most effective without becoming too disconcerting? Mori's "Uncanny Valley" maintains that as robots take on more human characteristics, there is a level at which people find the robot creepy and eerie. Incorporating multiple robot conditions enacting varying degrees of social cues and features may identify significant shifts in expectations along with a range of anthropomorphism. Research on the design of both the physical robot and the message features will aid to reduce the adverse effects of being the "uncanny valley." This research would also serve to extend the work of Baylor and Kim (2004) and Behrend and Thompson (2011), by addressing to what degree behavior and personality similarity between robot and human, rather than appearance alone, affect perceptions of liking and performance outcomes.

Conclusion

The current chapter serves to further our understanding of how individuals anticipate interactions with robots and potentially other machine agents. Specifically, the study highlights a current limitation of robotics in providing a better and less stressful learning experience for students. Not only does the idea of having a robot evaluate one's speech lack the ability to enhance a speaker's confidence, but it also has potentially detrimental effects on student performance outcomes. Educators and scholars of communication pedagogy should heed this research as a jumping off point for better understanding how students perceive the role of robot evaluators and their corresponding costs and benefits. As social robotics expands to contexts such as the classroom, it is important to understand better the role that pedagogical HMC might have in the classroom. How might the perceptions of robots in teaching roles change as the idea becomes more commonplace? What are the educational differences and implications for the human-to-human interaction script as students are evaluated by teachers, robots, and AI, or even a hybrid teaching team of both humans and machines?

These findings are not restricted simply to education either. Knowing that the mere anticipation of human-machine communication can elicit feelings of anxiety has far reaching implications as researchers and designers consider the best means of introducing these tools in context. This speaks to a larger cultural perception of social machines—perceptions driven by a vast array of influences such as media portrayals, decades of pop-culture representations, limited direct exposure, and conflicting views of automation. This anxiety is likely pervasive throughout society, or at least within the United States. How do we address this anxiety? What are the gateway contexts through which social robots can achieve early adoption and begin to shift people toward a more welcoming position? These questions are relevant as HMC becomes more commonplace, diminishing the novelty of machine presence and significantly changing the perceptions of their roles. We wish to encourage more research programs to tackle these difficult questions by studying social robots in context. Places to start include the areas where research has already begun such as education and within the home, but it is important for both researchers and designers to extend what we already know about HMC into new and unfamiliar contexts.

Note

1. www.interviewstream.com

References

Baylor, A. L, & Kim, Y. (2004). Pedagogical agent design: The impact of agent realism, gender, ethnicity, and instructional role. In J. Lester, R. Vicari & F. Paraguaçu (Eds.), *Intelligent Tutoring Systems* (Vol. 3220, pp. 592–603). Berlin: Springer.

Behrend, T. S., & Thompson, L. F. (2011). Trainer-trainee similarity effects in web-based training. *Computers in Human Behavior*, 27(3), 1201–1207.

Bridgeman, B., Trapani, C., & Attali, Y. (2012). Comparisons of human and machine scoring of essays: Differences by gender, ethnicity, and country. *Applied Measurement in Education*, 25(1), 27–40. doi:10.1080/08957347.2012.635502

Chang, C. W., Lee, J. H., Chao, P. Y., Wang, C. Y., & Chen, G. D. (2010). Exploring the possibility of using humanoid robots as instructional tools for teaching a second language in primary school. *Educational Technology & Society*, 13(2), 13–24.

Cooper, M., Keating, D., Harwin, W., & Dautenhahn, K. (1999). Robots in the classroom: Tools for accessible education. In Buhler, C. & Knops, H. (Eds.), *Assistive Technology on the Threshold of the New Millennium* (pp. 448–452). Amsterdam: IOS Press.

Edwards, A., Edwards, C., Spence, P. R., Harris, C., & Gambino, A. (2016a). Robots in the classroom: Differences in students' perceptions of credibility and learning between "teacher as robot" and "robot as teacher". *Computers in Human Behavior, 65,* 627–634. doi:10.1016/j.chb.2016.06.005

Edwards, C., Edwards, A., Spence, P. R., & Westerman, D. (2016b). Initial interaction expectations with robots: Testing the human-to-human interaction script. *Communication Studies, 67*(2), 227–238. doi: 10.1080/10510974.2015.1121899

Edwards. C., Edwards, A. H., Myers, S. A., & Wahl, S. T. (2003). The relationship between student pre-performance concerns and evaluation apprehension. *Communication Research Reports, 20*(1), 54–61. doi:10.1080/08824090309388799

Eisner, S. (2010). Grave new world? Workplace skills for today's college graduates. *American Journal of Business Education, 3*(9), 27–50.

Fogg, B. J. & Nass, C. (1997). Do users reciprocate to computers? *Proceedings of the CHI Conference,* Atlanta, GA.

Heider, F. (1958). *The psychology of interpersonal relations.* New York: Wiley.

Kyllonen, P. C. (2013, November 20). Soft skills for the workplace. *Change: The Magazine of Higher Learning, 45*(6), 16–23. doi:10.1080/00091383.2013.841516

Lehmann, H., Iacono, I., Robins, B., Marti, P., & Dautenhahn, K. (2011). 'Make it move': Playing cause and effects games with a robot companion for children with cognitive disabilities. *Proceeding ECCE '11: Proceedings of the 29th Annual European Conference on Cognitive Ergonomics,* 105–112. New York, NY. doi:10.1145/2074712.2074734

Lue, R. (2013, April 10). edX's expansion—and issues. *Harvard Magazine.* Retrieved from: http://harvardmagazine.com

MacIntyre, P. D., & Thivierge, K. A. (1995a). The effects of audience pleasantness, audience familiarity, and speaking contexts on public speaking anxiety and willingness to speak. *Communication Quarterly, 43*(4), 456–466. doi:10.1080/01463379509369992

MacIntyre, P. D., & Thivierge, K. A. (1995b). The effects of speaker personality on anticipated reactions to public speaking. *Communication Research Reports, 12*(2), 125–133. doi:10.1080/08824099509362048

Markoff, J. (2013, April 4). Essay grading software offers professors a break. *The New York Times.* Retrieved from: https://www.nytimes.com/2013/04/05/science/new-test-for-computers-grading-essays-at-college-level.html

McCroskey, J. C. (1970). Measures of communication-bound anxiety. *Speech Monographs, 37*(4), 269–277. doi:10.1080/03637757009375677

Miller, D. T., Downs, J. S., & Prentice, D. A. (1998). Minimal conditions for the creation of a unit relationship: The social bond between birthmates. *European Journal of Social Psychology, 28,* 475–481.

Mori, M. (1970). The uncanny valley. *Energy, 7*(4), 33–35.

Nass, C., Moon, Y., & Carney, P. (1999). Are respondents polite to computers? Social desirability and direct responses to computers. *Journal of Applied Social Psychology*, 29(5), 1093–1110. doi:10.1111/j.1559-1816.1999.tb00142.x

Nass, C., Steuer, J., & Tauber, E. R. (1994). Computers are social actors. *Proceedings of the CHI Conference*, 72–77. Boston, MA.

Neer, M. R., Hudson, D. E., & Warren, C. (1982, November). Instructional methods for managing speech anxiety in the classroom. *Proceedings of the annual meeting of the Speech Communication Association*, Louisville, KY.

Nomura, T., Suzuki, T., Kanda, T., & Kato, K. (2006). Measurement of negative attitudes toward robots. *Interaction Studies*, 7(3), 437–454. doi:10.1075/is.7.3.14nom

Nomura, T., Kanda, T., Suzuki, T., & Kato, K. (2008). Prediction of human behavior in human--robot interaction using psychological scales for anxiety and negative attitudes toward robots. *IEEE Transactions on Robotics*, 24(2), 442–451.

Proctor, R. F., Douglas, A. T., Garera-Izquierdo, T., & Wartman, S. L. (1994). Approach, avoidance, and apprehension: Talking with high-CA students about getting help. *Communication Education*, 43(4), 312–321. doi:10.1080/03634529409378989

Reich-Stiebert, N., & Eyssel, F. (2016). Robots in the classroom: What teachers think about teaching and learning with education robots. In *International Conference on Social Robotics* (pp. 671–680). Springer International Publishing. doi: 10.1007/978-3-319-47437-3_66

Robins, B. Dautenhahn, K. & Dickerson, P. (2009). From isolation to communication: A case study evaluation of robot assisted play for children with autism with a minimally expressive humanoid robot. *Proceedings from ACHI 2009, Second International Conference on Advances in Human-Computer Interactions*. Cancun, Mexico. 205–211. doi:10.1109/ACHI.2009.32

Robles, M. M. (2012). Executive perceptions of the top 10 soft skills needed in today's workplace. *Business and Professional Communication Quarterly*, 75(4), 453–465. doi:10.1177/1080569912460400

Schank, R. & Abelson, R. (1977). *Scripts, plans, goals, and understanding: An inquiry into human knowledge structure*. Hillsdale, NJ: Lawrence Erlbaum Associates.

Scheufele, D. A. (2000). Agenda-setting, priming, and framing revisited: Another look at cognitive effects of political communication. *Mass Communication & Society*, 3(2/3), 297–316. https://doi.org/10.1207/S15327825MCS0323_07

Schleuder, J. D., White, A. V., & Cameron, G. T. (1993). Priming effects of television news bumpers and teasers on attention and memory. *Journal of Broadcasting & Electronic Media*, 37(4), 437–452.

Serholt, S., Barendregt, W., Vasalou, A., Alves-Oliveira, P., Jones, A., Petisca, S., & Paiva, A. (2016). The case of classroom robots: Teachers' deliberations on the ethical tensions. *AI & SOCIETY*, 32(4),1–19. doi: 10.1007/s00146-016-0667-2

Spence, P. R., Westerman, D., Edwards, C., & Edwards, A. (2014). Welcoming our robot overlords: Initial expectations about interaction with a robot. *Communication Research Reports*, 31(3), 272–280. doi: 10.1080/08824096.2014.924337

Tesser, A. (1988). Toward a self-evaluation maintenance model of social behavior. *Advances in Experimental Social Psychology, 21,* 181–227.

Wardrope, W. J. (1996, November). Student attributions of pre-course expectations: What are they thinking when they take our courses? *Proceedings from the annual meeting of the Speech Communication Association,* San Diego, CA.

Wang, T. (2013). Web-based answering robot: Designing the instant questioning-answering system for education. *British Journal of Educational Technology, 44*(5), E143–E148. doi: 10.1111/bjet.12012

You, Z. J., Shen, C. Y., Chang, C. W., Liu, B. J., & Chen, G. D. (2006). A robot as a teaching assistant in an English class. *Proceedings from Advanced Learning Technologies, 2006. Sixth International Conference.* Kerkrade, The Netherlands. 87–91. doi:10.1109/ICALT.2006.1652373

5. Presence Past and Future: Reflections on 25 Years of Presence Technology, Scholarship, and Community

Matthew Lombard

Since conducting research (including my dissertation) at Stanford University in the early 1990s, through 25 years as a professor, and since 2002 as president of the International Society for Presence Research (ISPR; ispr.info), I've been fascinated by the concept and phenomena of telepresence, usually referred to simply as presence. Although it has been defined in (too) many ways, ISPR (2000) defines presence as

> a psychological state or subjective perception in which even though part or all of an individual's current experience is generated by and/or filtered through human-made technology, part or all of the individual's perception fails to accurately acknowledge the role of the technology in the experience.

Basically, even though we know we're using a technology, at some level we ignore that and just experience the people, places and events the technologies provide.

Presence experiences are very common. When we become emotionally involved in the lives of fictional characters in (even cliché filled) novels, television programs and movies; when we spend hours navigating environments, accomplishing tasks and competing against computer-generated avatars of other people or fictional characters in videogames and virtual worlds; when we enter the Haunted Mansion or Pirates of the Caribbean at Disneyland or the Wizarding World of Harry Potter at Universal Studios and feel immersed in a fictional world; when we enjoy paintings, graphic designs and optical illusions on flat surfaces that somehow seem to have depth; when we use virtual or augmented reality and feel like we're looking around and moving within another place or that virtual objects have become part of the place we're in;

when we talk to friends and family on the phone or via Skype or FaceTime and feel like we're together, or to Siri, Alexa and other virtual assistants and feel like they're independent social beings; when we treat our cars, computers, clocks, toys, robots, vacuum cleaners and all kinds of other technologies as if they have personalities of their own; when we have any of these and many other experiences, we've experienced presence.

Although it's often associated with the sense of "being there" offered by virtual reality, presence takes all of these forms. And although presence experiences aren't inherently positive or negative, many or most are entertaining, useful or both—there is something intensely satisfying about using technologies (defined broadly) that provide the illusion of being more than they are, that fade into the background as they take you somewhere else, to be alone or with others, or as they become your partner or friend. On the other hand, even if we may have to be willing to "suspend disbelief" to experience presence, it is a form of illusion, and that raises the prospect of unethical and even dystopian deceptions.

We live in an exciting era in human history, when technology and so much else seems to change so fast we barely have time to adjust before the next change arrives. At least in part as a result of this tumult, we often become so enmeshed in the present we rarely take the broader perspective. In this chapter, I reflect on how presence-evoking technologies, research and theory about presence, and the professional and especially the academic communities interested in presence, have evolved over the last quarter century. Aside from the general value of perspective about how far we've come, this reflection is intended to help us look ahead and, rather than passively accept the future of presence, shape it for our own and the greater good.

Technology

It's easy to forget that through the vast majority of the time humans have existed, media technologies were limited to drawing pictures and telling stories. Even considering just the five and a half centuries since the invention of the printing press, most of the mediated experiences we have today have only become widely available very recently. For example, twenty-five years ago, in 1992, as I completed my doctoral studies, we read only printed copies of newspapers, magazines and books; we listened to radios that only received local AM and FM broadcasts; we watched television sets that were bulky CRT boxes that displayed small-to-medium square images usually with monaural sound; we recorded TV shows on Beta and VHS VCRs; 70 mm (2D) celluloid films were state-of-the-art except for IMAX theaters at museums (which presented only documentaries); most people used corded landline telephones; computers sat on or under desks and had floppy drives; the first version of Windows had just replaced DOS; the World Wide Web had just become available to the public and the graphical internet as well as videogames, massively multiplayer online role-playing games (MMORPGs) and interactive toys were rudimentary versions of their current incarnations. Smartphones and laptop and tablet computers with multi-touch screens, streaming video, Skype and FaceTime, virtual and augmented reality, virtual worlds, social media, AI-based digital assistants like Siri and Amazon Echo, robots and androids, and Alternate Reality Games (ARGs) existed mostly in labs, if at all. And in addition to all the advancements and innovations in the forms of media, in just two and a half decades came more diverse and, especially in the case of television, more sophisticated stories and characters.

Today all of these media technologies and the experiences they provide us continue to evolve (along with the industries that produce them). But that evolution is part of the much larger evolution from cave paintings and smoke signals through the printing press and today's (and tomorrow's) media, and it represents not just a continuing improvement in terms of convenience, efficiency, potential value or affordability. Mediated experiences are evolving to become increasingly natural, intuitive, comfortable, easy, automatic, vivid and realistic because, for the user, technology seems increasingly less like technology—in other words, media technologies are increasingly capable of evoking a sense of presence. The types of changes that drive this evolution can be seen in the changes since just 1992: increased resolution/detail and speed; more immersiveness, interactivity and control; more natural inputs and outputs, such as haptics and voice; less obtrusive boxes, dials, and wires; more personalization; more sophisticated and subtle special effects; more mixing of the "real" and the "virtual"; and less reliance on media conventions for storytelling. Although we live in the present and quickly come to take these and related changes for granted, together they have substantially altered our mediated experiences of the world, providing us more and richer presence experiences in a wider variety of contexts than ever before.

As managing editor of the ISPR Presence News (n/d) and its predecessor, the Presence-L electronic list (n/d), I've had the opportunity to observe and publicize the increasing diversity of presence-evoking technologies and their applications in nearly every aspect of modern life, from the arts and entertainment to health and medicine to education and training and much more. The remarkable evolution of the technologies and how they're used represents a fascinating and important topic for study.

Scholarship

Along with our media technologies, the study of presence has evolved a great deal in the last 25 years. Although the identification and study of presence arguably began with Marvin Minsky's (1980) *Omni* magazine article "Telepresence" or Short, Williams, and Christie's (1976) book *The Social Psychology of Telecommunications,* or Alan Turing's (1950) article "Computing machinery and intelligence," Horton & Wohl's (1956) article on parasocial interaction, or Sutherland's (1965) "The Ultimate Display," among others, a milestone in presence scholarship occurred in 1992 when MIT Press launched the journal *Presence: Teleoperators and Virtual Environments. Presence* remains a valuable quarterly hard-copy publication "devoted to research into teleoperation and virtual environments (3D virtual reality worlds)" with a focus on fundamental research and particular appeal to computer scientists, psychologists and mechanical and electrical engineers.

In June 1998, about 50 people gathered at BT Labs in Ipswich, England (about 60 miles northeast of London) for "a workshop on Presence in Shared Virtual Environments." That event was followed by more-or-less annual Presence conferences and led in 2002 to the founding of the International Society for Presence Research (ISPR), which organizes the conferences and provides various resources to the presence community.

Beginning in 2002, a major stimulus for presence research took place when the European Community launched a series of multi-year, multi-million Euro funding initiatives explicitly focused on developing basic and applied knowledge about presence in its Information Society Technologies (IST) program on Future and Emerging Technologies (FET).

During the years since 1992, in addition to the work reported in presence conferences and journals, presence scholarship has become increasingly represented in diverse generalist conferences including those in Communication (e.g., the International Communication Association [ICA] and National Communication Association [NCA]), Psychology (American Psychological Association [APA]) and Computer Science (ACM Conference on Human Factors in Computing Systems [CHI]).

As all this suggests, the biggest change in presence scholarship since 1992 is the amount of scholarship produced. Literature searches using generalist databases WorldCat and Google Scholar and field-specific databases for Psychology, Communication, and Computer Science, both using the specific term "telepresence" and a set of 16 terms related to presence, all reveal that the vast majority of journal articles, books and dissertations related to presence have been published in the last quarter-century (see Figures 5.1 and 5.2).

Figure 5.1. Number of Search Results for "Telepresence" in Scholarly Databases by Year (as of June 2017).

Source: Credit and appreciation to SongYi Lee, Kun Xu and Hocheol Yang.

Note: The number of search results for the two generalist databases (WorldCat and Google Scholar) are represented using the scale at the left of the figure; the number of search results for the three field-specific databases are represented using the scale at the right of the figure..

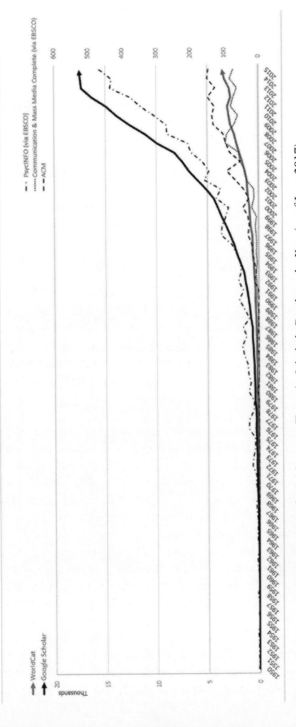

Figure 5.2. Number of Search Results for 16 Presence Terms in Scholarly Databases by Year (as of June 2017).

Source: Credit and appreciation to SongYi Lee, Kun Xu and Hocheol Yang.

Note: The number of search results for the two generalist databases (WorldCat and Google Scholar) are represented using the scale at the left of the figure; the number of search results for the three field-specific databases are represented using the scale at the right of the figure.

In 2001, IJsselsteijn, Lombard, and Freeman identified a "core literature" in presence, with 78 of 94 works (83%) coming between 1992 and 2001. Just a few of the key contributions to the presence literature during that period and beyond are Steuer's (1992) explication; Reeves and Nass' (1996) book *The Media Equation: How People Treat Computers, Television, and New Media Like Real People and Places*; Lombard and Ditton's (1997) literature review and unifying explication; Biocca's (1997) consideration of presence and embodiment; Biocca, Harms, and Burgoon's (2003) explication of social presence; Bracken and Skalski's (2010) book about presence and popular media, and the contributions to measurement and theory cited below.

Many of the other ways the scholarship has changed can be seen in the focus of the Presence conferences. The early ones were neatly organized, with a first segment lasting as long as a day considering what exactly presence is; another long segment focused on how to measure it; a third on theorizing about its causes, nature and consequences; and a fourth describing and demonstrating hardware and software applications of presence. A major step toward explicating the concept took place in 2000 as a result of a wide-ranging discussion among scholars on the Presence-L e-list, resulting in what is now the ISPR definition cited above (International Society for Presence Research, 2000). And several standardized questionnaire instruments to measure presence, e.g., the PQ (Witmer, Jerome, & Singer, 2005), ITC-SOPI (Lessiter, Freeman, Keogh, & Davidoff, 2001), MEC-SPQ (Vorderer et al., 2004), and Temple Presence Inventory (Lombard, Ditton, & Weinstein, 2009) were developed. Although much more can be done to refine our definitions and measurement tools, later Presence conferences focused less on these issues and more on developing, testing and refining theories and applications of not just presence generally but specific types of presence.

The major emphasis in the early conferences, and in much of the other scholarship on presence, was on virtual reality (so much so that our studies with television were considered out of the norm when Theresa Ditton and I were invited to give a keynote talk at the 1999 conference). And there was much more concern with the sense of presence involving "being there" in a media-generated environment (spatial presence) rather than "being with" people there (social presence). Even less attention was given early on to a type of presence Lombard and Ditton (1997) identified as medium-as-social-actor presence, in which the social responses are not to people or characters within a medium, but to the medium itself. I was fortunate to be a doctoral student at Stanford while Cliff Nass was developing the early, innovative program of research he called CASA—Computers Are Social Actors—in which he and his team demonstrated that even expert users respond to computers in unexpect-edly social ways (e.g., following politeness and gender-based norms).

The evolution and diversification of technologies available to the public drove a broadening of the scholarship. At Presence 2007, there was resistance to the idea that an Apple iPod's 2.5 inch video screen could evoke a sense of presence (see Bracken & Pettey, 2007) and the CASA paradigm was limited to desktop computers and in one study (Nass & Moon, 2000), television sets. CISCO's (2006) introduction of high-end telepresence suites (Cisco, n/d), the lower quality and cost Skype and FaceTime, and social media, all helped shift the focus toward social presence. Today, scholars are exploring presence responses to technologies from smartphones (e.g., Czaja, 2011; Richardson, 2005) to robots (e.g., Leite, Castellano, Pereira, Martinho, & Paiva, 2014), and Kun Xu and Lombard (2016) have proposed a detailed expansion of CASA to MASA—Media technologies Are Social Actors. As video games and virtual worlds evolved, Ratan (2012) explicated and he and others explored self-presence, in which users feel connected to their avatar or other mediated representation. As the lines between real and virtual blurred, Timmins and Lombard (2005) identified an unusual variant of traditional presence they called inverse presence, in which instead of the mediated seem-ing to be nonmediated, (usually intense) nonmediated experiences seem to be mediated (as in feeling like you're in a movie or videogame).

During the quarter century our models and theories about how presence works have grown more sophisticated, though this aspect of presence scholar-ship is still in its early stages. While there have been many proposed explana-tions for how presence (mostly spatial presence) occurs in different contexts and for different people, few are detailed enough to be considered complete, testable theories and none of them are truly comprehensive (for a review see Lombard, Lee, Sun, Xu, & Yang, 2017). Spatial presence has received the most attention. Nunez (2003) and Hartmann et al. (2015) provide useful reviews of both their own work on spatial presence theories, the Measures, Effects, Conditions (MEC) and Capacity Limited, Cognitive Constructionist (CLCC) models, respectively, and the work of others. While early theories of social presence were developed in the 1970s (Short et al., 1976) and 1980s (Daft & Lengel, 1986), more recently Biocca et al. (2003) proposed a more comprehensive if preliminary theory. The same can be said of theories regard-ing social responses to media themselves—the Media technologies Are Social Actors (MASA) theory (Xu & Lombard, 2016) expands on the basic argument of the earlier Computers Are Social Actors (CASA) paradigm and includes spe-cific, testable but so far untested propositions. Some of the most interesting theories about presence consider and apply to not just technology-mediated experiences but nonmediated ones as well, addressing fundamental assumptions about the nature of reality and our embodied experience (Gamberini & Spagnolli, 2015; Mantovani & Riva, 1999; Zahorik & Jenison, 1998). At the core of all presence theories is the idea that while our technologies have changed in dramatic ways in the last several decades, our minds and bodies have evolved slowly over millennia and have not (yet?) adapted to equip us with the ability to automatically and consistently distinguish between what we experience in our nonmediated environment and what we experience via our new media technologies.

As presence theories have evolved, we've gained a lot of knowledge from specific studies (mostly experiments) that examine the role of different factors in creating presence responses. Enough of these studies have now been completed, and they are rigorous enough, that Cummings and Bailenson (2016) were able to conduct a meta-analysis to examine the relative impact of many different factors, finding that user-tracking, stereoscopic images and wide fields of view are particularly impactful; more meta-analyses are likely on the way.

Many more application areas have been explored by presence scholars as well. These include health and medicine (e.g., Conde et al., 2010; Riva, 2016), organizational communication (Lee & Takayama, 2011; Standaert, Muylle, & Basu, 2016), advertising and marketing (Lombard & Snyder-Duch, 2017), education (Mikropoulos & Natsis, 2011; Selverian & Lombard, 2010), politics (Shane, Muhlberger & Cavalier, 2004; Mason, 2015 illustrates the need for more study), social change and activism (Ahn, Bailenson, & Park, 2014; Jo, 2010; Skwarek, 2014), art (Grau, 2003; Kac, 2005) and of course entertainment (Bracken & Skalski, 2010; Klimmt & Vorderer, 2003), among many others.

One program of research that I find particularly interesting and impressive has both expanded presence theory and pointed to extremely valuable applications. Jeremy Bailenson and his colleagues argue that the increasingly customizable digital avatars in online environments (video games, virtual worlds, etc.) means there is more potential for the Proteus Effect, in which users "make inferences about their expected dispositions from their avatar's appearance and then conform to the expected attitudes and behavior" (Yee, Bailenson, & Ducheneaut, 2009, pp. 293–294). So people using taller avatars behave more confidently in negotiations and those using more attractive avatars disclose more about themselves and maintain closer interpersonal distances (Yee & Bailenson, 2007; Yee et al., 2009); users of more sexualized avatars report more body-related thoughts and greater acceptance of myths about rape (Fox, Bailenson, & Tricase, 2013); users of avatars who exercise and are rewarded engage in more exercise themselves (Fox & Bailenson, 2009); seeing a virtual version of oneself consume soft drinks and gain weight leads to the intention and behavior that reduces soft drink consumption (Ahn, 2015); seeing an older version of oneself in a virtual mirror (or a photograph) makes users focus on financial planning for the future (Hershfield et al., 2011); and perceiving a virtual version of oneself as a member of a different race impacts users' implicit racial bias (see Hasler, Spanlang, & Slater, 2017). The exact roles of spatial, social and self-presence in these findings and others need to be explored further, but the implications for individuals and society are substantial.

While these are all examples of the positive uses of presence, as technologies have evolved, particularly artificial intelligence and robotics, there has also been an increased focus on the ethics of presence. It's a clichéd and arguable point that all technology is neutral, but presence is by most definitions a type of illusion, which suggests the possibility of deception. In Philosophy and Computer Science, as well as the public sphere, concern has grown recently about the dangers of developing artificially intelligent robots to create medium-as-social-actor presence experiences (e.g., in which they become our "servants," "co-workers," "friends," even "lovers"). Among the chief concerns is that they might evolve beyond human intelligence and morality (see Bostrom & Yudkowsky, 2014; Future of Life Institute, 2015; and Russell, Hauert, Altman, & Veloso, 2015). But ethical concerns are associated with many types and applications of presence. Increasingly entertaining and immersive simulations may distance us from the natural world and create confusions about what is real and artificial; virtual product demonstrations and training experiences that don't fully and accurately capture their non-mediated counterparts may lead to disappointing and even dangerous expectations; technologies that allow users to manipulate their appearance but can't provide the many subtle social cues of face-to-face interaction may limit our ability and desire for full human-to-human relationships; technologies that let us care for the sick at a distance may lead to a reduced concern about caring for them directly (see Lombard, 2009 for a detailed review).

I find nearly every topic related to presence interesting, but as with the ethical concerns, I find the larger implications of presence technologies and phenomena the most compelling. Three examples that stand out for me are the intersections of presence with sex, death and the nature of our existence. In "Telepresence and sexuality: A review and a call to scholars" (Lombard & Jones, 2013) we argued that simulating this basic but complex aspect of human life with actual or virtual people provides the greatest technical challenge for presence creators (who have a long and increasingly fascinating

history of attempts), an important opportunity for presence and communication theorists, and a myriad of implications for ethicists and futurists. In
"Telepresence after death" (Lombard & Selverian, 2008) we considered the
many ways humans have used technology to evoke a sense of the presence of
those who have died, from paintings and statues to audio and video record-
ings to the nascent use of holograms, digital "clones" and androids. Realistic
reproductions of those we've lost may provide great comfort and/or disrupt
the grieving process, and they again raise many practical, legal and ethical
concerns. And in "(Tele)Presence and simulation: Questions of epistemology, religion, morality, and mortality" (Jones, Lombard, & Jasak, 2011) we
reviewed the Simulation Argument (Bostrom, 2003) that we all may be living
within a simulation and considered the implications of six hypothetical scenarios that describe the true nature of our existence. The scenarios and the
possible means of coming to perceive their existence provide new ways of
thinking about the challenges of designing seamless presence illusions. And
more broadly, considering presence illusions as a guiding metaphor for the
functioning of our universe and ourselves (replacing the clock, locomotive
and computer) raises the most fundamental questions about how we (think
we) know our world (e.g., for each possible scenario, how might we come
to realize its true nature?), who or what created and controls it (e.g., could
it/they be powerful but not have ultimate power? to what extent do we ourselves have "god-like" free will?), how we should behave (e.g., what responsibilities does each scenario suggest for its creator(s) and inhabitants?), and
the nature of death (e.g., if the nature of our existence is not what it seems, is
there greater reason to believe in some form of existence beyond (after) it?).
To me, these and related topics illustrate the great value and richness of the
presence concept.

Community

The first presence conference I attended was Presence 1999 at the University
of Essex in Colchester, UK. Beyond the revelation that nearly every paper
at a conference could hold my interest, what made that conference and all
of the ones that followed so valuable and enjoyable were the other attendees. Because the study of presence touches nearly every field and discipline,
the academic presence community, relatively small but growing, is extremely
diverse. Members come from all over the world and have very different backgrounds, expertise areas, approaches to scholarship, and research interests but
have overlapping interest in one or more presence phenomena. Often they
had been studying what we know as presence phenomena but they hadn't

been familiar with the term or community. For whatever reason, the some-times extreme diversity not only doesn't interfere with productive presenta-tions and enjoyable conversations but encourages them. Maybe it's because, in my experience, presence scholars are unusually nice and interesting peo-ple. Ironically, I don't think we use presence technologies more than other scholars to stay in touch between in-person gatherings, but a primary mission of ISPR is to serve as a hub for the community via its conferences, website, ISPR Presence News and the ISPR Presence Community Facebook page (see http://ispr.info for details and links).

There is also an industry-based community of presence experts. In con-trast to the broader focus of the academic presence community, this group has had a more specific focus on visual collaboration technology for the world of business. The leading organization in this community is the Human Pro-ductivity Lab. As its website notes, "What began in 2005 as Human Produc-tivity Lab founder Howard Lichtman's personal blog on telepresence and visual collaboration grew into one of the world's most widely read publica-tions focused on telepresence, videoconferencing, and visual collaboration" (HPL, n/d). In addition to that online publication, Telepresence Options (http://www.telepresenceoptions.com/), HPL provides organizations with consulting and advising services for their selection, design and implemen-tation of visual collaboration technology. With the increased interest and likely growth in markets for virtual and augmented reality as well as robots, the industry-based presence community will likely grow and diversify in the coming years. While the academic and industry presence communities share important interests and goals, intermittent efforts to bring them together for professional and social events have had limited success, but the potential benefits to both mean we need to keep trying.

Future Presence

Based on the developments over the last 25 years, what might lie ahead for presence technology, scholarship and community? The future is obviously uncertain and it verges on foolhardy to make formal predictions, but it's a useful exercise to consider the possibilities ahead, in part to devise strategies to avoid the less pleasant ones.

Technology

In 1992, few if any people accurately predicted the presence-evoking tech-nologies of 2017, but the trends discussed above accelerated during that time and will likely continue to do so. I expect more blurring of mediated and nonmediated, real and fake, authentic and artificial. At least in the developed world, not only will we continue to spend more and more of our time in fully mediated experiences like television, movies and videogames, elements of technology-generated content will seep into the rest of our lives so that "mixed reality" will become increasingly common both for work and play. Technology will allow us to more conveniently and seamlessly communicate with each other, making face-to-face communication more rare and valued, but also increasing social anxieties. Technologies themselves will continue to become less obtrusive and to present more realistic and engaging experiences, raising the likelihood for greater entertainment and delight along with misperception, ethical and unethical persuasion, and escape and addiction. I believe presence will have enormously positive impacts in nearly every aspect of life in the developed world and many aspects of life elsewhere, but that it will have increasingly dangerous potential for deception and distraction in the interest of profit and without users knowing about or regulators limiting it.

Scholarship

The only prediction I feel confident in making about presence scholarship is that as presence becomes ever more relevant to modern life and nearly every field, the scholarship will continue to grow. It will very likely remain a literature dispersed across many disciplines and therefore a niche, interdisciplinary field of study, but it has the potential to be an essential one.

At least five factors could increase the value and impact of presence scholarship. First, we need to continue the process of refining terminology and disentangling definitions of types of presence so that we can speak and write about presence in an explicit if not standardized way (see Lombard & Jones, 2015 for a progress report). Second, the painstaking work of untangling and clarifying the role of the many characteristics of technology, content, user and context that contribute to presence and its nature and effects (immediate and short and long term) may lead to a useful set of guidelines for presence designers (a "handbook" of presence). Third, for these studies to be valid and useful we need to develop new, multi-faceted, multi-method approaches to measuring presence—already augmented and mixed reality technologies are making many of the standardized presence questionnaire instruments scholars use inadequate, and I would argue that any study that utilizes only closed-ended survey or questionnaire items, or any single method of assessing presence, can only capture a small portion of the phenomena being studied. Rather than manipulating versions of a media experience in the laboratory and asking indirect questions without mentioning presence, Lombard and Sun (2017) directly explained what presence is for study participants and used an online survey with closed and open-ended questions along with in-depth interviews to explore the nature of the presence experiences they have in their daily lives. The use of many other creative alternatives to the standard social science lab study are already providing the insights we need to advance our knowledge (see Wagner et al., 2009). Fourth, we need to continue to refine and test theories of presence. As Lombard et al. (2017) argue,

> The ultimate goal is a smaller set of theories that together are more comprehensive (account for more forms of presence across more people in more contexts), that are successful in both predicting and explaining presence phenomena, and that are as parsimonious and straightforward as possible while generating testable and falsifiable propositions and raising provocative new research questions regarding presence. (p. 1592)

Finally, and as, if not more, important than the other four factors, presence scholarship has to maintain and expand its focus on ethical issues. More people experiencing more, and more compelling and convincing, presence illusions means more opportunities for deception, invasion of privacy, and complex questions of legality and morality. Rather than taking an outside observer's perspective, presence scholars should try to predict and promote thoughtful discussion and solutions to the many ethical issues that presence raises for all of us. One way to be more proactive and hopefully prevent some of the negative, even dystopian, results of presence as it expands and evolves in the future is to study the many popular culture portrayals of that future to see what possibilities—both good and bad—might await us if we don't act (we've been doing this in a fun long-term web-based project; see Lombard et al., n/d). We also need to produce ethical guidelines for those who create, distribute and use presence-evoking technologies (see Lombard, 2009 for a very preliminary draft).

Community

I predict steady growth for both the academic and industry-based presence communities. It's always seemed sadly ironic that the people who create and study technologies that convey experiences across time and distance have had to travel to the same physical location to meet. But that is beginning to change with the use of higher quality videoconferencing and new telepresence robots, and I think it'll become even easier and more common for us to meet via presence technologies. Social media and social VR will also make it ever more convenient to stay in touch and collaborate. And ISPR is launching a new open-access online journal, the International Journal of

Telepresence (IJT; http://ijtelepresence.org) with a mission to serve as a home for scholarship by the extended presence community; the goal is to build on the staid, text-dominated traditional journal format by using presence evoking multi-media technology to illustrate what we study.

Conclusion

After 25 years I continue to be excited by the topic of presence. The technologies that evoke it, the scholarship of those who study it, and the academic and industry communities focused on it have all grown and evolved substantially in this relatively short period of time. The ways we use technology to shape our experiences of the world and of each other are changing more quickly than ever, with the prospect for hard-to-imagine developments and impacts in the future. There's never been a more important, challenging, and exciting time to study presence.

References

Ahn, S. J. (2015). Incorporating immersive virtual environments in health promotion campaigns: A construal level theory approach. *Health Communication, 30*(6), 545–556.

Ahn, S. J. G., Bailenson, J. N., & Park, D. (2014). Short-and long-term effects of embodied experiences in immersive virtual environments on environmental locus of control and behavior. *Computers in Human Behavior, 39*, 235–245.

Biocca, F. (1997). The cyborg's dilemma: Progressive embodiment in virtual environments. *Journal of Computer-Mediated Communication, 3*(2). Retrieved from https://doi.org/10.1111/j.1083-6101.1997.tb00070.x

Biocca F., Harms C., & Burgoon, J. K. (2003). Toward a more robust theory and measure of social presence: Review and suggested criteria. *Presence: Teleoperators and Virtual Environments, 12*(5), 456–480.

Bostrom, N. (2003). Are you living in a computer simulation? *Philosophical Quarterly, 2003, 53*(211), 243–255. Retrieved from http://www.simulation-argument.com/simulation.html

Bostrom, N., & Yudkowsky, E. (2014). The ethics of artificial intelligence. In K. Frankish & W. M. Ramsey (Eds.), *The Cambridge handbook of artificial intelligence* (pp. 316–334). Cambridge, UK: Cambridge University Press.

Bracken, C. C., & Pettey, G. (2007). It is REALLY a Smaller (and Smaller) World: Presence and small screens. *Proceedings of PRESENCE 2007: The 10th Annual International Workshop on Presence*, October 25–27, Barcelona, Spain. Available at http://astro.temple.edu/~lombard/ISPR/Proceedings/2007/Bracken and Pettey.pdf

Bracken, C. C., & Skalski, P. (Eds.). (2010). *Immersed in media: Telepresence in everyday life*. New York: Routledge.

Cisco (n/d). Cisco immersive telepresence. Retrieved from http://www.cisco.com/c/en/us/products/collaboration-endpoints/immersive-telePresence/index.html

Conde, J. G., De, S., Hall, R. W., Johansen, E., Meglan, D., & Peng, G. C. (2010). Telehealth innovations in health education and training. *Telemedicine and e-Health*, *16*(1), 103–106.

Cummings, J. J., & Bailenson, J. N. (2016). How immersive is enough? A meta-analysis of the effect of immersive technology on user presence. *Media Psychology*, *19*(2), 272–309.

Czaja, J. (2011). The cyborg habitus: Presence, posthumanism and mobile technology. In *Proceedings of 2011 International Society of Presence Research Annual Conference*. Available at https://astro.temple.edu/~lombard/ISPR/Proceedings/2011/Czaja.pdf

Daft, R. L., & Lengel, R. H. (1986). Organizational information requirements, media richness and structural design. *Management Science*, *32*(5), 554–571. doi: 10.1287/mnsc.32.5.554

Fox, J., & Bailenson, J. N. (2009). Virtual self-modeling: The effects of vicarious reinforcement and identification on exercise behaviors. *Media Psychology*, *12*(1), 1–25.

Fox, J., Bailenson, J. N., & Tricase, L. (2013). The embodiment of sexualized virtual selves: The Proteus effect and experiences of self-objectification via avatars. *Computers in Human Behavior*, *29*(3), 930–938.

Future of Life Institute. (2015). An open letter. Research priorities for robust and beneficial artificial intelligence [Position statement]. Retrieved from http://futureoflife.org/misc/open_letter

Gamberini, L., & Spagnolli, A. (2015). An action-based approach to presence: Foundations and methods. In M. Lombard, F. Biocca, J. Freeman, W. IJsselsteijn, & R. J. Schaevitz (Eds.), *Immersed in media: Telepresence theory, measurement & technology* (pp. 101–114). London, UK: Springer.

Grau, O. (2003). *Virtual Art: From illusion to immersion*. Cambridge, MA: MIT press.

Hartmann, T., Wirth, W., Vorderer, P., Klimmt, C., Schramm, H., & Böcking, S. (2015). Spatial presence theory: State of the art and challenges ahead. In M. Lombard, F. Biocca, J. Freeman, W. IJsselsteijn, & R. J. Schaevitz (Eds.), *Immersed in media: Telepresence theory, measurement & technology* (pp. 115–135): London, UK: Springer.

Hasler, B. S., Spanlang, B., & Slater, M. (2017). Virtual race transformation reverses racial in-group bias. *PLoS ONE*, *12*(4), e0174965. http://doi.org/10.1371/journal.pone.0174965

Hershfield, H. E., Goldstein, D. G., Sharpe, W. F., Fox, J., Yeykelis, L., Carstensen, L. L., & Bailenson, J. N. (2011). Increasing saving behavior through age-progressed renderings of the future self. *Journal of Marketing Research*, *48*(SPL), S23–S37.

Horton, D., & Wohl, R. (1956). Mass communication and para-social interaction: Observations on intimacy at a distance. *Psychiatry*, *19*(3), 215–229.

HPL. (n/d). About the Human Productivity Lab. Human Productivity Lab [website]. Retrieved from http://www.humanproductivitylab.com/en/category/about-the-lab/

IJsselsteijn, W., Lombard, M., & Freeman, J. (2001). Toward a core bibliography of Presence. *CyberPsychology & Behavior, 4*(2), 317–321.

International Society for Presence Research. (2000). *The Concept of Presence: Explication Statement*. Retrieved from https://ispr.info/about-presence-2/about-presence/

ISPR Presence News (n/d). Retrieved from https://ispr.info/posts/

Jo, D. (2010). Real-time networked media activism in the 2008 Chotbul protest. *Interface, 2*(2), 92–102.

Jones, M. T., Lombard, M., & Jasak, J. (2011). (Tele)Presence and simulation: Questions of epistemology, religion, morality, and mortality. *PsychNology Journal, 9*(3), 193–222.

Kac, E. (2005). *Telepresence & bio art: Networking humans, rabbits, & robots.* Ann Arbor, MI: University of Michigan Press.

Klimmt, C., & Vorderer, P. (2003). Media psychology "is not yet there": Introducing theories on media entertainment to the presence debate. *Presence: Teleoperators and virtual environments, 12*(4), 346–359.

Lee, M. K., & Takayama, L. (2011, May). "Now, I have a body": Uses and social norms for mobile remote presence in the workplace. In *Proceedings of the SIGCHI Conference on Human Factors in Computing Systems* (pp. 33–42). ACM.

Leite, I., Castellano, G., Pereira, A., Martinho, C., & Paiva, A. (2014). Empathic robots for long-term interaction. *International Journal of Social Robotics, 6*(3), 329–341.

Lessiter, J., Freeman, J., Keogh, E., & Davidoff, J. (2001). A cross-media presence questionnaire: The ITC-Sense of Presence Inventory. *Presence: Teleoperators and virtual environments, 10*(3), 282–297.

Lombard, M. (2009). The promise and peril of telepresence. In C. Bracken & P. Skalski (Eds.), *Immersed in media: Telepresence in everyday life* (pp. 197–228). New York: Routledge.

Lombard, M., & Ditton, T. (1997). At the heart of it all: The concept of presence. *Journal of Computer-Mediated Communication, 3*(2). Retrieved from https://doi.org/10.1111/j.1083-6101.1997.tb00072.x

Lombard, M., Ditton, T. B., & Weinstein, L. (2009, November). Measuring presence: The Temple Presence Inventory. In *Proceedings of the 12th Annual International Workshop on Presence* (pp. 1–15). Available at https://astro.temple.edu/~lombard/ISPR/Proceedings/2009/Lombard_et_al.pdf

Lombard, M., & Jones, M. T. (2013). Telepresence and sexuality: A review and a call to scholars. *Human Technology, 9*(1), 22–55. Available at http://humantechnology.jyu.fi/archive/vol-9/issue-1/lombard-jones9_22-55/@@display-file/fullPaper/Lombard_Jones.pdf

Lombard, M., & Jones, M. T. (2015). Defining presence. In M. Lombard, F. Biocca, W. A. IJsselsteijn, J. Freeman, & R. Schaevitz (Eds.), *Immersed in media: Telepresence theory, measurement and technology* (pp. 13–34). London: Springer.

Lombard, M., Lee, S., Sun, W., Xu, K., & Yang, H. (2017). Presence theory. In P. Rössler, C. A. Hoffner, & Liesbet van Zoonen (Eds.), *The International encyclopedia of media effects* (pp. 1583–1595). Hoboken, NJ: Wiley-Blackwell.

Lombard, M., & Selverian, M. E. (2008). Telepresence after death. *Presence: Teleoperators and Virtual Environments, 17*(3), 310–325.

Lombard, M., Selverian, M. E., Xu, K., Yang, H., Horvath, K., Park, S. B., & Hwang, H. S. (n/d). Telepresence in Media Environments [website]. Retrieved from https://smcsites.com/telepresence/

Lombard, M., & Snyder-Duch, J. (2017). Digital advertising in a new age: The power of (tele)presence. In S. Rodgers & E. Thorson (Eds.), *Digital Advertising: Theory and research* (3rd Edition) (pp. 169–187). New York: Routledge.

Lombard, M., & Sun, W. (2017). Examining telepresence experiences in everyday life: A direct, mixed-method approach. Unpublished manuscript.

Mantovani, G., & Riva, G. (1999). "Real" presence: How different ontologies generate different criteria for presence, telepresence, and virtual presence. *Presence: Teleoperators and Virtual Environments, 8*(5), 540–550.

Mason, W. (2015, July 19). How Virtual Reality Will Influence the 2016 Presidential Election. Upload VR. Retrieved from https://uploadvr.com/virtual-reality-2016-presidential-election/

Mikropoulos, T. A., & Natsis, A. (2011). Educational virtual environments: A ten-year review of empirical research (1999–2009). *Computers & Education, 56*(3), 769–780.

Minsky, M. (1980, June). Telepresence. *Omni magazine*, pp. 44–52.

Nass, C., & Moon, Y. (2000). Machines and mindlessness: Social responses to computers. *Journal of Social Issues, 56*(1), 81–103.

Nunez, D. (2003). *A connectionist explanation of presence in virtual environments* (Doctoral dissertation, University of Cape Town). Available at http://pubs.cs.uct.ac.za/archive/00000109/01/dnunez_thesis.pdf

Presence-L electronic list (n/d). [List archives]. Retrieved from https://listserv.temple.edu/archives/presence-l.html

Ratan, R. (2012). Self-presence, explicated: Body, emotion, and identity. In R. Luppicini (Ed.), *Handbook of research on technoself: Identity in a technological society* (pp. 322–336). Hershey, PA: IGI Global.

Reeves, B., & Nass, C. (1996). The *media equation: How people treat computers, television, and new media like real people and places*. New York: Cambridge University Press.

Richardson, I. (2005). Mobile technosoma: Some phenomenological reflections on itinerant media devices. *Fibreculture Journal*, (6).

Riva, G. (2016). Embodied medicine: what human-computer confluence can offer to health care. *Human Computer Confluence: Transforming Human Experience Through Symbiotic Technologies, 181*, 55–78.

Russell, S., Hauert, S., Altman, R., & Veloso, M. (2015). Ethics of artificial intelligence. *Nature, 521*, 415–418.

Selverian, M. E. M., & Lombard, M. (2010). Telepresence: A "real" component in a model to make human-computer interface factors meaningful in the virtual learning environment. *Themes in Science and Technology Education, 2*(1–2), 31–58. Retrieved from http://earthlab.uoi.gr/theste/index.php/theste/article/view/21/16

Shane, P. M., Muhlberger, P., & Cavalier, R. (2004, May). ITR: Developing and testing a high telepresence virtual agora for broad citizen participation: a multi-trait, multi-method investigation. In *Proceedings of the 2004 annual national conference on Digital government research* (p. 24). Digital Government Society of North America.

Short, J. A., Williams, E., & Christie, B. (1976). *The social psychology of telecommunications.* London: Wiley.

Skwarek, M. (2014). Augmented reality activism. In V. Geroimenko (Ed.), *Augmented reality art* (pp. 3–29). Basel, Switzerland: Springer International Publishing.

Standaert, W., Muylle, S., & Basu, A. (2016). An empirical study of the effectiveness of telepresence as a business meeting mode. *Information Technology and Management, 17*(4), 323–339.

Steuer, J. (1992). Defining virtual reality: Dimensions determining telepresence. *Journal of communication, 42*(4), 73–93.

Sutherland, I. E. (1965). The ultimate display. *Proceedings of the International Federation of Information Processing Congress, 2*, pp. 506–508.

Timmins, L. R., & Lombard, M. (2005). When "real" seems mediated: Inverse presence. *Presence: Teleoperators and Virtual Environments, 14*(4), 492–500.

Turing, A. M. (1950). Computing machinery and intelligence. *Mind, 59*, 433–460.

Vorderer, P., Wirth, W., Gouveia, F. R., Biocca, F., Saari, T., Jäncke, F., … Jäncke, P. (2004). Development of the MEC Spatial Presence Questionnaire (MEC-SPQ). Unpublished report to the European Community, Project Presence: MEC (IST-2001-37661). Hannover, Munich, Helsinki, Porto, Zurich.

Wagner, I., Broll, W., Jacucci, G., Kuutii, K., McCall, R., Morrison, A., … Terrin, J. J. (2009). On the role of presence in mixed reality. *Presence: Teleoperators and Virtual Environments, 18*(4), 249–276.

Witmer, B. G., Jerome, C. J., & Singer, M. J. (2005). The factor structure of the presence questionnaire. *Presence: Teleoperators and Virtual Environments, 14*(3), 298–312.

Xu, K., & Lombard, M. (2016). *Media are social actors: Expanding the CASA paradigm in the 21st century.* Presented at the 2016 annual conference of the International Communication Association (ICA), Fukuoka, Japan.

Yee, N., & Bailenson, J. (2007). The Proteus effect: The effect of transformed self-representation on behavior. *Human Communication Research, 33*(3), 271–290.

Yee, N., Bailenson, J. N., & Ducheneaut, N. (2009). The Proteus effect: Implications of transformed digital self-representation on online and offline behavior. *Communication Research, 36*(2), 285–312.

Zahorik, P., & Jenison, R. L. (1998). Presence as being-in-the-world. *Presence: Teleoperators And Virtual Environments, 7*(1), 78–89.

6. *Theorizing Verbally Persuasive Robots*

S. Austin Lee and Yuhua (Jake) Liang[1]

Robots carry a tremendous persuasive potential to influence their human partners. Research has already demonstrated the effectiveness of robots as persuaders in a variety of contexts, including soliciting donations at a museum (Siegel, Breazeal, & Norton, 2009), increasing awareness for energy conservation (Ham & Midden, 2014), and encouraging people to lead a healthy life (Kidd & Breazeal, 2007). Robots can function as compelling persuaders because when people interact with technology, such as robots, computers, and agents, they often treat those machines as social beings and apply social rules to their interaction (Nass & Moon, 2000; Reeves & Nass, 1996). This human tendency allows robots to capitalize on message strategies to increase their persuasiveness toward human partners.

The robots' ability to persuade humans becomes increasingly important when humans and robots collaborate as a team (i.e., co-roboting; National Science Foundation, 2016). Robots already occupy a wide range of application space, which includes co-defender, co-explorer, and co-worker. In those settings, the team's performance depends partly on how well robots can persuade their human partners to achieve the team's goal. It is because successful collaboration builds upon a symbiotic relationship where both communicators leverage their relative strengths in the planning and execution of tasks. In the manufacturing environment, for example, collaborative activities between humans and robots can be cost-effective and appreciably more productive than activities involving either group working alone. To provide favorable results toward that end, robots should be able to communicate their intentions, such as asking their fellow human workers to give clearer instructions or to help with certain tasks (Fong, Thorpe, & Baur, 2003). Similarly, human partners must be able to interpret the robots' intentions and modify the tasks accordingly. For service robots that assist people in their daily lives and work, communication and persuasion are important components in the overarching approach to robust social behavior. To construct intuitive and effective user interfaces, robots need not only to comprehend verbal and nonverbal messages, but also to build trust and develop social relationships (Hegel, Muhl, Wrede, Hielscher-Fastabend, & Sagerer, 2009). An understanding of these aspects of human-robot communication will enable robots to effectively operate in collaboration with their human partners.

To enable such collaboration, the process of human-robot interaction needs to be interactive and transactional. The traditional model of human-robot interaction was largely limited to "master-slave" commanding and monitoring: a robotic system is designed as "a 'slave' to do the dangerous or less intellectually demanding parts of a task" (Rosen, 1985, p. 25) and a human operator communicates with the machine to gain information and issue commands while the machine implements these commands (Sheridan, 1984). Within this control schema, the interaction model is essentially one-way: humans "speak" and robots "listen." Robots were conceptualized and treated as the silent and passive receivers of communication, even though the actual exchanges between humans and robots can be much more complex and have implications beyond the task itself (Guzman, 2016). In this paradigm, robot performance is strictly bound to human skill and the quality of the user interface. To improve system capability and increase flexibility, human-robot communication should occur in both directions: robots should be able to initiate the communication allowing the human and robot to support each other in different ways as needs and capabilities change throughout a task.

Persuasion is a skill that facilitates such collaboration in human-robot teams. Collaboration requires both humans and robots (1) to leverage each other's strengths effectively, (2) to communicate and coordinate their actions, (3) and to respond quickly and help the other resolve issues as they arise. To achieve this, the robots should possess the ability to take initiative in task performance by asking for and making use of human expertise and assistance, or when needed, even by assigning tasks to their human partners (Bruemmer, Marble, & Dudenhoeffer, 2002). The robots need to convince the human partners to understand and accept robot initiative and to trust the information and decisions that they made (Marble, Bruemmer, Few, & Dudenhoeffer, 2004).

In addition to facilitating human-robot collaboration, the persuasive ability of robots offers a number of potential benefits in a variety of contexts. First, it enables technology to complete its task more efficiently and effectively. A robotic health coach, for example, can better assist people reach their fitness goals by employing diverse persuasive strategies (Kidd & Breazeal, 2007).

Second, it helps technology build credibility and earn trust from humans. A search-and-rescue robot, for instance, can better convince disaster victims to follow its instructions by establishing credibility and gaining trust (Wang, Lewis, & Scerri, 2006). Finally, it benefits our society by promoting prosocial behavior among people, such as a robotic agent increasing awareness for energy conservation by using carefully designed messages (Ham & Midden, 2014).

Those potential benefits have stimulated recent research on robot persuasion, which builds upon the literature on persuasive technology. Since the seminal work conducted at Stanford University (e.g., Fogg & Nass, 1997), several terms were used to denote persuasion through technology (for a review, see Kegel & Wieringa, 2014). For example, Fogg (2003) coined the term CAPTology, which stands for Computers As this Persuasive Technologies. Atkinson (2006) proposed an alternative term, compusuasion (computer + persuasion), which expanded the scope of persuasion to unintended behavioral changes but failed to gain widespread currency. Siegel et al. (2009) devised the term persuasive robotics, focusing on robots instead of computer systems in general.

In this chapter, we will use the term robot persuasion, instead of persuasive robotics, with an emphasis on "persuasion" rather than "robotics." Thus far, the lion's share of research in persuasive robotics has been focused on nonverbal cues, including gestures, eye gaze, proximity, and touch, as well as vocalics, including vocal tones and the gender of voice, (Chidambaram, Chiang & Mutlu, 2012; Ham, Bokhorst, Cuijpers, van der Pol & Cabibihan, 2011; Siegel et al., 2009). While those nonverbal behaviors are potentially important, scant attention has been paid to the core of persuasion: message strategies. Persuasion occurs mainly through verbal messages, and therefore how robots utilize the messages is of ultimate importance.

This chapter illuminates the persuasive message strategies of robots by reviewing and synthesizing our line of research on this topic. To better understand the symbiosis between collaborative robotic systems and humans, it is necessary to conceptualize robots as a source of messages and utilize this conceptualization to test and theorize about the robots' persuasiveness potential. To provide the theoretical background, we will first discuss a transactional model of communication that illustrates the process of persuasion in human-robot communication. Afterward, we will introduce our recent work that demonstrates the efficacy of message strategies used by robots. We will elucidate the mechanism of persuasion, extrapolating from research on computer agents. The Computers Are Social Actors (Nass & Moon, 2000) paradigm and the functional triad of persuasive technology (Fogg, 2003) will provide theoretical bases. Finally, we will conclude the chapter with future directions for research, such as expanding the scope of persuasion strategies and investigating the novel concept of robot credibility.

With this synthesis of our research, we hope to examine the current state of scholarship, provide directions for future research, and ultimately, contribute to strengthening the theoretical foundations of research in human-machine communication, which is an umbrella term encompassing human-robot interaction, human-computer interaction, human-agent interaction, and interactions with other technologies. Although robots, computers, and agents differ in their presence and embodiment, the implications from human-robot interaction will be applicable to interaction with other types of technology. Indeed, our argument will build upon theories from human-computer interaction literature and evidence from human-agent interaction research.

Transactional Model of Human-Robot Communication

Traditionally, messages from humans to robots occur in the form of commands. Robots passively listen to the speech, recognize the intention, and carry out the command accordingly. In this process, the robots' response to human requests is a technological problem, defined by hardware and software capabilities (Hoffman & Breazeal, 2004; Huang & Mutlu, 2012). However, successful collaboration requires more than unidirectional communication. As Fong et al. (2003) pointed out, in a traditional view of human-robot interaction, a robot has "limited freedom to act and will perform poorly whenever its capabilities are ill-suited for the task at hand. Moreover, if a robot has a problem, it has no way to ask for assistance" (p. 255).

In a setting where humans and robots work together to contribute their differing roles and capabilities, the robots should be able to persuade human partners to clarify instructions, modify tasks, enhance safety, make decisions, and help the robots if needed. Unlike robots simply carrying out human commands, human partners may not follow the robots' requests, resulting in suboptimal performance as a team. From this perspective, a large portion of the robots' success depends on human compliance. In this respect, collaboration between humans and robots is not merely a technological problem, but a communication problem as well.

The transactional model of communication (Liang & Walther, 2015; Shannon & Weaver, 1949) is useful for theorizing such interaction. The primary elements of this communication model include the source, receiver, message, channel, effect, and context. In an environment where humans and robots collaborate, both parties can be the senders who express needs, share information, give commands, or attempt to persuade. In this chapter, we will focus on robot-generated messages, where robots actively take initiative in communication and generates messages to perform aforementioned functions. Especially in the context of persuasion, the messages are designed to achieve desired effects, such as changing the attitudes, beliefs, or behaviors of receivers (i.e., human partners). The messages generated by robots can be transmitted verbally or nonverbally. In this chapter, we will examine the verbal channels (e.g., synthesized voice or text on a screen) of persuasion. When a message is delivered through the channel, its transmission can be interfered by noise. The noise may be physical (e.g., robots' whirring noise as they move), semantic (e.g., robots' limited capability in natural language processing or text-to-speech generation), or psychological (e.g., humans' fear or distrust toward the robot). Addressing these noises is necessary for achieving desired communicative outcomes. Robots may use redundant channels (e.g., generating synthesized voice while displaying text on a screen), rephrase the message, monitor the receiver's feedback such as a nod or a raised eyebrow, or ask questions to ensure understanding. The communication process described so far occurs in a face-to-face, virtual, or teleoperated environment where humans and robots coexist and collaborate (i.e., co-roboting environment). It is also embedded in physical locations such as a factory floor, office, and home, as well as social contexts such as the roles of robots and human operators and the relationships between them, which together provide certain norms of operation and interaction. Finally, communication flows continually back-and-forth between humans and robots. Both humans and robots can simultaneously engage in the sending and receiving of messages, making the communication transactional (Barnlund, 2008).

Based on this conceptualization, robot persuasion can be defined as an ongoing process where robots send specific requests to human partners through voice or text to create, change, or reinforce the attitudes, beliefs, and behaviors of humans in a given physical and social context.

Figure 6.1 describes the transactional model of human-robot communication conceptualized in this chapter. It should be noted that the model is simplified for brevity. Communication between humans and robots develops over time and becomes more complex and convoluted. In addition, the model does not explain how meanings are created, coordinated, and managed in the process of communication, how identities are symbolically constructed, or how power and relationships are negotiated between humans and machines (Guzman, 2016). For example, instead of transmitting information that is fixed in advance, the meaning of the message may emerge out of the dynamic process of communication between humans and robots (Sandry, 2015). Nevertheless, the simplicity of the transactional model makes it useful

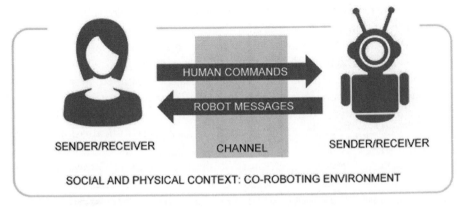

Figure 6.1. Transactional Model of Human-Robot Communication.
Source: Authors.

for examining the robots' potential to initiate communication and persuade their human partners.

Persuasive Potential of Robots

Based on this conceptualization of robots as the source of communication, we examined if robots (i.e., sender) can utilize verbal (i.e., channel) persuasive strategies (i.e., message) to gain compliance (i.e., effect) from human partners (i.e., receiver) in a collaborative task (i.e., context). Our investigation is focused on the verbal message strategies, which deserve more academic scrutiny. To date, we have examined a pre-giving strategy and a sequential-request persuasive strategy employed by robots.

Pre-giving Strategy

Among a vast array of persuasion and compliance gaining strategies examined in the human communication literature, we decided to first test a pre-giving strategy, which involves giving a target of persuasion a small gift or favor in advance before asking for compliance. Common examples are free samples at grocery stores or retail shops. If customers take the free sample, they are more likely to purchase the product even when they do not need it. In this sense, these free samples are not so free (Cialdini, 2008).

The reason we first chose a pre-giving strategy is that it capitalizes on the norm of reciprocity, which is one of the most fundamental and robust norms in human society. Reciprocity is based on the sense of obligation created by exchanges of benefits or favors among people. The recipients feel indebted to the giver until they repay the benefits or favors (Gouldner, 1960). As Cicero noted, "there is no duty more indispensable than that of returning a kindness" (1897, p. 27). Because reciprocity is the "vital principle of society" (Hobhouse, 1906, p. 12), one who deviates from this norm is often adorned with shameful labels, such as a moocher or an ingrate, and is excluded from future exchanges (Cialdini, 2008). Based on the universality and robustness of this norm, reciprocity may apply even when humans interact with machines (Fogg & Nass, 1997).

Our experimental design was inspired by Regan's (1971) classic study. In this study, participants were invited to rate paintings with their partner, who was actually a confederate (i.e., a research assistant acting as a participant). In the experimental condition, the confederate left the room during the art appreciation task and returned after a few minutes with two bottles of Coca-Cola: one for himself and one for the participant. In the control condition, the confederate left the room briefly but returned empty-handed. When the task was over, the confederate told the naïve participant that he was selling raffle tickets. Participants who received a bottle of Coke bought twice as many raffle tickets than participants in the control condition.

Originally, we sought to replicate this seminal study in the context of human-robot interaction. However, a robot would not be able to offer a can of Coke—it would look suspicious even if it did. Accordingly, we had to modify the manipulation of pre-giving. We eventually got an idea from an episode of the popular TV game show *Jeopardy!* where IBM's artificial intelligence, Watson, defeated human contestants. In our experiment, however, a robot helped human contestants instead of competing against them.

In this study (Lee & Liang, 2016), a total of 60 participants were invited to a trivia game with an ostensibly autonomous robot partner named CHRIS (Collaborative Human Robot Interaction System). Unbeknownst to participants, CHRIS was a Double Robotics telepresence robot with a synthesized voice and an animated face on the screen, operated by another research assistant behind a one-way mirror. To enhance the realism of the experiment, participants were explained the ostensible mechanism of CHRIS, which involved extracting keywords from each question, retrieving information from the database, and suggesting the most probable answer.

Participants were told that their task was to evaluate this newly developed robotic system. However, the true purpose of the experiment was to examine if participants reciprocated the robot's favor. Half of the participants were randomly assigned to the helpful robot condition, where it suggested mostly correct answers. The rest of the participants were assigned to the unhelpful robot condition, where it suggested irrelevant answers or failed to retrieve information. At the end of the five-minute trivia quiz, the experimenter stepped into the room and announced that the experiment was over and participants were free to go after filling out a short survey, and then left the room again. The questionnaire asked participants' evaluation toward CHRIS, including perceived expertise, sociability, and trustworthiness. When participants completed the questionnaire and stood up from the chair, CHRIS prompted a compliance gaining request, asking if they would complete 30 pattern recognition tasks that would take about 15 minutes. If participants agreed, they read a series of distorted CAPTCHA (Completely Automated Public Turing test to tell Computers and Humans Apart) letters on the robot's screen. This task would make sense to participants as CATPCHA is devised to prevent robots and computers from solving it without human assistance.

The result was unequivocal. When participants did not receive help from the robot, only 33% agreed to help. By contrast, when participants received help from the robot, 60% complied with the request. This clearly shows that robots can effectively gain human compliance by capitalizing on the norm of reciprocity and following with a verbal request. In other words, robots can afford social dynamics and serve to influence human behaviors.

We compared this result to a previous study using a computer agent with the same experimental procedure and a comparable participant pool (Lee, Liang, & Cho, 2016). The main differences between robots and computer agents lie in embodiment and presence: while robots are physical and mechanical entities presented in front of participants, agents are virtual entities presented on the screen. Accordingly, participants evaluated the robot as being more likeable and friendly than the virtual agent. Nevertheless, participants' compliance to the pre-giving strategy did not differ (robot 60.0% vs. agent 57.0%). In both studies, participants' evaluation toward the robots and agents, such as expertise, sociability, and trustworthiness, did not influence compliance. The only significant predictor was whether participants received help or not (Figure 6.2).

This finding is consistent with the human communication literature, where the norm of reciprocity operates independently from source evaluations (Boster, Rodriguez, Cruz, & Marshall, 1995). For example, in Regan's (1971) original experiment, the likability of the confederate was manipulated by acting in a normal and polite way versus in a rude and unpleasant way to a third person. However, the effect of manipulated liking was fairly weak. More importantly, the finding suggests that the norm of reciprocity may be a general principle where humans feel obligated to return a favor when the favor is given by machines.

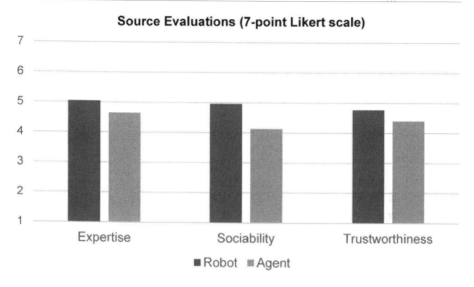

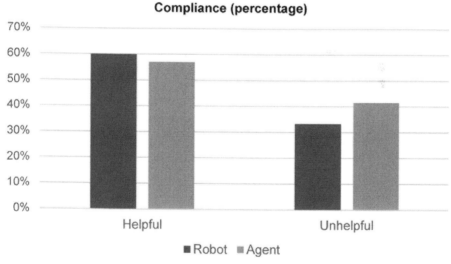

Figure 6.2. Comparison of Robots and Agents.
Source: Authors.

Sequential-Request Persuasive Strategy

In addition to the pre-giving strategy, we recently examined a sequential-request persuasive strategy employed by robots. Sequential-request strategies are a class of persuasive methods where requests are carried out in a specific sequence (Cialdini & Guadagno, 2004). For example, a foot-in-the-door strategy begins with a small initial request followed by a larger second request (Freedman & Fraser, 1966). After accepting the small initial request, respondents are more likely to agree with the larger second request than if that same large request is made in isolation.

The study examined this foot-in-the-door strategy used by robots (Lee, Liang, & Thompson, 2017), and was the first of its kind. Previous research examined the foot-in-the door strategy in a computer-mediated communication environment, where confederates worked as the sender of the message and solicited participants' compliance through email (Guéguen 2002; Guéguen & Jacob, 2001). This "electronic foot-in-the-door" strategy should be differentiated from the "robotic foot-in-the-door" strategy where robots function as the source of the persuasive message, as described in the transactional model of human-machine communication.

The study utilized and extended the experimental paradigm from our previous study (Lee & Liang, 2016). At the end of the trivia game, the robot asked participants to complete a series of pattern recognition tasks, either by requesting directly or by starting with a small request, then following with a larger request. The results (Figure 6.3) clearly demonstrated a robotic foot-in-the-door effect: 72% of participants who complied with the smaller initial request (helping the robot for 15 minutes) agreed to do the larger second request (helping the robot for 25 minutes). When only the larger request was presented (i.e., direct request condition), only 14% agreed to help. Whether the robot was helpful or not was not a significant predictor of compliance. The only significant predictor of compliance was the message strategy (i.e., foot-in-the-door vs. direct request).

The findings from both the pre-giving study and the foot-in-the-door study attest to the robots' potential to persuade humans using message strategies. These message strategies can be applied in a variety of contexts. For example, a salesbot may increase sales by giving out free samples. A robotic fundraiser may increase donation by starting with a small request, such as signing a petition, followed by a larger and actual request, such as making a gift. The findings also suggest that we may apply a wider variety of message strategies to robot persuasion.

Mechanism of Robot Persuasion

Our studies demonstrated that robots can effectively gain compliance from humans using message strategies. However, the human compliance to the robots' request is somewhat perplexing. If we think logically, humans do not

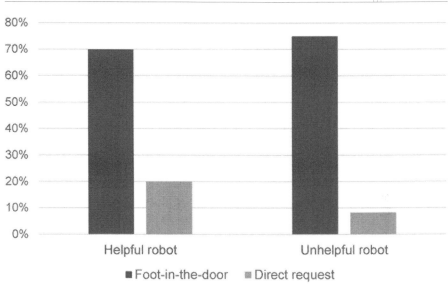

Figure 6.3. Compliance Rate to the Larger Request.
Source: Authors.

have any reason to feel obligated to robots. In our pre-giving study, there were multiple reasons for participants not to comply: 1) participants were aware that the robot's helping behavior was simply a programmed response, not an altruistic favor; 2) the experimenter announced that participants were free to go and left the lab to eliminate normative pressure; 3) participants did not expect any future interaction with the robot; 4) the robot would not blame participants or feel angry even if participants did not return its favor. Nonetheless, 60% of participants helped the robot for 15 minutes, simply because they were helped previously by the robot for 5 minutes. Hence, an arising question is why humans apply the norm of reciprocity when they interact with non-human entities such as robots.

Our foot-in-the-door study may also reflect how people perceive robots. According to self-perception theory (Bem, 1972), people often determine their attitudes and preferences by observing their own behavior. When applied to the foot-in-the-door strategy (Beaman, Cole, Preston, Klentz, & Steblay, 1983; Burger, 1999; DeJong, 1979), people may infer their attitudes as a result of seeing themselves agree to the trivial initial request. They may perceive themselves as more helpful and caring, and behave consistently with this self-perception, and thus become more compliant with the second, larger request. This self-perception, however, would be possible only when people treat robots as social entities worthy of help and care. For example, most people would not see themselves as helping and caring after charging a laptop or changing engine oil, even though the message on the screen or dashboard asked the owners to do so. In this regard, we may ask why people respond to the robots differently from machines that do not possess social cues.

Robots Are Social Actors

We may find answers from the human-computer interaction literature, especially the Computers Are Social Actors (CASA) paradigm based on the media equation theory. The late Clifford Nass at Stanford University asserted that humans treat computers as if they were social beings (Nass & Moon, 2000; Reeves & Nass, 1996). For example, research showed that people apply gender stereotypes to computers, even though machines do not possess any gender. Participants were more likely to follow advice from male-voiced computers than female-voiced computers (Nass, Moon, & Green, 1997). Interestingly, though, if the topic was about love and relationships, participants were more likely to listen to female-voiced computers (Lee, 2003). People also follow social rules, such as a politeness norm, when they interact with computers. For example, most participants responded to a computer in a polite manner, trying not to hurt its feelings (Nass, Moon, & Carney, 1999).

Fogg's (2003) conceptualization of the functional triad builds upon this CASA paradigm (Figure 6.4). This framework outlines the three basic ways

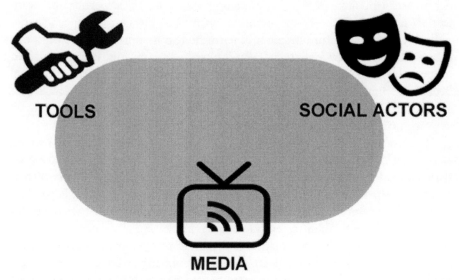

TOOLS   **SOCIAL ACTORS**

MEDIA

Figure 6.4. Functional Triad of Persuasive Technology.
Source: Authors (adopted from Fogg, 2003, p. 25).

that humans respond to persuasive technology, which can function as tools, media, or social actors—or combinations of them. This classification can be applied to robots. *Tool* refers to the robots' functional capabilities, *medium* refers to the robots' ability to serve as a conduit for certain experiences (e.g., co-roboting experience), and *social actor* refers to the robots' ability to relate to humans interpersonally.

Based on this framework, we conducted an experiment (Lee & Liang, 2015) that further investigates why humans comply with requests from machines. Based on the functional triad, we hypothesized three possible reasons for compliance: evaluations toward the source as a *tool*, affective state experienced through a *medium*, and normative influence that applies to an interaction with a *social actor*. More specifically, we expected that participants might comply (1) because the machine is useful and likable as a tool (source-based explanation), (2) because they are in a good mood, especially after a success in a trivia quiz (affect-based explanation), or (3) just because they were helped by the machine (norm-based explanation).

To test these competing hypotheses, we conducted an experiment using an animated virtual agent on a computer screen, instead of a physical robot. Although computer agents and robots differ in terms of their presence and embodiment, since they both possess certain levels of social cues, the findings from human-agent interaction may apply to human-robot interaction. Indeed, as described previously, the findings from our computer agent study (Lee et al., 2016) were highly comparable with those from our robot study (Lee & Liang, 2016).

A relatively large data set of 664 participants was collected. A path analysis assessed the effects of these factors on human compliance with the request originating from a computer. Figure 6.5 presents a simplified version of the hypothesized path model. Although this study used a computer agent, the design of the experiment and the persuasive messages were identical to the robot experiment.

The results showed that participants' evaluations toward the machine as a tool in light of their trivia game performance, were mostly unrelated to compliance. Although the computer's helpfulness was a strong predictor of its perceived competence, which in turn predicted its perceived compliance, the former was unrelated to compliance and the latter was weakly and, to our surprise, negatively associated with compliance. Participants' positive mood, elicited by receiving help from the machine, was minimally related to compliance. While these source-based and affect-based explanations did not account for compliance, the computer's helping behavior was the significant predictor

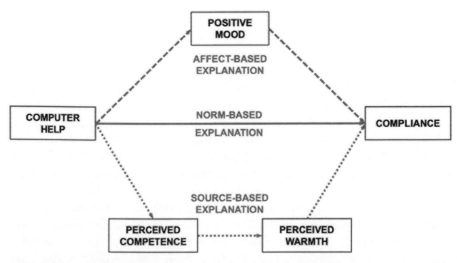

Figure 6.5. A Hypothesized Path Model.
Source: Authors.

of compliance, suggesting that the norm of reciprocity was the driving force that compelled participants to reciprocate (i.e., norm-based explanation).

The findings suggest that humans treat machines as if they were social beings and follow social norms, such as reciprocity. This human tendency allows robots and computer agents to function as the senders of messages in the transactional model of human-machine communication and utilize messages strategies for persuasion.

Mindlessness

Now that we know that robots and computer agents can effectively persuade humans because people treat machines as social actors, a subsequent question would be why humans treat machines as such. A plausible explanation involves mindlessness, which is analogous to going into an "auto-pilot" mode. Mindlessness is not necessarily a negative state. It occurs when a behavior is often scripted and does not require careful consideration of the information received from the environment (Langer, Blank, & Chanowitz, 1978). Mindlessness serves an important function of conserving cognitive resources, as humans are cognitive misers who prefer to think and solve problems in a simpler and less effortful way (Fiske & Taylor, 2013).

A body of literature suggests that when people interact with machines, they are often in a mindless state (Kim & Sundar, 2012; Lee, 2008; Nass & Moon, 2000; Sundar & Nass, 2000). People tend to focus too much on humanlike attributes, such as visual cues, voice, and interactivity, while not attending to the fact that the machines are not humans. As a result, people often overuse social categories, such as gender, and exhibit overlearned social responses, such as politeness and reciprocity, even when they interact with machines.

The influence of mindlessness on persuasion was examined in Langer et al. (1978)'s classical study. In this filed experiment, an experimenter asked subjects at the library waiting to use the copy machine if he or she may go in front of them. The experimenter's requesting messages varied based on the types of reasoning: sufficient, placebic, and direct. In the sufficient condition, a legitimate reason was provided: "May I use the Xerox machine, because I am in a rush?" In the placebic condition, only a pseudo-reason was provided with a trigger word: "May I use the Xerox machine, *because* I have to make copies?" In the direct condition, the confederate asked directly without any reasoning: "May I use the Xerox machine?" Langer et al. also varied the motivation to process the request by changing the amount of commitment: allowing the confederate to copy 5 pages versus 20.

The results showed that when 5 pages were asked, placebic and sufficient requests led to more compliance than direct requests, as the request was trivial and participants lacked the motivation to process the information. When participants heard the word "because," they mindlessly assumed that the experimenter had a reason to go before them. When 20 pages were asked, however, only sufficient requests resulted in more compliance compared to direct and placebic requests, because participants mindfully evaluated the legitimacy of the requests.

We applied and extended this experimental paradigm to examine mindlessness as an explaining mechanism. In this study (Liang, Lee, & Jang, 2013), we found that participants' compliance was a function of motivation and message type. Under a low motivational state (i.e., small request), both legitimate ("Could you please help complete pattern recognition tasks because this is needed to find the answers faster and more accurately?") and placebic ("Could you please help complete pattern recognition tasks *because* there's a need to recognize patterns?) requests were equally effective, yielding higher compliance than direct requests ("Could you please help complete pattern recognition tasks?"). This suggests that even when the reason was bogus, the trigger word "because" was enough to elicit an automatic response. However, as the motivation increased, participants complied more with the legitimate requests than the placebic requests. When the request size was extremely high (50 pattern recognition tasks for 25 minutes), both messages backfired: participants were in a fully mindful state and possibly realized the insensible.

The overall findings attest mindlessness as a compelling mechanism for the Computers (or Robots, or Machines in general) Are Social Actors effect. When interacting with machines, people often lack motivation to carefully process and integrate all relevant information, including the fact that they are interacting with machines, not humans. This tendency amplifies when machines display more anthropomorphic, or human-like cues (Lee, 2008; Schaumburg, 2001). Our study advances previous research on mindlessness that focused on the cognitive deficit (i.e., people are unable to process information fully when they have competing cognitive demands), which partially supported the CASA effect (Lee, 2010), by examining the motivational deficit, which is more likely to happen in day-to-day interaction with machines.

The fact that the CASA effect is activated in a mindless mental state (i.e., when people are too busy or do not care enough to process information) may imply that persuasion through robots may rely somewhat on heuristic or peripheral processing of human receivers elicited by the anthropomorphic cues of machines (Lee, 2010), rather than systematic or central processing (Chaiken & Trope, 1999). In our study (Lee et al., 2016), however, the varying degree of anthropomorphism did not influence compliance rate. In the robotic foot-in-the-door study (Lee et al., 2017), the perceived human-likeness of the robot did not predict participants' compliance to the second, larger request. It is possible that minimum cues of human-likeness are sufficient to elicit mindlessness required for persuasion. If this is true, the focus of robot persuasion should be on utilizing compelling message strategies based on robust social norms, rather than creating more humanlike robots that emulate nonverbal behaviors.

Future Directions

To date, we have documented the persuasive potential of robots and examined its mechanism based on the Computers Are Social Actors paradigm, as well as the functional triad of persuasive technology. Still, our research is in its infancy. There is much work to be done to fully understand the mechanisms of persuasion using robots, computers, and other machines. In this final section, we will discuss two of the most important directions for future research: expanding the scope of persuasion strategies and investigating the new concept of robot credibility.

More Persuasion Strategies

Our research so far has focused on the pre-giving and foot-in-the-door strategies. A wide array of persuasion strategies need to be examined in the future. As robots are the unique source of influence, some persuasive strategies may be more effective, while some may be less, compared to humans as the source of messages. Finding what strategies work and what does not will help researchers find boundary conditions and practitioners design message strategies for collaborative robots. In the sections below, we provide some examples of persuasive strategies that require attention.

Door-in-the-Face
A door-in-the-face strategy is the opposite of the foot-in-the-door. A persuader first makes a large request that is likely to be turned down, much like a metaphorical slamming of a door in his or her face, and then makes a second, more reasonable request (Cialdini et al., 1975). This message strategy operates by asking the target (i.e., a human receiver) a larger initial request (e.g., "Can you please help complete 500 pattern recognition tasks?"), followed by a second, actually desired request (e.g., "Can you please help complete 50 pattern recognition tasks?"). The strategy is effective because the receiver feels an obligation to reciprocate the sender (i.e., robot) concession with a concession of his/her own (Cialdini & Goldstein, 2004). Reciprocal concession is no longer effective when a different sender provides the request, supporting that reciprocal concession rests on the obligation to the sender (O'Keefe & Hale, 2001). Therefore, the requests should be made by the same robot.

Altruism
Altruistic behaviors occur when people feel empathetic toward a person of need and act toward helping the person (Batson & Shaw, 1991). Altruism does not occur merely out of willingness to help another; the research clearly shows that empathy is a necessary condition. For example, if a robot is shown to need human help and makes a request to the receiver to take some particular action, the human receiver is more likely to accept the request if the receiver feels empathic toward the robot (e.g., trying to understand from the robot's point of view and capabilities). Although the altruism effect has been established in the interpersonal context, it is unclear if robots are sources that are able to elicit credible responses such that empathy affects the compliance behavior.

Guilt
Guilt occurs in interpersonal contexts when the receiver's action results in the sender's negative emotional state (Baumeister, Stillwell, & Heatherton, 1994; Boster et al.,1999). Usually guilt arises when the receiver perceives that he/she has transgressed in some way (e.g., perceived harm, failure to take

the expected actions). Guilt produces a higher likelihood of receiver compliance. Guilt in the interpersonal context is common, but a human partner may
feel guilty toward a robot when his/her actions resulted in some negative
outcome for the robot. One possibility could be if a robot points out the
incorrect actions taken by the human partner, and these actions have detrimental effects on the robot in a collaborative task. If guilt indeed functions in
human-robot interaction, when a robot asks the human partner to correct the
action and/or take additional actions, the partner should be more likely to
comply compared to when the robot does not point out the incorrect actions
and the negative outcomes. In human-robot interaction, guilt should only
work if individuals regard robots as a legitimate communication source and
feel empathetic transgressing against the robots.

Robot Credibility

While expanding the scope of persuasion strategies, another focal area of
research should be the credibility of robots. Credibility is a quintessential
dimension of persuasion (Hovland & Weiss, 1951). Robots may not be able
to achieve desired task outcomes without establishing their credibility first
with human partners. For example, a search-and-rescue robot may need to
establish credibility quickly in order to convince disaster victims to follow
important instructions (Murphy, 2004). In health contexts, patients' willingness to interact with healthcare robots, accept their advice, and alter health
behavior may rest on the robots' ability to establish credibility and sustain the
patients' trust.

How human receivers perceive robots as a source determines the robot's
ability to persuade them (Wilson & Sherrell, 1993). Traditionally, source
credibility encompasses different dimensions, including perceived expertise, trustworthiness, and goodwill (McCroskey & Teven, 1999). However,
robots clearly differ from humans, and this requires an original reconceptual-
ization and development of how humans perceive robots as a source. We will
elucidate this source perception based on the functional triad (Fogg, 2003).

Robot as Social Actors

As people share an inherent affinity to seek relational development in communication contexts (Liang & Walther, 2015), they tend to develop social
and interpersonal connections with robot partners (Sauppe & Mutlu, 2015).
Given this, the extent to which they believe in robots' credibility relates to
their perception of the robots' ability to have a social connection. Given that
people treat robots as social beings, it will be interesting to examine whether
robots possess the fundamental dimensions of source credibility that are

comparable to those of humans (Pornpitakpan, 2004), as well as generalized liking toward a source (Cialdini, 2008).

Robot as Tools

Robots' primary function is to conduct their assigned tasks and, accordingly, robot credibility depends on the robots' capabilities to carry out such tasks. Theories of how people accept and adopt new technologies (e.g., Technology Acceptance Model; Venkatesh & Davis, 2000) hypothesize people's perception of the technology's usefulness and ease of use as important predictors of actual usage and adoption behaviors. Usefulness refers to the extent to which a person believes that using a machine will enhance task performance; ease of use refers to the limited efforts placed on using the machine. We assume that these constructs will be analogous to the task attraction dimension of interpersonal attraction (McCroskey, McCroskey, & Richmond, 2006). This dimension will essentially reflect people's affinity toward robots given the robots' performance and ability to collaborate.

Robot as Media

Fogg (2003) emphasized the importance of the interaction experience with persuasive technologies as media. The interaction with robots may elicit positive or negative moods. Certainly, a positive mood has been shown to enhance persuasion (Milberg & Clark, 1988). However, people often hold negative attitudes toward robots that may deteriorate their interaction experience (Nomura, Kanda, & Suzuki, 2006). Our recent work (Liang & Lee, 2017) found that 26% of the U.S. population report a heightened level of fear toward autonomous robots and artificial intelligence. Females, older people, people with less education, and people with lower income were more afraid of robots. For those people, robots need to provide positive interaction experience and elicit a positive mood, in order to gain trust and build credibility (Liang & Lee, 2016). Given such, including mood will be important in predicting and assessing human responses to interacting with robots.

Based on the discussion above of conceptualizing robots as social actors, tools, and media, future studies need to develop and validate the measure of robot credibility.

Conclusion

Thus far, we have learned that robots can effectively gain compliance from human partners, as the sender of persuasive messages in the transactional model of human-machine communication. We envision that in the near future, the persuasive potential of robots will be widely utilized in various sectors including industry, health, education, and service. Actually, this is already happening. For example, a robot is currently used to persuade children with cerebral palsy to follow a physical therapy regimen on a daily basis (Knight, 2017). In Japan, one hundred units of the humanoid robot Pepper are being deployed to sell life insurance (Macdonald, 2016). Understanding the mechanism of robot persuasion will help develop robots that can perform more effectively, provide more positive interaction experience, and function as social actors that are capable of collaborating with us in such contexts. We hope our work contributes to this end.

Note

1. In memoriam.

References

Atkinson, B. M. (2006). Captology: A critical review. In W. IJsselsteijn. Y. de Kort, C. Midden, & B. Eggen (Eds.), *Persuasive technology: First International Conference on Persuasive Technology for Human Well-Being, PERSUASIVE 2006* (pp. 171–182). New York, NY: Springer.

Barnlund, D. C. (2008). A transactional model of communication. In C. D. Mortensen (Ed.), *Communication theory* (2nd ed., pp. 47–57). New Brunswick, NJ: Transaction.

Batson, C. D., & Shaw, L. L. (1991). Evidence for altruism: Toward a pluralism of prosocial motives. *Psychological Inquiry, 2*(2), 107–122.

Baumeister, R. F., Stillwell, A. M., & Heatherton, T. F. (1994). Guilt: An interpersonal approach. *Psychological Bulletin, 115*(2), 243–267.

Beaman, A. L., Cole, C. M., Preston, M., Klentz, B., & Steblay, N. M. (1983). Fifteen years of foot-in-the door research a meta-analysis. *Personality and Social Psychology Bulletin, 9*(2), 181–196.

Bem, D. J. (1972). Self-perception theory. *Advances in Experimental Social Psychology, 6*, 1–62.

Boster, F. J., Mitchell, M. M., Lapinski, M. K., Cooper, H., Orrego, V. O., & Reinke, R. (1999). The impact of guilt and type of compliance-gaining message on compliance. *Communication Monographs, 66*(2), 168–177.

Boster, F. J., Rodriguez, J. I., Cruz, M. G., & Marshall, L. (1995). The relative effectiveness of a direct request message and a pregiving message on friends and strangers. *Communication Research, 22*(4), 475–484.

Bruemmer, D. J., Marble, J. L., & Dudenhoeffer, D. D. (2002). Mutual initiative in human-machine teams. In *Proceedings of the IEEE 7th Conference on Human Factors and Power Plants* (pp. 22–30). IEEE.

Burger, J. M. (1999). The foot-in-the-door compliance procedure: A multiple-process analysis and review. *Personality and Social Psychology Review, 3*(4), 303–325.

Chaiken, S., & Trope, Y. (1999). *Dual-process theories in social psychology*. New York, NY: Guilford Press.

Chidambaram, V., Chiang, Y. H., & Mutlu, B. (2012). Designing persuasive robots: How robots might persuade people using vocal and nonverbal cues. In *Proceedings of the 7th Annual ACM/IEEE International Conference on Human-Robot Interaction* (pp. 293–300). IEEE.

Cialdini, R. B. (2008). *Influence: Science and practice* (5th ed.). Boston, MA: Allyn & Bacon.

Cialdini, R. B., & Goldstein, N. (2004). Social influence: Compliance and conformity. *Annual Review of Psychology, 55,* 591–621.

Cialdini, R. B., & Guadagno, R. E. (2004). Sequential request compliance tactics. In R. H. Gass & J. S. Steiter (Eds.), *Perspectives on persuasion, compliance-gaining, and social influence* (pp. 207–222). Boston, MA: Allyn & Bacon.

Cialdini, R. B., Vincent, J. E., Lewis, S. K., Catalan, J., Wheeler, D., & Darby, B. L. (1975). Reciprocal concessions procedure for inducing compliance: The door-in-the-face technique. *Journal of Personality and Social Psychology, 31*(2), 206–215.

Cicero, M. T. (1897). *Cicero's three books of offices, or moral duties; also his cato major, an essay on old age; laelius, an essay on friendship; paradoxes; scipio's dream; and letter to quintus on the duties of a magistrate.* (C. R. Edmonds, Trans.). New York, NY: Harper & Brothers Publishers.

DeJong, W. (1979). An examination of self-perception mediation of the foot-in-the-door effect. *Journal of Personality and Social Psychology, 37*(12), 2221–2239.

Fiske, S. T., & Taylor, S. E. (2013). *Social cognition: From brains to culture* (2nd ed.). New York, NY: McGraw-Hill.

Fogg, B. J. (2003). *Persuasive technology: Using computers to change what we think and do.* San Francisco, CA: Morgan Kaufmann Publishers.

Fogg, B. J., & Nass, C. (1997). How users reciprocate to computers: An experiment that demonstrates behavior change. In *CHI'97 extended abstracts on Human Factors in Computing Systems* (pp. 331–332). Atlanta, GA: Association of the Computing Machinery.

Fong, T., Thorpe, C., & Baur, C. (2003). Collaboration, dialogue, human-robot interaction. In R. A. Jarvis & A. Zelinsky (Eds.), *Robotics research* (pp. 255–266). Berlin-Heidelberg, Germany: Springer.

Freedman, J. L., & Fraser S. C. (1966). Compliance without pressure: The foot-in-the-door technique. *Journal of Personality and Social Psychology, 4*(2), 195–202.

Gouldner, A. W. (1960). The norm of reciprocity: A preliminary statement. *American Sociological Review, 25*(2), 161–178.

Guéguen, N. (2002). Foot-in-the-door technique and computer-mediated communication. *Computers in Human Behavior, 18*(1), 11–15.

Guéguen, N., & Jacob, C. (2001). Fund-raising on the web: the effect of an electronic foot-in-the-door on donation. *CyberPsychology & Behavior, 4*(6), 705–709.

Guzman, A. L. (2016). The messages of mute machines: Human-machine communication with industrial technologies. *Communication +1, 5,* Article 4.

Ham, J., Bokhorst, R., Cuijpers, R., van der Pol, D., & Cabibihan, J. J. (2011). Making robots persuasive: The influence of combining persuasive strategies (gazing and gestures) by a storytelling robot on its persuasive power. In B. Mutlu, C. Bartneck, J. Ham, V. Evers, & T. Kanda (Eds.), *Proceedings of the 3rd International Conference on Social Robotics* (pp. 71–83). Amsterdam, The Netherlands: Springer-Verlag Berlin Heidelberg.

Ham, J., & Midden, C. J. H. (2014). A persuasive robot to stimulate energy conservation: The influence of positive and negative social feedback and task similarity on energy consumption behavior. *International Journal of Social Robotics, 6*(2), 163–171.

Hegel, F., Muhl, C., Wrede, B., Hielscher-Fastabend, M., & Sagerer, G. (2009). Understanding social robots. In *Proceedings of the 2nd International Conference on Advances in Computer-Human Interactions* (pp. 169–174). Cancun, Mexico: IEEE.

Hobhouse, L. T. (1906). *Morals in evolution: A study in comparative ethics.* London, UK: Chapman and Hall.

Hoffman, G., & Breazeal, C. (2004). Collaboration in human-robot teams. In *Proceedings of AIAA. 1st Intelligent Systems Technical Conference.* Chicago, IL: American Institute of Aeronautics and Astronautics.

Hovland, C. I., & Weiss, W. (1951). The influence of source credibility on communication effectiveness. *Public Opinion Quarterly, 15*(4), 635–650.

Huang, C., & Mutlu, B. (2012). Robot behavior toolkit: Generating effective social behaviors for robots. In *Proceedings of the 7th ACM/IEEE Conference on Human-Robot Interaction (HRI 2012)* (pp. 25–32). ACM.

Kegel, R. H. P., & Wieringa, R. J. (2014). *Persuasive technologies: A systematic literature review and application to PISA.* (CTIT Technical Report Series; No. TR-CTIT-14-07). Enschede, the Netherlands: Centre for Telematics and Information Technology (CTIT).

Kidd, C. D., & Breazeal, C. L. (2007). A robotic weight loss coach. In *Proceedings of the National Conference on Artificial Intelligence* (pp. 1985–1986). Menlo Park, CA: ACM Press.

Kim, Y., & Sundar, S. S. (2012). Anthropomorphism of computers: Is it mindful or mindless? *Computers in Human Behavior, 28*(1), 241–250.

Knight, W. (2017, February 16). A robot physical therapist helps kids with cerebral palsy. *MIT Technology Review.* Retrieved from https://www.technologyreview.com/s/603614/a-robot-physical-therapist-helps-kids-with-cerebral-palsy/

Langer, E., Blank, A., & Chanowitz, B. (1978). The mindlessness of ostensibly thoughtful action: The role of "placebic" information in interpersonal interaction. *Journal of Personality and Social Psychology, 36*(6), 635–642.

Lee, E.-J. (2003). Effects of "gender" of the computer on informational social influence: The moderating role of task type. *International Journal of Human-Computer Studies, 58*(4), 347–362.

Lee, E.-J. (2008). Gender stereotyping of computers: Resource depletion or reduced attention? *Journal of Communication, 58*(2), 301–320.

Lee, E.-J. (2010). What triggers social responses to flattering computers? Experimental tests of anthropomorphism and mindlessness explanations. *Communication Research*, *37*(2), 191–214.

Lee, S. A., & Liang, Y. (2015). Reciprocity in computer-human interaction: Source-based, norm-based, and affect-based explanations. *Cyberpsychology, Behavior, and Social Networking*, *18*(4), 234–240.

Lee, S. A., & Liang, Y. (2016). The role of reciprocity in verbally persuasive robots. *Cyberpsychology, Behavior, and Social Networking*, *19*(8), 524–527.

Lee, S. A., Liang, Y., & Cho, S. (2016). *Effects of anthropomorphism and reciprocity in persuasive computer agents*. Paper presented at the 102nd annual convention of the National Communication Association, Philadelphia, PA.

Lee, S. A., Liang, Y., & Thompson, A. M. (2017). *Robotic foot-in-the-door: Using sequential-request persuasive strategies in human-robot interaction*. Paper presented at the 67th annual convention of the International Communication Association, San Diego, CA.

Liang, Y., & Lee, S. A. (2016). Advancing the strategic messages affecting robot trust effect: The dynamic of user- and robot-generated content on human-robot trust and interaction outcomes. *Cyberpsychology, Behavior, and Social Networking*, *19*(2), 538–544.

Liang, Y., & Lee, S. A. (2017). Fear of autonomous robots and artificial intelligence: Evidence from national representative data with probability sampling. *International Journal of Social Robotics*, *9*(1), 379–384.

Liang, Y., Lee, S. A., & Jang, J. (2013). Mindlessness and gaining compliance in computer-human interaction. *Computers in Human Behavior*, *29*(4), 1572–1579.

Liang, Y., & Walther, J. B. (2015). Computer-mediated communication. In *International encyclopedia of social and behavioral sciences* (2nd ed., pp. 504–509). Waltham, MA: Elsevier.

Marble, J. L., Bruemmer, D. J., Few, D. A., & Dudenhoeffer, D. D. (2004). Evaluation of supervisory vs. peer-peer interaction with human-robot teams. In *Proceedings of the 37th Hawaii International Conference on System Sciences*. IEEE.

McCroskey, L. L., McCroskey, J. C., & Richmond, V. P. (2006). Analysis and improvement of the measurement of interpersonal attraction and homophily. *Communication Quarterly*, *54*(1), 1–31.

McCroskey, J. C., & Teven, J. J. (1999). Goodwill: A reexamination of the construct and its measurement. *Communications Monographs*, *66*(1), 90–103.

Macdonald, C. (2016, July 21). Pepper gets another job: Softbank robot to sell life insurance at 80 stores in Japan. *Daily Mail*. Retrieved from http://www.dailymail.co.uk/sciencetech/article-3702381/Pepper-gets-job-Softbank-robot-sell-life-insurance-80-stores-Japan.html

Milberg, S., & Clark, M. S. (1988). Moods and compliance. *British Journal of Social Psychology*, *27*(1), 79–90.

Murphy, R. R. (2004). Human-robot interaction in rescue robotics. *IEEE Transactions on Systems, Man, and Cybernetics*, *34*(2), 138–153.

Nass, C., & Moon, Y. (2000). Machines and mindlessness: Social responses to computers. *Journal of Social Issues, 56*(1), 81–103.

Nass, C., Moon, Y., & Carney, P. (1999). Are respondents polite to computers? Social desirability and direct responses to computers. *Journal of Applied Social Psychology, 29*(5), 1093–1110.

Nass, C., Moon, Y., & Green, N. (1997). Are computers gender-neutral? Gender stereotypic responses to computers with voices. *Journal of Applied Social Psychology, 27*(10), 864–876.

National Science Foundation. (2016). *National robotics initiative: The realization of co-robots acting in direct support of individuals and groups.* Washington, DC: NSF. Retrieved from https://www.nsf.gov/pubs/2016/nsf16517/nsf16517.htm

Nomura, T., Kanda, T., & Suzuki, T. (2006). Experimental investigation into influence of negative attitudes toward robots on human–robot interaction. *AI & Society, 20*(2), 138–150.

O'Keefe, D. J., & Hale S. L. (2001). An odds-ratio-based meta-analysis of research on the door-in-the-face influence strategy. *Communication Reports, 14*(1), 31–38.

Pornpitakpan, C. (2004). The persuasiveness of source credibility: A critical review of five decades' evidence. *Journal of Applied Social Psychology, 34*(2), 243–281.

Reeves, B., & Nass, C. (1996). *The media equation: How people treat computers, televisions, and new media like real people and places.* New York, NY: Cambridge University Press.

Regan, D. T. (1971). Effects of a favor and liking on compliance. *Journal of Experimental Social Psychology, 7*(6), 627–639.

Rosen, C. A. (1985). Robots and machine intelligence. In S. Y. Nof (Ed.), *Handbook of Industrial Robotics* (pp. 21–28). New York, NY: John Wiley & Sons.

Sandry, E. (2015). *Robots and communication.* New York, NY: Palgrave Macmillan.

Sauppe, A., & Mutlu, B. (2015). Effective task training strategies for human and robot instructors. *Autonomous Robots, 39*(3), 313–329.

Shannon, C. E., & Weaver, W. (1949). *The mathematical theory of communication.* Urbana, IL: University of Illinois Press.

Schaumburg, H. (2001). Computers as tools or as social actors?—The users' perspective on anthropomorphic agents. *International Journal of Cooperative Information Systems, 10*, 217–234.

Sheridan, T. B. (1984). Supervisory control of remote manipulators, vehicles and dynamic processes: Experiments in command and display aiding. In W. B. Rouse (Ed.), *Advances in man-machine systems research* (Vol. 1, pp. 49–173). Greenwich, CT: JAI Press.

Siegel, M., Breazeal, C., & Norton, M. I. (2009) Persuasive robotics: The influence of robot gender on human behavior. In *Proceedings of IEEE/RSJ International Conference on Intelligent Robots and Systems* (pp. 2563–2568). IEEE.

Sundar, S. S., & Nass, C. (2000). Source orientation in human-computer interaction programmer, networker, or independent social actor. *Communication Research, 27*(6), 683–703.

Venkatesh, V., & Davis, F. D. (2000). A theoretical extension of the technology acceptance model: Four longitudinal field studies. *Management Science, 46*(2), 186–204.

Wang, J., Lewis, M., & Scerri, P. (2006). Cooperating robots for search and rescue. In *Proceedings of the Agent Technology for Disaster Management Workshop at the 5th International Joint Conference on Autonomous Agents and Multi-agent Systems (AAMAS)*. ACM.

Wilson, E. J., & Sherrell, D. L. (1993). Source effects in communication and persuasion research: A meta-analysis of effect size. *Journal of the Academy of Marketing Science, 21*(2), 101–112.

7. *Communicating With Robots: ANTalyzing the Interaction Between Healthcare Robots and Humans With Regards to Privacy*

Christoph Lutz and Aurelia Tamò

In the coming years, we are expected to see a massive diffusion and adoption of artificial intelligence (AI) and robots (Gupta, 2015; van den Berg, 2016). In fact, robots are already heavily used in industrial settings and increasingly so for service tasks (Garmann-Johnsen, Mettler, & Sprenger, 2014; Lin, 2012). Gradually, they will be moving into our homes and institutions. The adoption of robots as new household members at home as well as the delegation of specific tasks to robots in nursing homes and in hospitals will importantly shape our attitudes towards our mechanical friends.

We address the topic of healthcare robots and privacy. Our choice of healthcare robots over other robots comes from the fact that they often deal with sensitive information and with vulnerable population groups (i.e., the elderly and/or ill individuals, see van Wynsberghe, 2013). This user segment might not always have the knowledge to give informed consent about data collection when interacting with robots. Moreover, it may lack the awareness to fully grasp the technological limits of the robots, leading to situations of potential dependency.

In this chapter, we will apply actor-network theory (ANT) to shed light on the privacy implications of healthcare robots. ANT strives to be a descriptive, constructivist approach that takes into account the agency of objects, concepts and ideas as well as the relationality of technology and the social (Latour, 1987). It has been applied to complex technological innovations, such as e-health systems (e.g., Muhammad & Wickramasinghe, 2014). We will use some of the main concepts of ANT to "map" the privacy ecosystem in robotic healthcare technology, analyzing (or ANTalyzing) the complex inter-play of robots and humans in that context.

The main contribution of the chapter is to contextualize the notion of privacy for healthcare robots by applying ANT. This reveals how a complex and fluid network of concrete and abstract actors is at play and forms the robotic privacy ecosystem. We will show how using key concepts from ANT illuminates important debates in the literature about robots and privacy in a healthcare setting. Thus, the chapter follows the general descriptive charac-teristic of ANT. Instead of prescribing what *should* be done, ANT often uses case studies and thick descriptions to illustrate what *is* actually done. "[ANT] tells stories about 'how' relations assemble or don't. As a form, one of several, of material semiotics, it is better understood as a toolkit for telling interesting stories about, and interfering in, those relations" (Law, 2009, p. 141–142).

The chapter contains three main parts in addition to the introduction and conclusion. First, we will provide our understanding of robots in the form of a working definition. We will also briefly survey the field of healthcare robotics. Second, we will elaborate on the privacy concerns that are specific to robots. Third, in the main section of the chapter, we will introduce actor-network theory. We will discuss the descriptive approach of the theory with two examples: Latour's (1994) gunman and the night walks from Beane & Orlikowski's study (2015). We will then introduce key concepts of ANT and apply them to the interaction between robots and humans. By doing so, we show how ANT can enrich our understanding of privacy in the context of healthcare robots. We conclude the chapter by discussing the theoretical implications of our analysis and by addressing the shortcomings of ANT as a framework for healthcare robots and privacy.

Robots in Healthcare

Defining the term robot has proven to be difficult and various authors have tried to establish a common understanding of what constitutes a robot (Bekey, 2012; Calo, 2016; Richards & Smart, 2016). Most definitions attribute a cer-tain agency[1] to robots (i.e., decision-making and versatility), indicating that robots are "constructed systems" or "organized" by engineers in a certain way, hence not completely self-governed. While Calo (2016) elaborates on the information processing capabilities of robots and ability of robots to (re-)act, Richards and Smart (2016) use the term "mental" agency which incor-porates information processing. We assume that the term "mental" implies a certain learning process of robots (e.g., machine-learning technology) and interactivity (i.e., learning from its environment and the social interactions).

Unlike Calo (2016), Richards and Smart (2016) distinctively highlight the physical embodiment of robots. In this chapter, robots are considered as physical objects, in contrast to "only" AI. In sum, key features associated with robots are agency, learning, and physical embodiment.

As our contribution focuses on healthcare robots, the question of how to categorize such robots arises. The Roadmap for US Robotics (2013) points out that robotic healthcare systems include a "wide range of environments (from the operating room to the family room), user populations (from the very young to the very old, from the infirm to the able-bodied, from the typically developed to those with physical and/or cognitive deficits), and interaction modalities (from hands-on surgery to hands-off rehabilitation coaching" (p. 29). A categorization of healthcare robots may be aligned to those modalities. Depending on the environment, the user, and the interaction modalities, healthcare robots can be further classified into different types. First, surgical robots support surgeons in their daily operations while still allowing the surgeons to override them when necessary (Roadmap for US Robotics, 2013). Second, robots can be directly implanted into humans as replacements for lost or malfunctioning body parts. Prosthetic devices which assist physical body functions (e.g. exoskeletons) are a typical example. Third, certain robots assist with patient rehabilitation and provide support for family members (Roadmap for US Robotics, 2013). Examples are RP-7 (Beane & Orlikowski, 2015) and patient transportation robots. The latter may offer ad hoc support for doctors and nurses (Garmann-Johnsen et al., 2014). The fourth type of robots is assistive robots that help with behavioral aspects (Roadmap for US Robotics, 2013). These robots target user behavior and tend to have intuitive interaction modalities (e.g., embracing a robot leads to a response via sound and movements). One example of such robots is therapy robots (e.g., *Paro* for animal therapy or *CosmoBot* for the tailored treatment of disabled children).[2]

On Healthcare Robots and Privacy

How do healthcare robots impact users' and bystanders' privacy?[3] How are their privacy implications different from those of other smart devices, such as smartphones, smartwatches, and fitness trackers? We argue that healthcare robots affect privacy in three distinct ways, when compared to other widely employed technologies such as smartphones:

(1) Robots have certain agency and are mobile: they can move by themselves from one room to another. As discussed below, this point is most closely connected to the dimension of physical privacy.

(2) Humans typically bond with humanoid or animal-like robots, sometimes even with less anthropomorphic or zoomorphic robots. They treat robots less as a tool and more as a being. As discussed below, this point is most closely connected to the dimension of social privacy.

(3) The technology on which robots rely is highly complex and not understandable for a layperson. The data processing is murky for users at best, a black-box at worst. These concerns already come up when analyzing smart devices and privacy, but with robots, they are likely to get intensified. As discussed below, this point is most closely connected to the dimension of informational privacy.

Privacy Issue 1: (Independent) Mobility of Robots and Access to Private Spaces

Robots reach out into the world. Their mobility comes with increased pervasiveness, in the form of an unprecedented potential for access to personal rooms and surveillance (Calo, 2012). A healthcare robot, for instance, can enter bedrooms while the tenants are awake or asleep. It can also move around houses and flats, monitor the individuals present, and, via face recognition and/or social media data analysis, attribute those faces to certain identities.

Calo (2012) identified surveillance and access as core privacy risks of robotic technology. Surveillance, in the context of robots, often involves a physical component as exemplified by drone spying in military contexts. Similarly, home healthcare robots could be (ab)used for surveillance purposes by the government, corporations, or private citizens. One can imagine a scenario where security services install tracking software into such an ostensibly harmless robot to monitor the whereabouts and habits of suspicious subjects. Similarly, access can have physical repercussions if, for example, a healthcare robot involuntarily enters an individual's bedroom or bathroom while they are in an intimate situation. Compared with other advanced forms of information technology in healthcare settings, such as wristbands, smart phones, or tablet-computers, the privacy consequences of robots are hence more far-reaching.

These concerns, linked to the mobility and surveillance capabilities of robots, are connected to the literature on *physical privacy*. Literature on physical privacy dates back at least to Warren and Brandeis (1890, p. 193), who defined privacy as "the right to be let alone." Thus, this conception of privacy is focused on the physical dimension, in the sense of freedom from intrusion into private spaces. With the advent of the Internet and other sophisticated information technology, the informational aspect of privacy has gained importance. Consequently, the vast bulk of privacy research in the context of the

Internet and computer technology focuses on informational privacy (see more on this below) and personal data as well as control over it (Smith, Dinev, & Xu, 2011). Here, the definitions of Westin[4] and Altman[5] are more appropriate as well as Petronio's (2002) privacy management theory (Margulis, 2011). Yet, with the advent of robots, the physical privacy discourse is again becoming more relevant. However, these dimensions of privacy are intrinsically intertwined and often coincide. For example, when a robot enters the bedroom of a person and records a private conversation, this could be seen as a violation of both physical and informational privacy.

Privacy Issue 2: Social Bonding With Robots

The second privacy issue is a result of the social bonding between humans and robots (Calo, 2012). Multiple studies in the field of human robot interaction have shown that humans tend to bond with humanoid (anthropomorphism) or animal-like (zoomorphism) robots (Breazeal, 2003; Darling, 2012, 2016; Duffy, 2003; Turkle, 2011). This tendency of humans to project emotions and feelings onto things is not new (Balkin, 2015). Yet, given the human tendency to bond with robots in a fashion similar to human bonding with other people, individuals might be inclined to discuss very personal and delicate topics with a robot such as emotional states, feelings, or even secrets. The robot, however, might not be designed to adequately deal with such sensitive topics. In this sense, healthcare robots such as therapy robots could be seen by some people as counsellors rather than assistants or servants (Rabbitt, Kazdin, & Hong, 2015).

The literature has discussed such issues under the term *social privacy*. Social privacy is concerned with control over interactions and both the proximity towards and distance between other individuals (Trepte & Reinecke, 2011). Since healthcare is, to a large extent, a social setting with specific actors co-operating, the element of communication and interaction should not be neglected. In a similar manner to virtual assistants on computers and smartphones (such as Siri, see Guzman, 2017), social robots often have sophisticated speech recognition and language capabilities which enable interaction and the establishment of intimate relationships.[6]

Privacy Issue 3: A Robot's Access to Data and the Black Box Problem

Robots can gather, analyze and act upon a vast body of data. The collection of identifiable user data (e.g., names, date of birth, eating preferences and cultural taste), location data or other types of sensitive information is, at its root, an issue of *informational privacy*. According to Alaiad & Zhou (2014), informational privacy is the most relevant form of privacy with respect to the acceptance of robot technology. Other authors agree that information processing is one of the core aspects of robotics (Felzmann, Beyan, Ryan, & Beyan, 2015). Thus, robots "do not just impact on the physical environment of their users or provide limited, task specific information, but control the informational environment for humans more comprehensively" (Felzmann et al., 2015, p. 3).

In this sense, additional concerns beyond those raised in HRI studies occur. The tracking of users and bystanders through robots is an example, leading us to question what information is obtained and how this information is to be used. One can imagine a scenario where a healthcare robot collects information not only about the patient to whom it has been designated, but also collects information about other individuals, such as children, in the vicinity without their knowledge. A further issue in the field of informational privacy is the sharing of data with third parties for unintended and non-consensual purposes (Felzmann et al., 2015). A study by Syrdal and colleagues (2007) showed that most participants felt uneasy when put in a scenario where robots had the power to disclose personal information, such as psychological or personality characteristics, to other individuals without their permission. They were also worried about the possibility of data about themselves being collected by robots of others (Pew Research Center, 2014).

The concept of contextual integrity or privacy in context (Nissenbaum, 2004) can be applied to informational privacy. We have to ask (1) to whom the information is communicated and whether this corresponds with the existing information norms in a given setting (e.g.., it might be appropriate to pass medical information on to a doctor but not to an employer) and (2) what conversations among individuals are recorded by the robot and how they are used. Robots' sensory capabilities and abilities to process real-time big data enable a multitude of services. For instance, in healthcare and elderly care, doctors and nurses can delegate particular duties to robots, such as reminding patients to take their medicine, checking patients' pulse rates, monitoring activities at home, monitoring eating habits as well as undertaking routine activities and social interactions (Felzmann et al., 2015). However, the delegation of such tasks to healthcare robots "raises significant issues regarding the role and use of information that underlies such decision-making" (Felzmann et al., 2015, p. 3).

In this regard, the aspect of black-boxing becomes important. Black-boxing implies a lack of transparency on the side of the data collectors but also a lack of knowledge and awareness on the side of the users. The issue has been increasingly investigated in the ethical and critical literature on algorithms (Mittelstadt, Allo, Taddeo, Wachter, & Floridi, 2016; Sandvig, Hamilton, Karahalios, & Langbort, 2014), with Pasquale (2015) aptly diagnosing today's information environment as a black box society. Like a variety of web services, robots are increasingly connected to the cloud and run on sophisticated, often black-boxed, algorithms. Many users, particularly non-technical and vulnerable users in healthcare settings, lack understanding about robots' background information collection and the privacy literacy necessary to avoid damage.

Interactions Between Humans and Machines: HMC

Establishing a relationship of trust between robots and machines involves correct assessments of human privacy expectations across different situations. Robots need to understand the signals and triggers that require them to adapt their communication. We think that a communicative approach to human-machine interaction can help illuminate these privacy dynamics. In the following paragraphs, we thus introduce the theory of human-machine communication (HMC).

When analyzing human-human interaction, our daily activities can be described as a bundle of social connections and interactions between them. Simple gestures, body language, and spoken language indicate to others what we think, feel, want. Similarly, in human-machine communication (HMC), robots need to acquire an understanding of such signals to smoothly adapt. They interact and communicate with humans in a variety of ways.

HMC is a relatively new and interdisciplinary field of communication studies (see Introduction, this volume). HMC can be seen "as an umbrella term encompassing HCI, HRI, and HAI" (Guzman, 2016, p. 2, fn. 7). It is not only interested in widely studied information and communication technologies such as social media and mobile media but also in more mundane and seemingly "mute" technology (Guzman, 2016). Industrial technologies such as industrial robots are an example. In a thorough analysis of industrial technologies, Guzman (2016) shows how HMC theory can point us to the communicative affordances of machines that are not primarily designed for communication. Extending cybernetic theory, the analysis convincingly argues for going beyond technological instrumentalism. HMC takes into consideration the role of the humans and machines. In the context of industrial technologies, depending on the role of the worker communicating with the machine (as an operator controlling the machine or as an assembly line worker being controlled by the machine), different relationships and meanings are conveyed. Thus, HMC invites us to think about communication more broadly than is usually done in communication and media studies.

In the following, we are very much interested in HMC-related questions and share its perspective. Privacy, as a social phenomenon, is strongly rooted in communication. Not surprisingly, communication research is one of the key disciplines that investigate privacy. For example, communication privacy management theory has emerged as a prominent privacy theory from a communication perspective (Petronio, 2002), proving useful across a range of contexts. However, traditional privacy research rooted in communication studies does often not consider the materiality and agency of non-human agents to a sufficient extent. To analyze the relationships between humans and machines, in our case between humans and healthcare robots in the context of privacy, we choose ANT—a framework with similarities to HMC. Before dwelling upon the topic of robot-human-relationships and privacy in healthcare settings, we illustrate how ANT operates with two examples. Then, we describe ANT itself and the common terminologies used within this framework, applying them to the healthcare robot-privacy ecosystem.

Actor Network Theory

Setting the Stage: Two ANT Examples

The first example comes directly from Bruno Latour, one of the founders of ANT. In his famous case study on guns, Latour (1994) argues that a gun itself can be seen not only as an object but also as a so-called "actant." As an actant, a gun pushes humans to pull the trigger. In this sense, humans and guns transform one another when combined—the object itself cannot kill. Humans might not feel the urge to kill and might not be able to do so. When in combination—the gun in an individual's hand—this initial setting changes: the interaction creates a "gunman." The feeling of a gun in their hands transforms humans as they enter a relationship with their gun (Latour, 1994). They become gunmen, which in itself is an actor-network. Therefore, Latour argues that the responsibility for actions must be shared among actants in a network.

While ANT has been used for seemingly arbitrary and diverse cases, from the Berlin key (Latour, 2000), to scallop domestication in the St. Brieuc Bay in Brittany (Callon, 1986), to the gun example mentioned above (Latour, 1994), it also proves to be valuable for describing new technologies in-situ. The second example serves to illustrate this. In a case study, Beane and Orlikowski (2015), in the tradition of socio-materiality, describe the introduction of the telepresence robot RP-7 in a post-surgical intensive care unit (SICU) of a mid-sized US hospital. The authors focus on so-called night walks: routine checks on patients that take place every evening at 9 pm and involve experienced attending physicians (APs), residents in training, and nurses. By comparing traditional night walks via landline telephone[7] to the new night walks via RP-7 robot,[8] they show how the materiality of the technologies (phone vs. robot) and the materiality of the preparation on the side of the residents (collecting hands-on evidence by talking to nurses and visiting the patients before the night walk vs. only going through their medical records) affects the coordination work in the SICU. The night walk as a specific practice can be interpreted as an actor-network itself, with the robots, individuals involved (APs, residents in training, nurses, and patients), and their outputs (e.g., patient records, data collected by RP-7) serving as the actants (see below for an explanation of this term). These actants perform diverse interactions and enter into coalitions with each other but also encounter conflicts. The authors show how the corresponding outcomes in the form of patient care quality vary according to the technology involved. The interactions are more standardized and less immediate in the case of traditional telephone night walks. They only involve APs and residents and are locally bound, leaving more responsibility for the residents and less room for intervention and scrutiny for the APs. By contrast, the RP-7 night walks are more open and complex, involve nurses and patients, and can thus partly enhance the quality of the patient care (but they also partly deteriorate it, depending on the residents' preparation). In terms of privacy, the introduction of the robot increases the potential of surveillance and control on the part of the APs, possibly decreasing the residents' and patients' perceived privacy.

These two examples help us to (re-)think the relationships between humans and things. They provoke us to consider matters of agency, the impact of technology as well as establishing culpability. In this sense, the descriptive angle of ANT motivates us to think differently about privacy. Both examples show how technology is not a neutral, independent entity but constantly enacted within pre-existing and evolving social settings. In other words, the social and technological/material are intrinsically interwoven (Orlikowski, 1992; 2007), making it necessary to consider the "bigger picture" or actor-network.

Networks as a Method of Analysis

ANT was developed in the mid-1980s by the sociologists Michel Callon, Bruno Latour and John Law. The theory argues that technology and the social environment interact with each other, forming complex networks. These networks consist of multiple relationships between the social, the technological or material, and the semiotic. It is important to recognize that the concept of a network in ANT does not refer to the analysis of technical networks such as power grids and flight connections. "An actor-network may lack all the characteristics of a technical network—it may be local, it may have no compulsory paths, no strategically positioned nodes" (Latour, 1996, p. 369). Neither is ANT an approach for the explanation of existing social networks such as Facebook friend networks, kinship networks, or intra-organizational networks, as would be the case in structural sociology and social network analysis (Latour, 1996). Rather than investigating technical or social network structures, ANT understands itself as an ontology and introduces a method with which something can be described. According to ANT, the world cannot simply be divided into either social or material aspects. Instead, ANT stresses the capacity of technology to be an actor in and of itself, one which influences and shapes other relations. ANT sees material objects as an element of a network. Illustrating the relationship between objects (amongst both other objects and humans) is the main aim of ANT.

In this sense, ANT is more of a *descriptive framework* than an explanatory theory. Instead of explaining relationships in terms of cause-and-effect, ANT describes the interactions between units or elements. It treats objects and subjects, both human and non-human, with the same vocabulary (see below). By focusing on the interaction between various actors and concepts, ANT describes the ordering of technological, social, and organizational developments. In the words of Latour: "Network is a concept, not a thing out there. It is a tool to help describe something and not what is being described." (Latour, 2005, p. 131). As the term "network"[9] illustrates, the interesting part of this descriptive process is the interaction, energy, flow and link between different actants (contrary to the human actors themselves). An actant can be anything which "influences the turn of events" in a particular setting (Krieger & Belliger, 2014, p. 92).

ANT employs different terms to describe particular aspects of the network. In the following sections, we will describe some of the most reoccurring terms in ANT and then apply them to the healthcare robot-privacy context.

What ANT Offers for the Analysis of Robot-Patient-Interactions

Actants

Frequently used terms in ANT are "actor" and "actant." The former relates mostly to human actors while the latter describes the ability of non-human objects to act. In other words, an actant is any participant in the network (human or non-human) which has a certain presence and can make a difference in a given situation.

In healthcare contexts, we can distinguish different actants. In line with HMC theory, not only interactive information and communication technologies, such as email, social media, and phones, but also "passive" and mute machines are of interest (Guzman, 2016). Actants can include patients, doctors, nurses, robots, medical instruments, regulators, equipment suppliers, pharmaceutical companies, and even abstract ideas, such as the concepts of care ethics (van Wynsberghe, 2013), privacy and patient rights, the Hippocratic Oath, and medical standards. None of these actants enjoys prevalence, as Callon (2007) notes: "ANT is based on no stable theory of the actor; rather it assumes the radical indeterminacy of the actor. For example, the actor's size, its psychological make-up, and the motivations behind its actions—none of these are predetermined" (p. 273).

Translation

The term translation describes the process of creating actor-networks as well as the formation of order among the actants. In a translation, the actors in a network influence each other in a process of association (Krieger & Belliger, 2014). Translation includes a strong process perspective with four characteristic phases that can overlap: problematization, interessement, enrolment, and mobilization (Callon, 1986). The network thus goes through phases of defining a central problem or agenda (problematization), recruiting outside actants into the network and assigning roles for them (interessement), bringing these actants together (enrolment), and mobilizing formerly passive actants to create alignment (i.e., aligned interests) in the network.

In the actor-network of privacy and healthcare robots, translation involves negotiation between additional actants beyond engineers, end-users, and the robot itself. Pharmaceutical and healthcare companies, for example, might want to use the robot as an advertising machine, which, based on the patients' own behavioral routines, could promote certain medications or therapies. To do so, such companies would require access to the robot by cooperating with the engineers or by updating the robot's software with a script. Thus, to use the robot as an advertising machine, they would have to enter various coalitions.

Translation is necessary to mediate[10] meaningfully between the various points in the network. Robotics engineers, for example, should think of consumer concerns such as privacy (Calo, 2012; Lutz & Tamò, 2015), security, and job replacement (Eurobarometer 427). They should also implement safeguards in ways accessible by both the end-users and the robots (Lederer, Hong,

Dey, & Landay, 2004). This would mean making the privacy and security-related aspects understandable, transparent, and easy to apply for the end-user. For the robot, it would mean using "sustainable" code, algorithms and stable hardware which minimizes privacy hazards and the overall damage potential.

Heterogeneous Networks
A heterogeneous network is one where the interests of the actants are aligned. In order to establish whether interests of actants align, we would need to conduct interviews with various participants of the network. For instance, we would need to assess the patients' points of view through interviews, assessing whether they value privacy, how they perceive it in relation to other actants (i.e., if they feel it is endangered by doctors or pharmaceutical companies spying on them via a robot), and what they do to protect their privacy. These interviews could be complemented with a document analysis of the robots, by studying user manuals, promotional materials, the internal project transcripts from the engineering team as well as its code and software. The walkthrough approach, based on Science and Technology Studies (STS) and ANT, presents a suitable methodological approach how this can be done for the analysis of apps (Light, Burgess, & Duguay, 2016). It could be applied to robots as well. Such analyses could also be enhanced with an ethnographic analysis of the robot in-action, specifically looking at how privacy is dealt with. Given the recent emergence of healthcare robots, their currently limited adoption, and the fact that they are still being developed and in processes of experimentation, carrying out an ANT study about such a research and development project could be a promising approach.

Tokens or Quasi Objects
Tokens are, in essence, the successful interactions of actors in an actor-network. They are being passed through the network. By being passed increasingly through a network, tokens get punctualized (see below), normalized, and are progressively taken for granted. By contrast, when tokens are transmitted less frequently or when errors in the transmission of tokens occur (e.g., because a bug interrupts normal routines), punctualization is decreased and the actor-network faces problems (Zwicker, Seitz, & Wickramasinghe, 2014).

Robots can be considered as hybrids, tokens or quasi-objects, which Latour (1993) defines as "simultaneously real, discursive and social" (p. 64). The discursive element is particularly interesting since it implies that robots are shaping the discourse around themselves and are shaped by it at the same time. If a majority of people, because of, say, press coverage about a robotic incident (e.g., a Fisher teddy bear or Barbie dolls exposing private data or a deadly incident involving a robot at Volkswagen; see Associated Press, 2015;

Franceschi-Bicchierai, 2015, 2016), perceive them as privacy-intruding, dangerous, malign or even creepy, this might feedback on the existing actor-network by inhibiting future purchases of robots or reducing public funding for the research and development of new robots. In fact, recent research shows that such perceptions of fear are widespread, with 26 percent of the US population experiencing high levels of "fear of autonomous robots and artificial intelligence" (Liang & Lee, 2017).

Punctualization
Punctualization is the viewing of a combination of actors as one actor. Punctualization corresponds with black-boxing. It describes how a combination of actants is seen as one actant in a larger network. Thus, punctualization can be considered a form of zooming out, where originally separated actants are seen as one unit. Punctualization is only questioned in moments of crisis and in situations which deviate from the normal functioning of the actor-network. In such instances, de-punctualization can occur and the punctualized actant is decomposed into its constituent parts.

To view healthcare robots as individual actants in an actor-network requires the application of punctualization. This is because such robots are in fact composed of numerous components, ranging from sensory parts such as cameras and microphones, to motorized elements such as arms, legs, or fingers, and even to processing hardware such as computer chips. The concept of punctualization is closely in line with Privacy Issue 3 discussed above (i.e., black-boxing). In the case of healthcare robots and privacy, robots and their roles in the actor-network might avoid scrutiny as long as they function properly and show no signs of violating the privacy of users. However, if a serious privacy breach should occur, punctualization might be dissolved and de-punctualization might occur. For example, if a healthcare robot inadvertently breaches patient privacy (e.g., by taking a compromising photo of its user), this would trigger suspicion as to the proper functioning of the robot. The patient might, for instance, scrutinize the robot's configuration and settings. The patient might even attempt to break open the robot's casing to reveal the underlying mechanics—showing that the robot is a composition of various individual components rather than an entity in its own right. In this sense, privacy breaches can be considered triggers for de-punctualization.

Obligatory Passage Point
According to Callon (1986), an obligatory passage point (OPP) is a critical incident where actants in a network converge around an important issue and the survival of the actor-network is at play. The OPP serves as a mediating and transforming element, including its own action program.

In the wider context of robots and privacy, an OPP could be a critical incident such as a publicly discussed privacy breach. For example, in the instance of the Barbie dolls which listened to the private conversations of children, the dolls were negatively perceived by parents. This, in turn, led the Barbie doll producer to rethink the technical functions of their toys. In this sense, the actants of a network have to adjust their interactions in order for the network to remain intact. OPP here necessitates discussions about the technologies integrated in products, the responsibilities of manufactures and the wishes of customers.

In the context of healthcare robots, the agreement needed by various actors to work with specific robots and the creation of data processing standards could be seen as an OPP necessary for establishing the presence of healthcare robots. In addition, legislation or court decisions concerned with how healthcare robots can be employed will impact the network and its actants.

Discussion and Conclusion

Theoretical Implications

Our analysis revealed a number of theoretical implications. An important take-away is that robots do not endanger privacy in a linear, predictable fashion. Instead, they are being embedded in existing and constantly evolving actor-networks of people, interest groups, ideas, social constructions, and evolving norms. Thus, they are, to a certain extent, socially shaped and constructed. ANT illustrates the reciprocal and dynamic nature of the robotic privacy ecosystem. Indeed, the notion of an ecosystem is perhaps the most fundamental takeaway of any ANT analysis. All actants interact with one another and are co-dependent upon one another. The ecosystem is constantly adapting and re-establishing its "inner balance." When applied to privacy and robots, we must take into account the delicate balancing needed between various actants' interests. This balancing, in turn, requires a prior assessment of the technologies, concepts and ideas at hand.

ANT maps the relationships, interactions, and dependencies among actants. It can be used to describe how relationships and responsibilities face alteration once healthcare robots become more present in our homes, nursing facilities, or hospitals. In the words of Van Wynsberghe (2013, p. 142): "Beyond the embedding of values and/or norms, once the robot enters a network it will alter the distribution of responsibilities and roles within the network as well as the manner in which the practice takes place." This change is described by ANT—the key term here being "translation." In the context of privacy, the descriptive analysis of relationships is thus key for a better understanding of the issues in question (see Beane & Orikowski, 2015 for a good example). ANT helps generate the right questions to ask actants in order to better understand the relationships between them. One such question is the extent of delegation accepted by actants: what factors influence the acceptance of robots as "nurses" or "doctors' assistants"? Linked to that, what data triggers which actions of robots? The more doctors, nurses, or patients delegate tasks to healthcare robots, the more we will be confronted with the question of how robots make decisions. As robots interact progressively more with complex processing systems, gain increased functional abilities and "make a wide range of decisions and apply them on behalf of the user, potentially bypassing active input by the user entirely," it is necessary to identify the underlying mechanisms and the role of user data (Felzmann et al., 2015, p. 282). This includes thinking about the code which robots use and its social implications, such as triggering discrimination or social bonding (Lutz & Tamò, 2015).

Moreover, ANT provides a framework and a common language for facilitating both the description and comparison of networks. For example, it is important to stress that, while considered to be single entities, robots are, in fact, composed of various units such as cameras, sensors, software, and cloud processing operations (see above on punctualization). Therefore, in the context of privacy, each unit might trigger different reactions among actants. Thus, before it is possible to examine the whole actor-network, single units should be analyzed.

The chapter is therefore a call to overcome the technological determinism prevalent in the discourse about robots and privacy (e.g., Carroll, 2015). ANT stresses that technology itself does not lead to certain outcomes in a deterministic fashion. Thus, it aligns with the socio-technical perspective which argues that technology is not an independent force but must be explained within its political and social context. However, ANT pushes further than the socio-technical view by proposing that the ecosystem as a whole is key. The ecosystem perspective provides a holistic view of the network and highlights the reciprocal nature of relationships among actants. In that manner, ANT can reconcile two primary paradigms in the context of robots and privacy, indeed also in the context of new technology more generally.

ANT reminds us that the application of new technologies depends on specific social settings, with the material aspects being of crucial importance. The users have a certain leeway how they employ the technology but are also constrained by the material properties of the technology, of the environment, and by the social situation. A new technology such as the RP-7 telepresence robots mentioned above (Beane & Orlikowski, 2015) can thus only be understood in relation to other actants in the actor-network, including technology (medical devices in the SICU, such as body sensors and measurement instruments, monitors, hospital beds and furniture, computers, the telephone etc.), semiotic concepts such as care ethics (Van Wynsberghe, 2013), and social relations and hierarchies between the people involved. This descriptive, non-normative approach of ANT can help us to take a step back and see the evolving privacy implications of robots in a more nuanced and empirical way.

Shortcomings of ANT for the Analysis of Privacy With Healthcare Robots

We see three shortcomings of applying ANT to healthcare robots and privacy. Firstly, ANT works best when applied to concrete scenarios and cases (e.g., Beane & Orlikowski, 2015). Qualitative and ethnographic methods in complex settings (such as research labs and hospitals) are especially suited to uncover the potential of the theory (Light et al., 2016). However, the context-sensitivity of ANT is one of its big strengths and weaknesses at the same time. Its descriptive approach only allows limited generalizability. Our chapter is an attempt to apply the theory to a relatively broad topic. More research—especially empirical research—is needed to uncover specific actor-networks around healthcare robots and privacy. One promising approach would be a comparative case study which looks at two different robot-privacy actor-networks in healthcare settings and compares them (e.g., assistive telepresence robots in SICUs vs. therapeutic interactive robots in nursing homes).

A second shortcoming concerns the type of technology at stake. ANT is particularly useful for taken-for-granted technologies that manifest themselves in concrete everyday practices such as doorknobs, tables, bridges, seatbelts, tunnels, fishing rods, and keys (Latour, 2000). In such contexts, ANT can shed new light on social practices. However, new technologies such as healthcare robots are in the spotlight per se and currently being investigated and questioned from different angles. Thus, an application of ANT might make more sense in 20 years when healthcare robots are widely accepted, used and take-for-granted, when they disappear into the background. At the moment, the analysis of industrial robots, which have been used for a longer time and are now taken-for-granted across many industries, could be an interesting avenue of inquiry (Guzman, 2016).

Third, ANT has been criticized by the research community for not being enough of a strong scientific method, remaining predominantly descriptive instead of providing explanations or making predictions. Some critics argue that ANT analysis leads to no objective insights and does not offer guidance on how to improve the status quo (Boltanski & Chiapello, 2005). Others are skeptical of the agency of things (Schaffer, 1991). However, we could argue that robots, especially healthcare robots, present a strong case for the agency of things. All three privacy issues discussed in this chapter—mobility, social bonding, and black boxing—indicate that healthcare robots are not only passive objects and neutral, uninvolved parties, but actants, with specific ingrained programs, interests and potentials for action.

Notes

1. Agency should not be confused with autonomy. Although both terms are sometimes used synonymously, autonomy goes a step further, indicating the ability of making one's own decisions, following one's own interests.
2. http://www.allonrobots.com/robotic-therapy.html
3. A philosophically interesting and futuristic question would be to ask the question in reverse: How do users and bystanders impact robots' privacy? With ongoing discussions about the legal personhood of robots, do we need to re-think the notion of privacy and consider ascribing some version(s) of it to robots?
4. Westin (1967, p. 7) defines privacy as "[...] the claim of individuals, groups, or institutions to determine for themselves when, how, and to what extent information about them is communicated to others. [Moreover] ... privacy is the voluntary and temporary withdrawal of a person from the general society through physical or psychological means."
5. Altman (1975, p. 24) defines privacy as "the selective control of access to the self."
6. This topic has been taken up by Hollywood and science-fiction writers. The movie *Her* is a good example for a narrative of the bonding between artificial intelligence and humans.
7. In the traditional telephone night walk, the AP, who is at that time at home or outside the hospital, calls the resident on a landline phone inside the SICU and they discuss each patient's status. In this type of night walk, only the AP and the responsible resident are involved (not the nurses or even the patients).
8. In the "new" night walk via RP-7, the AP remotely controls the RP-7 robot and goes from patient bed to patient bed with it, engaging in conversation over the patients' health status with both the nurses and residents via the robot.
9. Latour's understanding of network goes back to the French word for network réseau, as inspired by Diderot, "in order to avoid the Cartesian divide between matter and spirit" (Latour, 1996, p. 170). In that sense, the notion of the network in ANT closely resembles the philosophical idea of the rhizome, as introduced by Deleuze and Guattari (1988).
10. ANT distinguishes between mediators and intermediaries. Mediators change the state of affairs in a network, while intermediaries only transport or pass on other actants without transforming them. Because of their potential of being anthropomorphized and their real-life agency, (social) robots are a prime example of mediators instead of just being an intermediary (Latour, 2005).

References

Alaiad, A., & Zhou, L. (2014). The determinants of home healthcare robots adoption: An empirical investigation. *International Journal of Medical Informatics, 83*(11), 825–840.

Altman, I. (1975). *The environment and social behavior: privacy, personal space, territory, crowding.* Monterey, CA: Brooks/Cole.

Associated Press (2015, July 2). Robot kills worker at Volkswagen plant in Germany. *The Guardian.* Retrieved from https://www.theguardian.com/world/2015/jul/02/robot-kills-worker-at-volkswagen-plant-in-germany

Balkin, J. (2015). The path of robotics law. *California Law Review Circuit, 6,* 45–60.

Beane, M., & Orlikowski, W. J. (2015). What difference does a robot make? The material enactment of distributed coordination. *Organization Science, 26*(6), 1553–1573.

Bekey, G. (2012). Current trends in robotics: Technology and ethics. In P. Lin, G. Bekey, & K. Abney (Eds.), *Robot Ethics: The Ethical and Social Implications of Robotics* (1st ed., pp. 17–34). Cambridge, MA: MIT Press.

Boltanski, L., & Chiapello, E. (2005). *The new spirit of capitalism.* London, UK: Verso. [First French edition: *Le nouvel esprit du capitalisme.* Paris, Gallimard 1999]

Breazeal, C. (2003). Toward sociable robots. *Robotics and Autonomous Systems, 42*(3), 167–175.

Callon, M. (1986). Some elements of a sociology of translation: Domestication of the Scallops and the Fishermen of St Brieuc Bay. In J. Law (Ed.), *Power, Action and Belief: A New Sociology of Knowledge?* (pp. 196–233). London, UK: Routledge.

Callon, M. (2007). Actor-network theory: The market test. In K. Asdal, B. Brenna, & I. Moser (Eds.), *Technoscience—The Politics of Intervention* (pp. 273–286). Oslo: Unipub.

Calo, R. (2012). Robots and privacy. In P. Lin, G. Bekey, & K. Abney (Eds.), *Robot Ethics: The Ethical and Social Implications of Robotics* (1st ed., pp. 187–202). Cambridge, MA: MIT Press.

Calo, R. (2016). Robots in American Law. *University of Washington School of Law Research Paper,* No. 2016–04.

Carroll, R. (2015, November 21). Goodbye privacy, hello 'Alexa': Amazon Echo, the home robot who hears it all. *The Guardian.* Retrieved from http://www.theguardian.com/technology/2015/nov/21/amazon-echo-alexa-home-robot-privacy-cloud

Darling, K. (2012). Extending legal rights to social robots. *SSRN Electronic Journal.* DOI: 10.2139/ssrn.2044797

Darling, K. (2016), Extending legal protection to social robots: The effects of anthropomorphism, empathy, and violent behavior towards robotic objects. In R. Calo, M. Froomkin, & I. Kerr. (Eds.), *Robot Law* (pp. 213–234). Northampton, MA: Edward Elgar Publishing.

Deleuze, G., & Guattari, F. (1988). *A thousand plateaus: Capitalism and schizophrenia.* New York, NY: Bloomsbury Publishing.

Duffy, B. R. (2003). Anthropomorphism and the social robot. *Robotics and Autonomous Systems, 42*(3), 177–190.

Felzmann, H., Beyan, T., Ryan, M., & Beyan, O. (2015). Implementing an ethical approach to big data analytics in assistive robotics for elderly with dementia. In *Proceedings of the 2010 ACM ETHICOMP Conference* (pp. 280–286), Leicester, 7–9 September.

Franceschi-Bicchierai, L. (2015, December 4). Bugs in 'Hello Barbie' could have let hackers spy on children's chats. *Vice Motherboard*. Retrieved from https://motherboard.vice.com/en_us/article/qkj4n7/bugs-in-hello-barbie-could-have-let-hackers-spy-on-kids-chats

Franceschi-Bicchierai, L. (2016, February 2). Internet-connected Fisher Price teddy bear left kids' identities exposed. *Vice Motherboard*. Retrieved from https://motherboard.vice.com/en_us/article/wnx5vw/internet-connected-fisher-price-teddy-bear-left-kids-identities-exposed

Garmann-Johnsen, N., Mettler, T., & Sprenger, M. (2014). Service robotics in healthcare: A perspective for information systems researchers? *Proceedings of the 2014 International Conference on Information Systems (ICIS)*, Auckland NZ, 14–17 December.

Gupta, S. K. (2015, September 8). Six recent trends in robotics and their implications. *IEEE Spectrum*. Retrieved from https://spectrum.ieee.org/automaton/robotics/home-robots/six-recent-trends-in-robotics-and-their-implications

Guzman, A. L. (2016). The messages of mute machines: Human-machine communication with industrial technologies. *Communication+ 1, 5*(1), 1–30. DOI: 10.7275/R57P8WBW

Guzman, A. L. (2017). Making AI safe for humans: A conversation with Siri. In R. Gehl, & M. Bakardjieva (Eds.), *Socialbots and their friends: Digital media and the automation of sociality* (pp. 69–85). London: Routledge.

Krieger, D. & Belliger, A. (2014). *Interpreting networks: Hermeneutics, actor-network theory & new media*. Bielefeld: Transcript Verlag.

Latour, B. (1987). *Science in Action: How to follow scientists and engineers through society*. Milton Keynes: Open University Press.

Latour, B. (1993). *We have never been modern*. Cambridge, MA: Harvard University Press.

Latour, B. (1994). On technical mediation—philosophy, sociology, genealogy. *Common Knowledge, 3*(2), 29–64.

Latour, B. (1996). On actor-network theory: A few clarifications. *Soziale Welt, 47*(4), 369–381.

Latour, B. (2000). The Berlin Key or how to do words with things. In P. M. Graves-Brown (Ed.), *Matter, Materiality, and Modern Culture* (pp. 10–21). London: Routledge.

Latour, B. (2005). *Reassembling the Social. An Introduction to Actor-Network-Theory*. Oxford: Oxford University Press.

Law, J. (2009). Actor network theory and material semiotics. In B. S. Turner (Ed.), *The New Blackwell Companion to Social Theory* (pp. 141–158). Hoboken, NJ: Wiley.

Lederer, S., Hong, J. I., Dey, A. K., & Landay, J. A. (2004). Personal privacy through understanding and action: Five pitfalls for designers. *Personal and Ubiquitous Computing, 8*(6), 440–454.

Liang, Y., & Lee, S. A. (2017). Fear of autonomous robots and artificial intelligence: Evidence from national representative data with probability sampling. *International Journal of Social Robotics, 9*(3), 379–384.

Light, B., Burgess, J., & Duguay, S. (2018). The walkthrough method: An approach to the study of apps. *New Media & Society, 20*(3), 881-900. doi: https://doi.org/10.1177/1461444816675438

Lin, P. (2012). Introduction to Robot Ethics. In P. Lin, G. Bekey, & K. Abney (Eds.), *Robot Ethics: The Ethical and Social Implications of Robotics* (1st ed., pp. 3–16). Cambridge, MA: MIT Press.

Lutz, C., & Tamò, A. (2015, August 21). RoboCode-Ethicists: Privacy-friendly robots, an ethical responsibility of engineers? In *Proceedings of the 2015 ACM SIGCOMM Workshop on Ethics in Networked Systems Research* (pp. 27–28), London.

Margulis, S. T. (2011). Three theories of privacy: An overview. In S. Trepte, & L. Reinecke (Eds.), *Privacy Online* (pp. 9–17). Heidelberg/Berlin, DE: Springer.

Mittelstadt, B. D., Allo, P., Taddeo, M., Wachter, S., & Floridi, L. (2016). The ethics of algorithms: Mapping the debate. *Big Data & Society, 3*(2). Available at http:// dx. doi.org/10.1177/2053951716679679

Muhammad, I., & Wickramasinghe, N. (2014). How an actor network theory (ANT) analysis can help us to understand the personally controlled electronic health record (PCEHR) in Australia. In A. Tatnall (Ed.), *Technological Advancements and the Impact of Actor-Network Theory* (pp. 15–34). Hershey, PA: IGI Global.

Nissenbaum, H. (2004). Privacy as contextual integrity. *Washington Law Review, 79*, 119–157.

Orlikowski, W. J. (1992). The duality of technology: Rethinking the concept of technology in organizations. *Organization Science, 3*(3), 398–427.

Orlikowski, W. J. (2007). Sociomaterial practices: Exploring technology at work. *Organization Studies, 28*(9), 1435–1448.

Pasquale, F. (2015). *The black box society: The secret algorithms that control money and information*. Cambridge, MA: Harvard University Press.

Petronio, S. (2002). *Boundaries of privacy: Dialectics of disclosure*. Albany, NY: State University of New York Press.

PEW Research Center (2014). Global opposition to U.S. surveillance and drones, but limited harm to America's image. Retrieved from http://www.pewglobal.org/2014/07/14/global-opposition-to-u-s-surveillance-and-drones-but-limited-harm-to-americas-image/

Rabbitt, S. M., Kazdin, A. E., & Hong, J. H. (2015). Acceptability of robot-assisted therapy for disruptive behavior problems in children. *Archives of Scientific Psychology, 3*(1), 101–110.

Richards, N., & Smart, W. (2016). How should the law think about robots? In R. Calo, M. Froomkin, & I. Kerr (Eds.), *Robot Law* (pp. 3–24). Northampton, MA: Edward Elgar Publishing.

Roadmap for US Robotics (2013). A roadmap for US robotics: From internet to robotics. *Robotics Virtual Organization*. Retrieved from http://www.roboticscaucus.org/Schedule/2013/20March2013/2013%20Robotics%20Roadmap-rs.pdf

Sandvig, C., Hamilton, K., Karahalios, K., & Langbort, C. (2014). Auditing algorithms: Research methods for detecting discrimination on internet platforms. Paper presented at "*Data and Discrimination: Converting Critical Concerns into Productive Inquiry*" Preconference of the 64th Annual Meeting of the International Communication Association. May 22, Seattle, WA.

Schaffer, S. (1991). The eighteenth brumaire of Bruno Latour. *Studies in History and Philosophy of Science, 22*(1), 174–192.

Smith, H. J., Dinev, T., & Xu, H. (2011). Information privacy research: An interdisciplinary review. *MIS Quarterly, 35*(4), 989–1016.

Special Eurobarometer 427 (2015). *Autonomous systems.* Report retrieved from http://ec.europa.eu/public_opinion/archives/ebs/ebs_427_en.pdf

Syrdal, D. S., Walters, M. L., Otero, N., Koay, K. L., & Dautenhahn, K. (2007). "He knows when you are sleeping"—Privacy and the personal robot companion. In *Proceedings of the 2007 AAAI Workshop Human Implications of Human–Robot Interaction,* (pp. 28–33), Washington DC, 9–11 March.

Trepte, S., & Reinecke, L. (2011). The social web as a shelter for privacy and authentic living. In S. Trepte, & L. Reinecke (Eds.), *Privacy Online* (pp. 61–74). Heidelberg/Berlin, DE: Springer.

Turkle, S. (2011). Authenticity in the age of digital companions. In M. Anderson, & S. L. Anderson (Eds.), *Machine Ethics* (1st ed., pp. 62–76). Cambridge: Cambridge University Press.

Van den Berg, B. (2016). Mind the air gap. In S. Gutwirth, R. Leenes, & P. De Hert (Eds.), *Data Protection on the Move: Current Developments in ICT and Privacy/Data Protection* (pp. 1–24). Dordrecht: Springer Netherlands.

Van Wynsberghe, A. (2013). Designing robots for care: Care centered value-sensitive design. *Science and Engineering Ethics, 19*(2), 407–433.

Warren, S., & Brandeis, L. (1890). The right to privacy. *Harvard Law Review, 4*(5),193–220.

Westin, A. F. (1967). *Privacy and freedom.* New York, NY: Atheneum.

Zwicker, M., Seitz, J., & Wickramasinghe, N. (2014). E-health in Australia and Germany. In A. Tatnall (Ed.), *Technological Advancements and the Impact of Actor-Network-Theory* (pp. 145–160). Hershey, PA: IGI Global.

8. My Algorithm: User Perceptions of Algorithmic Recommendations in Cultural Contexts

TERJE COLBJØRNSEN

In the culture industries, discovery and recommendation have tradition-ally been the tasks of critics and insiders, be they professional or amateur (Hesmondhalgh, 2007; Maguire & Matthews, 2014). Today, the recommen-dations provided by cultural critics, reviewers, store clerks and knowledgeable fans are increasingly supplemented, enhanced and occasionally supplanted by automated services. If you wonder what to read, view or listen to, digital plat-forms are ready at hand with suggestions seemingly tailored specifically for you. These recommendations are the work of what are typically referred to as *algorithms*. In contexts of cultural consumption, algorithms offer targeted suggestions and cultural guidance based on computations of input from large reservoirs of user data. Automated functions for discovery and recommen-dations are important features of all the major players in digital media and culture. Spotify, Netflix and Amazon, arguably among the dominant cul-tural distributors in the digital sphere, all make recommendations based on your and your network's listening, viewing and reading habits and expressed preferences: Spotify's personalized Discover Weekly playlist is compiled by sourcing listening patterns of individual users as well as preferences logged by other users. Netflix offers automated recommendations by giving prominent display to certain titles from its vast catalogue based on calculations of ratings and usage. Amazon provides recommendations of the "you might also like"-kind by analysing purchase patterns across its millions of users and product categories.

For the most part, algorithms remain unavailable for further scrutiny or comprehensive understanding, which is why they are often referred to as *black boxes* (Pasquale, 2015). As Latour (1999) has pointed out, obfuscation or black-boxing may contribute to the success of a technology, by avoiding a complicating presentation of the inner workings of the machine. In other words, automated recommendations may have infused our media culture precisely because their inner workings do not get in the way of the presentation of outputs. Nonetheless, certain events and disputes allow us to glimpse into the closely guarded algorithms, such as when Hallinan & Striphas (2016) use the algorithm improvement competition initiated by Netflix to examine the logic of algorithms. Patents and publications by the companies themselves provide another entry point (Gomez-Uribe & Hunt, 2015). I make the case here that we can also study how algorithms perform their tasks by looking at what users express about these services. The pros and cons of different digital media services are a constant source of debate which can, as I will demonstrate in the following, be employed for research purposes.

Thus, this chapter sets out to explore algorithms in cultural contexts at the reception end, looking at how users perceive and relate to online automated discovery and recommendation services for cultural products and services.[1]

Culture, Taste, Quality, and Digital Media

This chapter discusses algorithms particularly in contexts of media and popular culture, examining how algorithms contribute to cultural discovery and the shaping of cultural taste. The study is rooted in the field of media and communication and in studies of popular culture and the so-called culture (or cultural) industries (cf. Hesmondhalgh, 2007). Thus, when the notion of "cultural algorithm" is applied in the following, it is within this frame of reference.[2]

The nature of aesthetical value judgements and the question of how taste is formed are long-standing academic debates, from the Kantian (1790/2007) view of disinterested pleasure to Bourdieu's (1984) perspective on how the expression of bourgeois taste is an exercise in making distinctions to uphold societal hierarchies, and further to Peterson & Kern's (1996) notion of an "omnivorous" taste in US high-status persons. These discussions of taste frequently intersect with discourses on cultural quality, and the implications of subjective, intersubjective and objective standards of what constitutes excellence in art and culture.

As mentioned, seeking out and recommending cultural experiences and artifacts have traditionally been the tasks of critics and insiders to the culture industries. Going back at least to the 1970s, the culture industries have increasingly relied on sophisticated marketing and measuring methods to shape tastes and stimulate purchases. The latest spin in this tale is the development of data analysis and especially the analysis of "big data," the enormous amounts of user data collected continuously as we go about our digital lives. Algorithms form essential parts in the data-driven culture industries, shaping cultural taste at both individual and social levels (Beer, 2013).

What Are Algorithms?

Formal understandings of algorithms, common to computer science, define them simply as descriptions of a step-by-step method by which a task is to be accomplished (Goffey, 2008). Gillespie's precise and technical definition suggests that algorithms are "encoded procedures for transforming input data into a desired output, based on specific calculations" (2014, p. 167). In cultural contexts, the algorithmic recommendation process typically takes the form of a search, a query or simply logging on to a service, prompting suggestions of what to devote your time to. Broadly speaking, algorithms have an input and an output function. What you have previously bought, looked at, recommended or rated forms the basis of what the algorithm will suggest for you. So-called collaborative filtering adds data from other users into the calculations. It has been noted that this filtering process may create what have been termed "filter bubbles" (Pariser, 2011), where old habits and preferences are reinforced and new expressions are effectively hindered. According to Uricchio (2015), the algorithms of Spotify, Pandora, Netflix and Amazon steer clear of surprises and provide access to "the desired, the familiar, and the reassuring" (2015, p. 8).

The prominence of algorithms is increasingly recognized in the academic literature, including the humanities and social sciences, to the extent that a notion of "algorithmic culture" has been proposed (Striphas, 2015). Studying software systems in relation their social and cultural contexts, algorithm studies can be considered a subgroup of so-called "software studies" (Chun, 2011; Fuller, 2008; Manovich, 2013). Studies of algorithms in media and communications contexts are now manifold, especially concerning social media (e.g., Bucher, 2012, 2016; Shaw, 2016) and search engines (e.g., Roberge & Melançon, 2017).[3] While some exceptions already exist (e.g., Bucher, 2016; Hagen, 2015), the research on user responses to algorithms is still emerging.

Responding to the increased centrality of algorithms in aspects of private and public life, communication scholars, new media theorists and media philosophers have suggested that we take into account the pragmatic dimension of algorithms in order to assess their cultural, political and social impact (Anannny, 2016; Beer, 2016; Gillespie, 2014; Goffey, 2008; Kitchin, 2016). Along this vein, algorithms "do things," and they exist in a material and concrete sense for us (Goffey, 2008, p. 17). According to Gillespie (2016), we may separate technical, popular and social scientific understandings of algorithms. These are often conflated and confused, with the result that "We find ourselves more ready to proclaim the impact of algorithms than to say what they are" (Gillespie, 2016, p. 18). Gillespie further urges researchers to "be cognizant of the multiple meanings of algorithm as well as the discursive work the term performs" (2016, p. 18).

The notion of "the algorithm" often comes to represent something other than the technical procedure, such as standing in for "Facebook" or "Spotify" (cf. Gillespie, 2016). While this may rest on simplistic understandings of how digital media platforms operate (cf. Bogost, 2015), the notion of "algorithm" seems nonetheless to have come to signify the black box and the automation of cultural discovery. To some extent and in certain situations, we have become aware that algorithms perform tasks such as filter our search results and our social networking feeds; that they make suggestions for us on digital media platforms and guide us in the content databases of Spotify, Netflix and Amazon. It follows that the way we talk about digital media platforms, is influenced by *the concept of the algorithm*. "Algorithm" in common parlance can be loosely defined as anything the service/platform/machine does to produce an output as a suggestion or recommendation to the user. "Cultural algorithms," then, provide output in the form of suggestions for music, movies, television shows, books etc.

How Users Perceive Algorithms

What can we expect to find in a study on how users relate to and perceive algorithmic recommendations? Users are likely to express opinions of how well the services' recommendation engines work, so issues of perceived quality and relevance are apparent concerns.

It could be argued that algorithmic recommendations generally operate under a paradox: As users feed the services with more information on their likes and dislikes, algorithms can suggest more of the same kind that they seem to like. For many people, cultural consumption is also about being genuinely surprised, encountering *serendipity* in cultural discoveries (Nowak, 2016). Hence, replicating serendipity in algorithms has become a crucial task for software engineers and programmers (Rond, 2014).[4]

In a related manner, algorithms may risk *apophenia*, perceiving patterns and connections where none actually exist (boyd & Crawford, 2012). As can be expected, the programmers working on algorithms are already working to detect outliers, that is, items which constitute obvious deviations from the overall taste pattern. If small children use an adult's Spotify account, the service will recognize the children's songs as outliers not to be taken into account for future suggestions.

A different issue regards the notion of online privacy and how users feel about services that are increasingly familiar with their likes and dislikes, habits and relationships. Studies have found widespread concern among users over how businesses monitor them (Pew Research Center, 2014). Analysts of increasingly personalized advertising in online media have noted the so-called "creepiness factor" (Thierer, 2013), the sense that marketers are capitalizing on personal or private information without due consent or transparency. Similar affective responses are likely to be found in cultural contexts as well. (However, a presumptively large group will probably be unconcerned or ignorant of how algorithms provide recommendations).

Looking specifically at active and reflective users (the ones who take to Twitter to express their opinion), we may expect them to take a personal interest in the recommendation algorithms, seeing them as parts of their online identities. After all, the user data we leave behind through interaction with Facebook, Google, Netflix, Spotify, Amazon and a host of other digital interlocutors has the potential to assemble into something resembling a *digital identity*. Cheney-Lippold (2011) has written about "A New Algorithmic Identity," understood as "identity formation that works through mathematical algorithms to infer categories of identity on otherwise anonymous beings" (p. 165). Hess (2014) has coined the term "digital rhetorical identification" as a way of conceptualizing what he terms "the blurred nature of identity across offline and online contexts" (p. 2). Bucher (2016) has looked at how Facebook algorithms trigger responses and reflections from users, brought together in what she has termed the "algorithmic imaginary": the way users think about algorithms, how they function and how they ought to function.

Along this line, studies of users and algorithms intersect with human-computer interaction (HCI) and human-machine communication (HMC, as elaborated in this volume). We may say that since algorithms provide users with feedback and respond to changes in input, they take part in a meaningful exchange, a form of communication. While this communication is encoded by nature of the computerization of algorithms, it is typically not presented to the user in computer code. Rather, algorithmic communication comes in verbal ("you may also like"/ "people also listened to") and visual (thumbnails presenting covers) modes and is often made to resemble the rhetoric of human communication, though without the use of an avatar, a robot or a spoken dialogue system. Examples of close identification with algorithms (Bucher, 2016; Cheney-Lippold, 2011; Hess, 2014)—or simply playing with algorithmic identification—indicate the permeability between human and machine in these contexts, a familiar concern for HMC research (Suchman, 2006). I hope that a study like the present may expand the HMC literature by including algorithmic feedback and human responses as a form of human-machine communication.

Method

To provide an answer to the question of how users relate to automated recommendations, this study starts out from a qualitative analysis of Twitter messages related to algorithms in cultural contexts.[5] The micro-blogging platform Twitter has some 300 million active users worldwide, employing the platform for a number of uses including reflections on media, culture and technology. For the purpose of this article, Twitter appeared a productive platform to investigate, as users often rejoice about newfound favourites or vent their frustrations with algorithm-based services there. Twitter feeds are hardly representative of any larger population but are rich sources of non-representative utterances on popular culture. And it is the goal of this study to explore everyday notions of algorithms in this kind of cultural talk.

Analysing tweets qualitatively, rather than subjecting them to a quantitative study, enables the researcher to grasp more of the variety and the complexity of irony, play and interplay in Twitter contexts. The relative shortage of previous research and established theories means a predominantly inductive approach is suited to the research question. The iterative coding approach employed here, is influenced by grounded theory (Glaser & Strauss, 1967) and more explicitly the constructivist variant, where data and theories are the result of the researcher's interactions with their participants and emerging analyses (Charmaz, 2006; Thornberg & Charmaz, 2014). Qualitative methods, such as grounded theory, have the benefit of not being dependent upon predefined categories and issues, allowing the researcher the flexibility to expand and adapt as new issues emerge (Charmaz, 2015). Conversely, this kind of research may identify themes and topics for broader and more comprehensive studies of user perceptions of algorithms.

To start, I decided on search criteria, looking at "algorithm," in combination with either "Spotify," "Amazon," or "Netflix." These queries could function as quite "neutral," i.e., not biased towards very critical or very supportive attitudes to the services. Spotify, Amazon and Netflix were selected as unquestionably among the dominant digital media providers, all three relying on algorithm-based recommendations.

I harvested tweets containing the abovementioned keywords for two periods: The first search, using the now defunct Topsy software, was conducted in November 2015 for the period September–November 2015. This data set was found to be insufficient (n = 294) but provided a general overview and coding criteria which were employed for the larger sample in data set 2. The second search, using the DiscoverText software, was conducted in real time 9th to 31st of August 2016 (data set 2, n = 1,434). This whole set was coded and analysed in DiscoverText.

Based on a first screening of the material in data set 2, about a third of the harvested tweets were categorized as irrelevant to the research question (e.g. links to news articles without adding any expressed sentiment or opinion; tips for authors or musicians to eschew the algorithms for professional purposes). The remaining 972 tweets were then first subject to an open *in vivo* coding process, moving in further steps to categorize and refine the categories, annotate and make connections across the sample. Instead of the standard line-by-line coding strategy, I opted to code each tweet independently. Basically, I was looking for verbal cues as to how users expressed sentiments and opinions about algorithms. Interesting and relevant quotes were highlighted for possible citation. In the following, all direct quotes from the material have been slightly altered to protect the identity and privacy of the Twitter user behind it.

After three rounds of coding and recoding, all relevant tweets had been assigned to one of seven categories.

(1) Quality and relevance: perceptions of how well the algorithm performs its tasks for the user in question

(2) Comparisons: expressed comparisons between different algorithms or algorithm-based services

(3) Strategies to control input or output: expressed approaches or desires to control or adjust the algorithm's performance

(4) Breaking or confusing: notions of either purposefully or unintentionally disrupting the algorithm's performance, resulting in unexpected or undesired output

(5) Identification or distancing: perceptions of user identification with or estrangement from the algorithm

(6) Humans and computers: expressed notions of the relationship between humans and computers/technology

(7) Privacy and surveillance: perceptions of how algorithm-based services collect information about the user and conflicting emotions resulting from this.

For the sake of a more coherent and readable presentation, findings are in the following grouped in three dimensions and presented in this order:

(A) Perceptions of quality and relevance (tweets assigned to categories 1–2 above)
(B) Perceptions of input/output mechanisms (categories 3–4)
(C) Identification and relationships with algorithms (categories 5–7)

Discussion of Findings

Perceptions of Quality and Relevance

Examining the Twitter responses to algorithmic recommendations, I found numerous examples of users responding with evaluations of whether the service in question performed its task satisfactorily: The algorithm(s) suggested this; I liked it (or not). There are only a very few direct mentions of either "quality" or "relevance"/ "relevant" in the material, so the following examples have been interpreted by me as indirect assessments of quality and relevance. A dominant category of tweets characterizes the recommendations made (especially by Spotify and Netflix, Amazon not so much) as "accurate," "amazing," "dead on" or "spot on." Negative evaluations characterize the algorithm as "broken" and its output as "off," "failure" or "garbage." However superficial such judgements may be, they can be said to constitute minimal assessments of quality and relevance. In turn, the various comments on the quality or relevance of algorithms (not limited to the above examples) can be divided into several groups: First, we have comments regarding the quality of the service/platform, more specifically pertaining to the perceived quality of either the compression algorithm, the shuffling algorithm (Spotify in particular), the advertising algorithm (Amazon and Spotify Free), the algorithm categorizations (Netflix) and the pricing algorithm (Amazon). Secondly, we find assessments regarding the quality of content, typically referring to some aspect of the size and profile of the database in question. Then finally, comments are made on the quality of curation or filtering. Praise or criticism is directed at the quality of the recommendation algorithm and its ability to find items to the user's liking or the ability to find new things that interest the user.

This latter set of responses quite clearly expresses relevance rather than quality in the sense of the traditional cultural critic understanding. Responses to recommendations take the form of subjective and individualized statements of taste: The algorithm is seen to perform well when it meets precisely the desired outcome of the user, expressed in terms such as "spot on," "dead on" or "nailed it." Taste, thus, comes to be described as something precisely defined.

Moreover, there is a wide range of responses that see the suggestions in comedic or ironic light, often pointing to the laughably malapropos or inexplicable suggestions made by algorithms:

> My Discover Weekly playlist is seriously confused. I think the algorithm may have a drinking problem.

Amazon in particular generates responses that brings to mind the notion of *apophenia* (boyd & Crawford, 2012), perceptions of patterns where none actually exist. Putting together items from across its mega-catalogue, Amazon's algorithms are occasionally prone to making bizarre connections in shopping suggestions. Surprising combinations also come forth within the cultural context:

> I just ordered Flaubert's Sentimental Journey. Amazon suggested I might also enjoy 50 Shades of Grey.

To some, these malapropos suggestions seem to relieve the tensions felt in connection with the impact of algorithms, machine learning and artificial intelligence (AI), as in this ironic remark:

> I was concerned about the rise of AI, then the Spotify algorithm suggested Mungo Jerry's In the summertime, which is literally my least favorite song.

In some cases, the irrelevance of the algorithmic suggestions strikes a more sinister note, as the two tweets cited below exemplify:

> Hi, amazon algorithm: you can stop suggesting guest books to me. One for my father's funeral was enough.

> Amazon, your life event algorithm is not working properly. I look at books on grief and you're trying to sell me a breast pump.

The sense conveyed by tweets such as the last one is that algorithms are assumed to be knowledgeable about most aspects of our lives, but fail to live up to these high expectations. Comments such as these can be read as exposés of the algorithm's inability to relate to complex social and emotional contexts. The Amazon rhetoric of employing phrases such as "You might also like" means the comparison with human communication is likely to happen and may, as the above goes to show, set the algorithm up for failure in the face of complex social situations.

Perceptions of Input/Output Mechanisms

Algorithms are, as I have briefly touched upon, dynamic entities capable of learning and improving performance. But what about the users' sense of agency with respect to improving the quality of suggestions?

The most conspicuous pattern emerging from the datasets is one of capitulating to the algorithm, for better or worse. Expressions such as "magical," "black magic" and "witchcraft" are used to signify the impenetrable workings of the algorithm, the sense of dealing with a black box. One user compares the Spotify recommendation algorithm to "a personally assigned wizard." Without actually referring to the notion of the black box, these users nevertheless perpetuate the myth of the algorithm as something out of our reach, something non-human and unattainable. While some acknowledge the process of coding behind the algorithms, the actual code and the data behind suggestions remains unseen, thus maintaining the veneer of mystery and magic:

> I'd love to see the amount of glorious data that goes into the magical Spotify algorithm.

Another comment on the taste-making skills of the Spotify Discover Weekly algorithm betrays the user's ambiguity in allowing an algorithm to anticipate what will be enjoyable:

> ... I surrender to being predictable by an algorithm and enjoy the tunes!

Building on findings in data set 1, and anticipating a growing user competency in algorithmic encounters, I was expecting to find users adopting strategies to control the algorithms, or to respond to suggestions in more nuanced and active ways. For instance, Bucher (2016) found strategic algorithmic behaviour among her sample of active Facebook users. Comparatively few such deliberate strategies emerge in this data set. Mainly, the sense of agency that is expressed vis-à-vis the automated suggestion is the notion that disparate input can "confuse" or "break" the algorithm, as evidenced in the following three tweets:

> My chief goal in life is to confuse the hell out of the Spotify algorithm

> I keep buying random things on Amazon in a desperate attempt to throw off their shopping suggestions algorithm

> After much committed genre hopping I'm pleased to say I've reached the limits of the Netflix algorithm. Recommendations just says "pass"

Also in non-deliberate settings, similar notions of breaking or disrupting the algorithm emerge, as when a user complains that her partner has "messed up" the Netflix algorithm, a well-known issue with shared accounts:

> I just had a serious conversation with my husband about messing up my Netflix algorithm.

Note here also the reference made to "my algorithm," an indication of the sense of ownership and identification we can find in these algorithmic contexts, to which the next section is devoted.

Identification, Relationships, and Communication With Algorithms

A striking feature in the material is the number of tweets articulating a sense of communicating or identifying with the algorithm. Granted, these comments are typically made tongue-in-cheek, but can nonetheless be interpreted as expressions of quite complex human-machine relationships. See for instance this tweet on the "exquisite taste" of an algorithm which is simultaneously recognized as personalized:

> It's narcissistic and dumb, I know, but I never fail to be impressed at the exquisite taste of the personalized Spotify playlist algorithm.

Here, studying the algorithm's output comes forth as equivalent to studying yourself (narcissism), all the while being impressed with its taste, as if the expression of taste were disembodied from you.

While there are instances of acknowledging the humans behind the algorithms (i.e. programmers or engineers), a more prominent feature is a personalization of algorithms. On the one hand, algorithms are perceived to "know me so well," even "better than I know myself." Conversely, when the algorithm seems not to know the user in question or makes an odd suggestion, it is thought to be intoxicated: "Go home, algorithm, you're drunk" appears several times in the material. This sentiment also exemplifies a direct communication with the technology, indicating how people who use media technologies do so as active participants who engage with technology in meaning-making processes. The algorithm can also resemble other characters and personas, such as the "smug older brother" or "a college freshman who just discovered [indie rock musician] Stephen Malkmus." We may recognize in these characterisations the taste-makers of analogue times.

While one user expresses a wish that the algorithm could be made "a little gayer," several others admit to being "in love with an algorithm," even ready to make a commitment:

> I know it's a computer algorithm, but seriously, can I get married to my Spotify Discover Weekly?

> Without a doubt, I'd marry the algorithm that makes the Discover Weekly playlists

Clearly, Spotify's Discover Weekly algorithm is an attractive partner, but a more turbulent relationship is demonstrated in this tweet:

> Oh sod off Spotify—you get me, babe, but you're just an algorithm. It's never going to work xo

The above quotes are clearly made jokingly or ironically, but nonetheless point towards users who single out *the algorithm* as something specific—and specifically alluring—to the service. They may not be able to marry the algorithm, but there are indications of a pseudo-intimacy in the articulation of opinions such as these. An even clearer indication of identification is found in the references to "my algorithm," the idea that a service which is (or claims to be) highly personalized, offers *an algorithm especially for you*. Articulations of "my algorithm" are indicative of Cheney-Lippold's (2011) "new algorithmic identity," as well as Hess's (2014) "digital rhetorical identification." The fact that the users themselves make the connections explicitly are a reminder of user reflexivity and symptomatic of Bucher's (2016) finding that active users are expressing notions of an "algorithmic imaginary."

Finally, I expected to find some references to the so-called creepiness factor (Thierer, 2013), or expressed apprehensions over privacy in these algorithm-based cultural contexts. However, there were, in fact, only a handful of such concerns, directly expressed. Notably, concerns over the algorithm's creepily intimate knowledge of taste preferences or other personal information are typically found to be coupled with notes on quality. In the words of one of the users: The algorithm is "so good it's borderline creepy." Another commenter is simultaneously "impressed/slightly unnerved" by the accuracy of the algorithm's suggestions. Similarly, this user does not seem to find a dissonance between "creepy" and "cool":

> I find it creepy, but even more cool how the @Spotify Discover Weekly algorithm is on point every single time.

While the extent to which the creepiness factor can be observed in cultural contexts is worthy of more research, it seems plausible that the digital cultural sphere is perceived as less risky than social media or news contexts.

Conclusion

As the world of online media is increasingly characterized by the visible and imperceptible work of algorithms, it becomes a task of communication scholars to examine the roles and responses of algorithm users, including in cultural contexts. This chapter has sought to elaborate on how users perceive and relate to automated discovery and recommendation services, looking at Spotify, Netflix and Amazon. Where in the past, a music aficionado or film buff might have sought out a specific record store clerk or a well-stocked video rental store to get precise and relevant suggestions,[6] these functions are now diminishing as digital, algorithm-based services are on the rise. You can talk to and relate to your local music, film or book store clerk, but how do you communicate with an algorithm? Do people have relations with algorithms? The findings presented here, suggest that people do communicate with algorithms, that they identify with them, argue and negotiate with them and speculate about their behaviour and characteristics.

Using a Twitter sample, I have categorized and discussed a certain genre of human-algorithm communication: tweets concerning algorithms and digital cultural services. I have presented three dimensions of user perceptions and relations to algorithms: The first, *perceptions of quality and relevance*, found cultural quality described as something precisely defined, in notions such as "spot on" or "off." Perceived failures of the algorithm are seen by users to indicate the inability of a technology to relate to complex social and emotional contexts. The second dimension, *perceptions of input/output mechanisms*, looked at how users conceive of the algorithms' actual workings. While there are very few instances of strategic behaviour vis-à-vis the algorithm, the notion of the black box is frequently invoked, both explicitly and implicitly. Here, we are reminded of the so-called third law of science fiction writer Arthur C. Clarke that, "Any sufficiently advanced technology is indistinguishable from magic" (1972/2013, p. 250). Finally, the chapter has looked at *identification and relationships with algorithms*. A large share of the analyzed tweets articulates a sense of communicating or identifying with the algorithm, ranging from tongue-in-cheek remarks about the algorithm being "drunk" and proclamations of love to more sober considerations of what algorithms can and cannot offer. Notably, a sense of algorithmic identification is present, as users not only have strong bonds with the services in question, but also make statements betraying a close and even intimate, or pseudo-intimate, association with algorithm-based services, as indicated by the notion of "my algorithm."

What does it mean to invoke the self ("my") in relation to the algorithm? Previous research has focused on the way in which algorithmic identities are assigned people by the companies behind the systems: For instance, Cheney-Lippold places the individual user in an entirely passive role and holds that "categories of identity are being inferred upon individuals based on their web use" (2011, p. 165). Similarly, Hess's (2014) notion of "digital rhetorical identification" as a "process of *technological unconscious consubstantiality*" (2014, p. 9) leaves little room for agency or reflexivity on the part of the user. Indeed, there is a need to maintain a critical—and sceptical—stance towards the companies that provide the algorithms that play important roles in so many aspects of our lives. Nonetheless, what the findings of this study indicate is the relationship and communication flows between humans and algorithms are not one-dimensional but a complex exchange in a network of human and non-human actors.

Moreover, there are users who do not simply accept their algorithmic fate, but (try to) make sense of algorithmic work and reflect on their power to inform everyday life and shape identity. In this, I agree with Bucher's contention that "the algorithmic imaginary is a powerful identification that needs to be understood as productive" (2016, p. 11). As researchers, we benefit from engaging with users in their speculations over what algorithms are and can do in at least two ways: Users can give insights about the way algorithms perform their tasks while simultaneously providing insights on how people relate to and communicate with these quite elusive entities.

Finally, a study such as this, based on a rather small sample from a specific communication platform, has clear limitations: The study is unable to offer clear results on how people relate to algorithms in general, but provides some novel insights and several inroads for further research into user perceptions of algorithms. Future research could seek to expand on the three dimensions highlighted here or take the user perspective into other contexts and examine perceptions of other popular notions such as artificial intelligence and machine learning. There is reason to believe that some of the perceptions will be different in other contexts than the cultural (e.g. news journalism; social networking systems), where the political and social stakes are more clearly in the balance.

Notes

1. The study forms part of a project funded by the Norwegian Arts Council on culture and the quality concept. My research deals with user experiences of algorithmic recommendations and how algorithms change notions of quality and relevance in digital cultural contexts.
2. "Cultural algorithm" is also used within computer science and the branch of evolutionary computing with a different meaning. See, for instance, Reynolds, R. G. (1994).

An introduction to cultural algorithms, in *Proceedings of the 3rd Annual Conference on Evolutionary Programming*, World Scientific Publishing, pp 131–139.

3. Tarleton Gillespie and Nick Seaver provide a continually updated list on http://socialmediacollective.org/reading-lists/critical-algorithm-studies/

4. As a Spotify engineer working on their Discover Weekly algorithm noted: "We've seen a lot of anxiety, like, if I only listen to Discovery Weekly, will the snake eat its own tail?", see http://qz.com/571007/the-magic-that-makes-spotifys-discover-weekly-playlists-so-damn-good/

5. The study was reported to the Norwegian Centre for Research Data and approved by its Data Protection Official for Research.

6. If this is unfamiliar terrain, please consult films such as *High Fidelity* (2000) and *Clerks* (1994).

References

Ananny, M. (2016). Toward an ethics of algorithms: Convening, observation, probability, and timeliness. *Science, Technology & Human Values, 41*(1), 93–117. https://doi.org/10.1177/0162243915606523

Beer, D. (2013). *Popular culture and new media*. London, UK: Palgrave Macmillan. Retrieved from http://link.springer.com/10.1057/9781137270061

Beer, D. (2016). The social power of algorithms. *Information, Communication & Society, 20*(1), 1–13. https://doi.org/10.1080/1369118X.2016.1216147

Bogost, I. (2015, January 15). The cathedral of computation. *The Atlantic*. Retrieved from http://www.theatlantic.com/technology/archive/2015/01/the-cathedral-of-computation/384300/

Bourdieu, P. (1984). *Distinction: A social critique of the judgement of taste*. London: Routledge & Kegan Paul.

boyd, danah, & Crawford, K. (2012). Critical questions for big data. *Information, Communication & Society, 15*(5), 662–679. https://doi.org/10.1080/1369118X.2012.678878

Bucher, T. (2012). Want to be on the top? Algorithmic power and the threat of invisibility on Facebook. *New Media & Society, 14*(7), 1164–1180. https://doi.org/10.1177/1461444812440159

Bucher, T. (2016). The algorithmic imaginary: Exploring the ordinary affects of Facebook algorithms. *Information, Communication & Society, 20*(1), 1–15. https://doi.org/10.1080/1369118X.2016.1154086

Charmaz, K. (2006). *Constructing grounded theory: A practical guide through qualitative analysis*. London: Sage.

Charmaz, K. (2015). Grounded theory: Methodology and theory construction. In J. D. Wright (Ed.), *International Encyclopaedia of the Social & Behavioral Sciences* (pp. 402–407). Amsterdam: Elsevier Ltd.

Cheney-Lippold, J. (2011). A new algorithmic identity: Soft biopolitics and the modulation of control. *Theory, Culture & Society, 28*(6), 164–181. https://doi.org/10.1177/0263276411424420

Chun, W. H. K. (2011). *Programmed visions: Software and memory* (Reprint edition). Cambridge, MA: The MIT Press.

Clarke, A. C. (1972/2013). *Profiles of the future: An enquiry into the limits of the possible* (Kindle edition). London, England: SF Gateway

Fuller, M. (2008). *Software studies: A lexicon.* Cambridge, MA: The MIT Press.

Gillespie, T. (2014). The relevance of algorithms. In T. Gillespie, P. J. Boczkowski & K. A. Foot (Eds.), *Media technologies* (Kindle edition, pp. 167–193). Cambridge, MA: The MIT Press.

Gillespie, T. (2016). Algorithm. In B. Peters (Ed.), *Digital keywords: A vocabulary of information society and culture* (pp. 18–30). Princeton, NJ: Princeton University Press.

Glaser, B. G., & Strauss, A. L. (1967). *The discovery of grounded theory: Strategies for qualitative research.* Chicago: Aldine.

Goffey, A. (2008). Algorithms. In M. Fuller (Ed.), *Software studies: A lexicon* (pp. 15–20). Cambridge, MA: The MIT Press.

Gomez-Uribe, C. A., & Hunt, N. (2015). The Netflix recommender system: Algorithms, business value, and innovation. *ACM Transactions Management Information System, 6*(4), 1–19. https://doi.org/10.1145/2843948

Hagen, A. N. (2015). The playlist experience: Personal playlists in music streaming services. *Popular Music and Society, 38*(5), 625–645. https://doi.org/10.1080/03007 766.2015.1021174

Hallinan, B., & Striphas, T. (2016). Recommended for you: The Netflix Prize and the production of algorithmic culture. *New Media & Society, 18*(1), 117–137. https://doi.org/10.1177/1461444814538646

Hesmondhalgh, D. (2007). *The cultural industries.* Los Angeles: Sage.

Hess, A. (2014). You are what you compute (and what is computed for you): Considerations of digital rhetorical identification. *Journal of Contemporary Rhetoric, 4*(1/2), 1–18.

Kant, I. (1790/2007). *Critique of judgement* (N. Walker Ed., and J. C. Meredith, Trans.). Oxford: Oxford University Press.

Kitchin, R. (2016). Thinking critically about and researching algorithms. *Information, Communication & Society, 20*(1), 14–29. https://doi.org/10.1080/13691 18X.2016.1154087

Latour, B. (1999). *Pandora's hope: Essays on the reality of science studies.* Cambridge, MA.: Harvard University Press.

Maguire, J. S., & Matthews, J. (Eds.). (2014). *The cultural intermediaries reader.* Thousand Oaks, CA: Sage.

Manovich, L. (2013). *Software takes command* (INT edition). New York; London: Bloomsbury Academic.

Nowak, R. (2016). When is a discovery? The affective dimensions of discovery in music consumption. *Popular Communication, 14*(3), 137–145. https://doi.org/10.1080 /15405702.2016.1193182

Pariser, E. (2011). *The filter bubble: What the internet is hiding from you* (Kindle edition). London: Viking/Penguin.

Pasquale, F. (2015). *The black box society: The secret algorithms that control money and information.* Cambridge, MA: Harvard University Press.

Peterson, R. A., & Kern, R. M. (1996). Changing highbrow taste: From snob to omnivore. *American Sociological Review, 61*(5), 900–907. https://doi.org/10.2307/2096460

Pew Research Center. (2014). *Public perceptions of privacy and security in the post-Snowden era.* Retrieved from http://www.pewinternet.org/2014/11/12/introduction-18/

Roberge, J., & Melançon, L. (2017). Being the King Kong of algorithmic culture is a tough job after all: Google's regimes of justification and the meanings of Glass. *Convergence: The International Journal of Research into New Media Technologies, 23*(3), 306–324. https://doi.org/10.1177/1354856515592506

Rond, M. de. (2014). The structure of serendipity. *Culture and Organization, 20*(5), 342–358. https://doi.org/10.1080/14759551.2014.967451

Shaw, D. (2016). Facebook's flawed emotion experiment: Antisocial research on social network users. *Research Ethics, 12*(1), 29–34. https://doi.org/10.1177/1747016 115579535

Striphas, T. (2015). Algorithmic culture. *European Journal of Cultural Studies, 18*(4–5), 395–412. https://doi.org/10.1177/1367549415577392

Suchman, L. (2006). *Human-machine reconfigurations: Plans and situated actions* (2nd ed.). Cambridge, England: Cambridge University Press.

Thierer, A. (2013). The pursuit of privacy in a world where information control is failing. *Harvard Journal of Law & Public Policy, 36*(2), 409–456.

Thornberg, R., & Charmaz, K. (2014). Grounded theory and theoretical coding. In U. Flick (Ed.), *The SAGE handbook of qualitative data analysis* (pp. 153–170). London: SAGE Publications Ltd.

Uricchio, W. C. (2015). Recommended for you: Prediction, creation and the cultural work of algorithms. *The Berlin Journal, 28.* 6–9. Retrieved 9 August 2016, from http://dspace.library.uu.nl/handle/1874/330722

9. A Robot Will Take Your Job. How Does That Make You Feel? Examining Perceptions of Robots in the Workplace

PATRIC R. SPENCE, DAVID WESTERMAN, AND XIALING LIN

The fourth industrial revolution has reshaped not only the public's life but also the global workforce. From intelligent digital agents to self-driving vehicles and semi-autonomous robots, the technology evolution enables robotics to perform human-like tasks with high facility. Algorithms and automation can connect vast amounts of information at a speed impossible for humans, optimizing resource collaborations. Robotics and artificial intelligence have permeated a wide range of industries such as customer service, healthcare, logistics, transportation, and home maintenance; it frees people from trifles and drudgery to more "creative" tasks, achieving work that is more efficient. Yet, instances such as the robot-staffed stores in Japan with cloud-based, emotion-sensing humanoid robots also highlight job displacement by robotics due to technology advances (Strange, January 27, 2016).

John Maynard Keynes warned of a new disease of technological unemployment (1963), and this was echoed by Minsky (1980), who suggested that teleoperators and automation might take the place of many human workers. This has already started taking place; although different countries have seen different rates of robotic worker adoption. For example, between 2008 and 2011, China saw a 210% increase in the number of robots per 10,000 employees in manufacturing, the United States saw a 41% increase, while Japan actually experienced a 1% decrease during the same timeframe. However, overall numbers remain low in China (21 robots per 10,000 employees as of 2011) and much higher in Japan (339 per 10,000), with the USA somewhere in the middle (135 per 10,000; as cited in Moniz & Krings, 2016).

A report by the McKinsey Global Institute suggests that although few occupations (less than 5 percent) could be fully automated utilizing current technologies, "almost every occupation has partial automation potential," with an estimate that 51% of activities in the U.S. economy could be automated with current technologies (Manyika, et al., 2017). Estimates for European Union countries suggest the percentages of jobs at risk range from the mid-40s to low 60s due to roboticization (Moniz & Krings, 2016). Instead of investing the current resources to accommodate the possibilities of human errors, organizations and companies prefer robots and automation that lower the employment cost as well as enhance work efficiency. This is especially true for jobs that focus on tasks that are "simple and repetitive" (Moniz & Krings, 2016, p. 6), and has already become a reality for jobs in "automotive, electronics, metal engineering and plastics." For instance, since the 1970s, self-serve gas pumps have replaced gas attendants in the majority area of the U.S and created new jobs required for workers that are more skilled within the past 40 years (Maney, November 11, 2016). Not only the automation of jobs is discussed regarding blue-collar workers and less skilled labor, organizational and business professionals are considering how to adapt robots to management-level positions (Chamorro-Premuzic & Ahmetoglu, December 12, 2016). Such discussions raise attention to robots and task automation that reduce labor cost as well as deliver increased performance for human workers. To better address automation and employee performances, it is necessary to explore how people view robots and their place in the workplace.

As robots continue to enter the workplace, people will increasingly come into contact with those who might end up taking their job (or at least, likely change their job). As Moniz and Krings (2016) state, "The more robots are introduced in work environments, the more human interaction with those systems becomes crucial" (p. 7). This interaction is likely to be driven by peoples' initial impressions of robots, as are other interactions (e.g., Sunnafrank & Ramirez, 2004). Thus, it is important to understand how people feel about the robots they will be working with, especially when those robots may be replacing them.

One potential major source of information about robots, especially in the workplace, which might lead to impressions of such robots, are media portrayals. For example, some research has shown a relationship between television viewing and anxiety toward technology in general (Nisbet, et al., 2002). This is likely due to the prominence of destructive technology narratives featured on television. Similarly, robots often appear as evil antagonists to humans in popular media (Syrdal, Nomura, Hirai, & Dautenhahn, 2011). However, a study of older adults that used cultivation theory to predict impressions of robots formed by movie portrayals found that the more films featuring robots that people remembered, the less anxious about social robots they were (Sundar, Waddell, & Jung, 2016). Notably, people also reported that the majority of robots that were remembered were remembered as good, rather than bad.

Cultivation theory relies upon the overall viewing of content to explain media effects. However, particular portrayals of robots might have differing effects. For example, Sundar, et al., (2016) also found that anxiety toward robots was lower when the robots remembered from movies had a more human-like appearance and elicited more sympathy in the storyline of the film. This suggests that the type of portrayal matters; and one theory that can help explain the effects of viewing news stories about robots in the workplace is exemplification theory (Zillmann, 1999, 2002; Zillmann & Brosius, 2000). Exemplification theory often is described as a theory of media influence that deals with media representations, or exemplars. The theory draws on principles from evolutionary psychology, cognitive psychology, media psychology and human communication. It postulates that three cognitive mechanisms (quantification, representativeness, and availability heuristics), and can be used to both explain and predict the type of information most likely to be remembered and recalled (Spence, Lachlan, Sellnow, Rice & Seeger, 2017).

There are various ways that a story can be told. For example, a story about workplace robots can focus on how many robots are actively "working," how many jobs are lost/created, how many robots are expected in the future, etc. This type of statistical information about the overall likelihood of a phenomenon is called base-rate information (Zillmann & Brosius, 2000). However, the story could also be showing an interview with a person whose job has been lost to a robot, while also showing footage of robots at work. This would be using exemplars to tell the story (Zillmann & Brosius, 2000). Exemplars are examples chosen to represent a phenomenon. Exemplars will share a variety of characteristics with other examples of the same phenomenon but are unlikely to share all characteristics (Zillmann & Brosius, 2000). Thus, when using exemplars to help tell a story, choices are made about the characteristics that are represented in the story, and these chosen exemplars drive judgments of a phenomenon more so than ones that are not. Certain exemplar portrayals have a higher likelihood to drive people's judgments and reactions to the social world (Sellnow-Richmond, George, & Sellnow, 2018). Exemplars that are concrete, iconic, and emotionally arousing influence issue perceptions more than portrayals which are abstract, symbolic, and emotionally inconsequential (Aust & Zillmann, 1996; Gibson & Zillmann, 1994; Spence et al., 2017; Zillmann, 2002; Zillmann, Gibson, & Sargent, 1999).

Pictures and quotations are common ways of exemplifying a phenomenon (Spence, Westerman & Rice, 2017), and both can easily provide concrete, iconic and emotional information within a news story (Westerman, Spence & Lachlan, 2009; Westerman, Spence, & Lin, 2015). Interestingly, exemplars seem more influential to peoples' judgments about a phenomenon than base-rate information, even if base-rate information is provided (Gibson, Callison, & Zillmann, 2011; Zillmann & Brosius, 2000). Overall, people are likely to pay attention to and remember exemplars over base-rate information, and more so, if those exemplars are concrete, emotional, and iconic, which also makes them more likely to be more likely to influence judgments and understanding of a given phenomenon.

The Study

Because robots themselves can be used as an exemplar or portrayed using exemplars a study was conducted to better understand these effects and perceptions. To this end, the study consisted of three experimental conditions. Two conditions focused on robots in the workplace. The first condition (non-humanoid condition) was a news report from a national news network. The report was edited and focused on the benefits of technological process and talked about how innovation with robots will hurt jobs and how new categories of jobs will be created. The central focus was how fast robots could replace humans in the workplace. There was also a discussion about ownership of robots and capitalism. The visual robots featured in the news report were non-anthropomorphic. The robots did not have human features, rather, they were portrayed as moving inventory in warehouses and packaging boxes.

In the second condition (humanoid condition), a news report from a national news network was also used. Many of the same facts and projections were reported, with a focus on replacing humans, the creation of new types of jobs and issues of capitalism, however, there were also exemplified commentary in the news feature. Terms such as "robots 2.0" and "the coming robotic revolution" were used. The robots featured in the news report were anthropomorphic and in addition to doing labor, the robots were seen interacting with humans.

The third condition was a control condition. Participants watched a TedEd video concerning "why Ketchup is so hard to pour?" The video was chosen because it was a similar length of time to the news reports used and didn't have a direct relationship to the questions being asked. After being randomly assigned to one of the conditions and viewing the video, a continue button appeared. Once respondents hit continue, they were taken to a series of questions asking different perceptions about interacting with robots, robots and the workforce and robots in the future. Given that there was some shared information across the two experimental conditions, the analyses are not fully crossed but are instead limited to comparisons of individual cell means, and all reports are one-way ANOVA. Results are discussed in the next section, and means for each condition and the test used can be found in Table 9.1.

There were 224 participants in the study. Participants came from Business and Communication classes at a larger mid-south research university. They were provided nominal course credit or extra credit for participation. Using college students for this study provides the potential for interesting comparisons in the future as the members of this sample are assumed to be technological adaptors, possess technological literacy and will potentially live and work through the adoption of robots in various aspects of the workplace and social life.

A few demographic questions were asked of the participants. Of the 224 participants, there was an even split in terms of biological sex with 112 reporting male and 112 reporting female. The reported range in age of participants was 18 to 53 years with a mean of 20.5 and a standard deviation of 2.97. The sample was predominantly Caucasian (83%) with 6.3% reporting Asian, 5.8% reporting African American, 2.2% reporting Latino/Hispanic and 2.7% indicating other. There were 225 participants in the study. However, one participant indicated their race as "other" and in the space provided to self-report race, the respondent entered "human." This respondent was removed from the data set. The following sections provide results from the study. In this exploratory research, each question was treated individually, and results are presented and discussed on a question by questions basis (See Table 9.1).

General Perceptions of Robots

Participants in the study were asked about their general perceptions of robots ranging on a scale from "very positive" to "very negative." Those in the control condition had the most positive perceptions of robots (as indicated by the reversed score) followed by those in the non-humanoid condition and finally those in the humanoid condition. Interestingly, the news story showing a humanoid robot led to more negative perceptions of robots than the news story with the non-human robot. Although there are other differences between the news stories, this is an interesting difference that is worthy of future research. One possible explanation for this pattern of data comes from an idea known as the uncanny valley (Mori, 1970). The uncanny valley is an idea in robotics that suggests the more human-like robots become, the more

Table 9.1. Results From Survey Questions.

Question	Control Condition	Non-Humanoid Condition	Humanoid Condition	p
Generally speaking, do you have a very positive, fairly positive, fairly negative or very negative view of Robots? 1–5, 1 being "very positive" and 5 being "very negative"	M (2.42) SD .77	M (2.75) SD 9.3	M (2.86) SD .92	.001
Robots are necessary as they can do jobs that are too hard or too dangerous for people 1–5, 1 being "totally disagree" and 5 being "totally agree"	M (3.94) SD .83	M (3.56) SD .95	M (3.87) SD .87	.05
Widespread use of Robots can boost job opportunities in the United States 1–5, 1 being "totally disagree" and 5 being "totally agree"	M (3.22) SD .90	M (2.85) SD .85	M (2.77) SD 1.1	.01
Widespread use of Robots can boost job opportunities in developing countries 1–5, 1 being "totally disagree" and 5 being "totally agree"	M (3.19) SD .86	M (2.88) SD .90	M (3.17) SD .86	.085 Non-significat
Robots are a form of technology that requires careful management 1–5, 1 being "totally disagree" and 5 being "totally agree"	M (4.10) SD .88	M (4.11) SD .83	M (4.11) SD .86	.996 Non-significat
With Robots present in the workplace I don't see an opportunity for advancement 1–5, 1 being "I agree a lot" and 5 being "I disagree a lot"	M (3.54) SD 1.01	M (3.08) SD 1.10	M (3.23) SD 1.32	.05
When communicating with Robots in the workplace I expect to feel 1 being "tense" and 7 being "relaxed"	M(4.31) SD 1.38	M (3.60) SD 1.56	M (4.21) SD 1.53	.01
When communicating with Robots in the workplace I expect to feel 1 being "Confident" and 7 being "Fearful"	M (3.42) SD 1.40	M (4.19) SD 1.36	M (3.46) SD 1.40	.001
When communicating with Robots in the workplace I expect to feel 1 being "Peaceful" and 7 being "Stressed"	M (3.90) SD 1.43	M (4.32) SD 1.34	M (3.76) SD 1.42	.05

Source: Authors.

we as humans start to like the robots. As Sundar et al., (2016) found, anxiety toward robots decreased when more human-like robots were the ones people remembered from movies. Also, if a robot is perfectly human-like, we find it familiar and are more likely to like it a great deal. However, there exists a point when a robot is pretty human looking, but not quite human enough, and then people start to be creeped out by them. This sharp decline in attitude is what is the uncanny valley; on a chart plotting how human looking a robot is on the x-axis and familiarity/likability on the y-axis, the drop in likability seen when a robot is pretty human looking but not human looking enough exists a valley between the two peaks of sort or human looking and incredibly human looking (Mori, 1970). Overall, there seems to be somewhat mixed support for the uncanny valley in the literature (e.g., Brenton, Gillies, Ballin, & Chatting, 2005; Burleigh, Schoenherr, & Lacroix, 2013). Thus, it is possible that the robot in the humanoid condition was a robot that fell into the uncanny valley for viewers of the newscast. This, as well as how the uncanny valley operates overall, is something that future research can examine.

Dangerous Jobs

Another item asked about the necessity of robots because they can perform jobs that are either too hard or dangerous for humans. The control condition reflected the strongest belief that this was a necessary feature of having robots in the workforce, followed by the humanoid condition and the non-humanoid condition. This may have been a result of viewing the anthropomorphized robots in the humanoid condition that pushed respondents to stronger perceptions. Research from social learning theory indicates that motivation is the perception of potential positive and negative outcomes that are believed to be likely to enhance or diminish the probability of an observer performing the observed behavior (Lachlan, Spence & Lin, 2013; Manz & Sims, 1981; Bandura, 1977). Behaviors that are viewed as leading to positive outcomes are more likely to be adopted by observers than behaviors with the potential of harmful outcomes (Bell, 1992; Nelson et al., 2009; McIntyre et al., 2012). Thinking about completing a hard or dangerous act after being primed by the exemplified condition may have created higher levels of motivation to avoid a hard or dangerous task because the respondent in this condition could vicariously imagine the anthropomorphized robot completing the task. Moreover, exemplification theory postulates that in the presence of a risk portrayed with exemplars, people will be motivated to take protective actions (Zillmann, 2006). The exemplified features of this condition, theoretically, should have motivated the respondents to see robots as an option for completing hard or dangerous occupational tasks.

Opportunities for Jobs in the U.S. and Developing Countries

There were two questions which centered on robots and job opportunities, either in the United States or in developing countries. For the ability of robots to boost job opportunities in the United States, those in the control condition were most optimistic, followed by the non-humanoid condition, and the least optimism was express by the participants in the humanoid condition. However, these differences in optimism disappeared when the question asked about developing countries, with the level of optimism rising in the experimental conditions, so that no significant differences existed among conditions. Moreover, it also follows that participants in the non-humanoid condition would have more optimism because they may not perceive robots as a threat to their job.

Concerning the question about job opportunities in the United States, responses follow what would be expected based upon exemplification theory. The more iconic image of a humanoid robot performing a job made it easier to remember and thus believe that robot could "be performing my job." Moreover, with the question framed as being in the United States (where the majority of the sample was drawn from) may have allowed more internalization. Some previous research has speculated that proximity might increase exemplification effects (Westerman et al., 2009). Thus, those who saw humanoid robots performing jobs may have internalized job loss or loss of opportunities to themselves, leading to the patterns seen in responses to this question.

Personal Advancement in the Workplace

The next item asked the participants to indicate their perception of advancement opportunities with robots in the workplace. The highest levels of perceived opportunity were in the control condition, followed by the non-humanoid condition and the least optimism for advancement was found in the humanoid condition. The responses to personal advancement in the workplace also make sense considering many of the theories discussed in this chapter. But an area to examine based off the characteristics of the sample may be the human emotion of envy. Envy, as described by Parrott & Smith (1993), is "the emotion that arises when a person lacks another person's quality, achievement or possession, and either desires it or wishes the other lacked it" (in Vidaillet, 2007, p. 1672). The exemplified condition with the humanoid robot may cause the respondent to resent the fact that this robot can work longer, without pay and perform at a higher level than the human. The anthropomorphized features of the robot and coupled with other exemplars highlight that this type of coworker would not supplement a white-collar job, but, rather, it may replace that job making the human obsolete. This may also be a case where people make estimations of the capabilities, abilities, and potential of robots based of scripts (Spence, Westerman, Edwards, C., & Edwards, A., 2014; Edwards, C., Edwards, A., Spence & Westerman, 2016). The more potential people see in humans, the more potential people will see in robots with human features. Whereas in the non-humanoid condition the robot is viewed as a helper, a tool and not as a co-worker or competition. Because of this, envy may be the more appropriate human emotion to study in these situations compared to fear.

Two findings from a study in 1985 (Shenkar, 1988) help to illustrate the findings in this study. Interviews concerning the introduction of additional robots to an industrial plant were undertaken. Senior management described the robots as similar to machinery and believed that others also held this view at the organization. However, middle management and other employees perceived the robots as replacing humans. The perspective changed based on the proximity of the robot to one's role in the organization. Similarly, the perspective changed as the robot becomes more human like coupled with exemplars indicating their ability to replace humans. This same study also outlined that among middle management and other organization employees existed a limited belief in the robot's ability to perform workplace tasks. This helped reduce the apprehensions of some who were concerned with the introduction of robots in the workplace. In the non-exemplified condition, the robot may not have been seen as having the ability to perform the tasks that the respondent believes he or she would conduct in day-to-day organizational life, thus explaining the difference between conditions.

Feelings When Communicating With Robots in the Workplace

Three questions were taken from a scale that asked about feelings of communicating with robots in the workplace. The first question asked participants to choose between the adjectives of "Tense" and "Relaxed." Participants in the control condition indicated that they would be most relaxed communicating with robots in the workplace followed by the humanoid condition and then the least relaxed (or most tense) perceptions were from those in the non-humanoid condition. A similar question provided the adjectives of "Confident" and "Fearful." Again, participants in the control condition indicated that they would have the highest levels of confidence when communicating with robots in the workplace followed by the humanoid condition and then the most fearful perceptions were from those in the non-humanoid condition. Last, the adjectives "Peaceful" and "Stressed" were used. As with the previous two questions about communicating with robots in the workplace participants in the control condition indicated that they would be most peaceful communicating with robots in the workplace followed by the humanoid condition and then the most stressed perceptions were from those in the non-humanoid condition.

This is another area that the uncanny valley (Mori, 1970) might help explain. One possible reason why the uncanny valley experience exists (to the extent that it does) is an expectancy violation. Looking pretty life-like leads a person to expect the robot to look VERY life-like. Thus, when it does not look as life-like as the expectations created, it is liked even less than it would have been if not for these expectations. In the current study, people seemed less positive about communicating with robots after viewing a story showing non-humanoid robots as compared to one showing humanoid robots. If people are basing their impressions from an exemplar showing a non-human robot, it is likely that their expectations of communication would be lowered, as we do not typically communicate with non-humans (or at least, we are more likely to expect interaction with humans). Given this possibility, it would make sense to see more negative feelings when thinking about communicating with robots under these circumstances, which seem like a possible interaction version of the uncanny valley. This is something that future research would need to examine to be able to make claims about.

Overall, the idea of the uncanny valley is an interesting one for exemplification theory and robots. For example, past research examining people's perceptions of interacting with a robot suggests that people have more generally negative impressions of doing it, compared to interacting with a human (Edwards, C., Edwards, A., Spence, & Westerman, 2016; Spence, Westerman, Edwards, C., & Edwards, A., 2014). These preconceptions about interacting with a robot may be driven by what people think of when they think "robot," and that may be a robot that falls into the uncanny valley, as many media portrayals of robots likely do. In that case, the exemplar that is driving peoples' perceptions of a robot and interacting with said robot is one that falls into the uncanny valley, and it would be expected that one might not be interested in interacting with a robot. However, actual interaction with that robot might overcome those initial fears if a) the actual robot was not uncanny, and/or b) the interaction itself helped overcome the initial fears (Spence, Edwards, A., & Edwards C., 2018). These are ideas that can and should be tested.

Implications and Future Research Directions

In most of the analysis, the control condition motivated respondents to have either the highest or lowest responses, perceptions and attitudes to the question. An argument can be made that this supports the strength of the other conditions to create change through priming and content in the respondents. Another argument could be made that these findings, may support the sleeper effect (although untested). It has been noted in Exemplification theory (Spence, Westerman, & Rice, 2017; Westerman, Spence & Lachlan, 2012) results immediately after exposure to experimental stimuli featuring both more and less threatening visuals resulted in seemingly equal amounts of impact on perceptions. However, when measuring these outcomes again after a two-week period, respondents who had seen been exposed to the more threatening visuals reported higher perceptions than time 1. Thus, the impact of the stronger, more iconic exemplar, was "asleep" and was only found later. Each question may have acted as a prime for the control group. Without an immediate referent to draw opinions from, the members of the control group recalled previous exemplars (either positive or negative to the question at hand) they were exposed to and used those to make judgments. This is an area that calls for future research. Studies might wish to move past only close-ended responses with a control group and ask what they envisioned when thinking about a robot in relation to the question.

Before addressing some of the implications of the research and future directions in research in robots, some limitations to this study will be outlined. This will allow the reader to consider the implications and future directions considering the limitations.

Ideally, the news features shown to participants would have had the same audio content and only the images would be different. Although ideal, this could not be done with an existing national network newscast. However, for an initial study such as this, the weakness in experimental content was deemed an acceptable tradeoff for the ecological validity of using existing newscasts.

Future research can more tightly control the robots shown, to manipulate features related to things like the uncanny valley, showing robots that are of varying degrees of humanness. This humanness could be exemplified in multiple ways. For example, in a classic uncanny valley sense, robots with varying degrees of looking human might impact people's perceptions in ways mentioned previously in this chapter. The communicability of a robot might also matter for this. Would the valley exist in a similar way, so that as communication skill improved, likability would as well, but only up to a point where the communication was human but not quite human enough (the valley), increasing again as communication got very human? Or is there a point where a robot communicates in a too-perfect manner, thus making it seem non-human? Moreover, what characteristics of communication (e.g., language use, tones of voice, use of facial expressions, etc.) would be most important for a robot to demonstrate in responding to news stories about robots? These are all questions that future research can examine. Other similar areas of research have begun to look at receiving instructions from robots compared to other media (Lachlan et al., 2016; Goble Beattie, & Edwards, 2016; Edwards, C., Edwards, A., Spence, & Shelton, 2014) and the noted future directions are a natural extension of this research.

Another interesting avenue of study here would be to show news reports about robots failing at the jobs they are designed for. This could take multiple routes. For example, industrial robots could be shown breaking and/or failing to perform the mechanical duties they are designed. For example, if a robotic arm was designed to move bottles from a conveyor belt to a capping device, then some participants could see the arm performing this job well, and other participants could see the video of the arm dripping bottles or failing to place them in the capping device properly. The effects of these different exemplars of occupational robots would be interesting to study, as it may be the case that exemplars of problematic robots create less concern than robots that are effective. This could also be applied to other types of robots as well. Perhaps robots designed for jobs where communication is a central component, such as robotic waiters, would be more impacted by "uncanny valley" issues in communication. Would worse communication skills be perceived as failing to be capable of doing a job, thus leading to less concern about robots in the workplace?

Another area to study that was briefly discussed in this chapter was the emotion of envy rather than fear concerning the introductions of robots in the workplace. Although fear of this phenomena is real and can explain reactions of humans in the workplace, technology and robotics have come to a place where people may be comfortable enough that fear is the unlikely emotion driving these reactions. Interesting work has begun to look at the area of guilt in robotic platforms (Stoll, Edwards C., Edwards, A., 2016) and envy is a worthwhile extension of such research. Studies examining how people perceive and react over time to robots in the workplace can help the scientific community better understand human emotions to robots.

Initially guided by the idea that exemplified portrayals of robots may have an effect on perceptions of robots the current study offers many insights within and outside the scope of exemplification theory, along with several avenues of future research directions. Page limitations and research limitations prevent more discussion in this present context. However, there is much to learn about perceptions, attitudes, and emotions associated with robots in the workforce. Scientists studying communication are in a unique position to conduct and disseminate such research. Such conversations on human-machine communication are needed in the present and should continue into the future to guide both policy and practice.

References

Aust, C. F., & Zillmann, D. (1996). Effects of victim exemplification in television news on viewer perception of social issues. *Journalism & Mass Communication Quarterly, 73*(4), 787–803. doi:10.1177/107769909607300403

Bandura, A. (1977). Self-efficacy: Toward a unifying theory of behavioral change. *Psychological Review, 84*(2), 191–215. http://dx.doi.org/10.1037/0033-295X.84.2.191

Bell, R. (1992). Using video-based behaviour modelling training to improve performance at work. *Training & Management Development Methods, 6*(1–4), 5–10.

Brenton., H; Gillies, M., Ballin, D., & Chatting, D. (2005). The uncanny valley: Does it exist and is it related to presence, Presence-Connect, 8. MIT-Press.

Burleigh, T. J., Schoenherr, J. R., & Lacroix, G. L. (2013). Does the uncanny valley exist? An empirical test of the relationship between eeriness and the human likeness of digitally created faces. *Computers in Human Behavior, 29*(3), 759–771. doi:10.1016/j.chb.2012.11.021

Chamorro-Premuzic, T., & Ahmetoglu, G. (2016, December 12). The pros and cons of robot managers. *Harvard Business Review.* Retrieved from https://hbr.org/2016/12/the-pros-and-cons-of-robot-managers

Edwards, C., Edwards, A., Spence, P. R., & Westerman, D. (2016). Initial interaction expectations with robots: Testing the human-to-human interaction script, *Communication Studies, 67*(2), 227–238. doi: 10.1080/10510974.2015.1121899

Edwards, C., Edwards, A., Spence, P. R., & Shelton, A. K. (2014). Is that a bot running the social media feed? Testing the differences in perceptions of communication quality for a human agent and a bot agent on Twitter. *Computers in Human Behavior, 33,* 372–376. doi: http://dx.doi.org/10.1016/j.chb.2013.08.013

Gibson, R., Callison, C., & Zillmann, D. (2011). Quantitative literacy and affective reactivity in processing statistical information and case histories in the news. *Media Psychology, 14,* 96–120. doi:10.1080/15213269.2010.547830

Gibson, R., & Zillmann, D. (1994). Exaggerated versus representative exemplification in news reports: Perception of issues and personal consequences. *Communication Research, 21*(5), 603–624. doi:10.1177/009365094021005003

Goble, H., Beattie, A. J., Edwards, C. (2016). The impact of twitterbot race on interpersonal impressions. *Iowa Journal of Communication, 48*(1), 23–35.

Keynes, J. M. (1963, original 1930). Economic Possibilities for our grandchildren *Essays in persuasion* (pp.358–373). New York, NY: W. W. Norton.

Lachlan, K. A., Spence, P. R., Rainear, A., Fishlock, J., Xu, Z., & Vanco, B. (2016). You're my only hope: An initial exploration of the effectiveness of robotic platforms in engendering learning about crises and risks. *Computers in Human Behavior, 65,* 606–611. doi:http://dx.doi.org/10.1016/j.chb.2016.05.081

Lachlan, K. A., Spence, P. R., & Lin, X. (2013). Self-efficacy and learning processes associated with the elderly during disasters and crises. In B. Raskovich & S. Mrdja (Eds), *Natural Disaster: Prevention, Risk Factors and Management* (pp. 327–338) New York, NY: Nova.

Maney, K. (2016, November 11). How artificial intelligence and robots will radically transform the economy. *Newsweek.* Retrieved from http://www.newsweek.com/2016/12/09/robot-economy-artificial-intelligence-jobs-happy-ending-526467.html

Manyika, J., Chui, M., Miremadi, M., Bughin, J., George, K., Willmott, P., & Dewhurst, M. (2017). *A future that works: Automation, employment, and productivity.* New York, NY: McKinsey Global Institute.

Manz, C. C., & Sims, H. P. (1981). Vicarious learning: The influence of modeling on organizational behavior. *Academy of Management Review, 6*(1), 105–113.

McIntyre, J. J., Lachlan, K., & Spence, P. R. (2012). Attending to the future: The role of learning in emergency response. *Journal of Emergency Management, 10,* 41–52. doi:10.5055/jem.2012.0085

Minsky, M. (1980). Telepresence, *Omni, 2,* 45–51

Moniz, A. B., & Krings, B.-J., (2016). Robots working with humans or humans working with robots? Searching for social dimensions in new human-robot interaction in industry. *Societies, 6*(3), 23. doi:10.3390/soc6030023

Mori, M. (1970). The uncanny valley. *Energy, 7*(4), 33–35.

Nelson, L. D., Spence, P. R., & Lachlan, K. A. (2009). Learning from the media in the aftermath of a crisis: Findings from the Minneapolis bridge collapse. *Electronic News, 3,* 176–192. doi:10.1080/19312430903300046

Nisbet, M. C., Scheufele, D. A., Shanahan, J., Moy, P., Brossard, D., & Lewenstein, B. V. (2002). Knowledge, reservations, or promise? A media effects model for public perceptions of science and technology. *Communication Research, 29*(5), 584–608. doi:10.1177/009365002236196

Parrott, W. G., & Smith, R. H. (1993). Distinguishing the experiences of envy and jealousy. *Journal of Personality and Social Psychology, 64*(6), 906–920. doi:10.1037/0022-3514.64.6.906

Sellnow-Richmond, D. D., George, A. M., & Sellnow D. D. (2018). An IDEA model analysis of instructional risk communication in the time of ebola. *Journal of International Crisis and Risk Communication Research, 1*(1), 135–166. https://doi.org/10.30658/jicrcr.1.1.7

Shenkar, O. (1988). Blue, white and steel collar: a case study of robot introduction. *New Technology, Work and Employment, 3*(1), 66–73. doi:10.1111/j.1468-005X.1988.tb00090.x

Spence, P. R., Edwards, A., & Edwards, C. (2018). Attitudes, Prior Interaction, and Petitioner Credibility Predict Support for Considering the Rights of Robots. In

Companion of the 2018 ACM/IEEE *International Conference on Human-Robot Interaction* (pp. 243–244). ACM. doi: 10.1145/3173386.3177071

Spence, P. R., Lachlan, K. A., Westerman, D., Lin, X., Harris, C. J., Sellnow, T. L., & Sellnow-Richmond, D. D. (2017). Exemplification effects: Responses to perceptions of risk. *Journal of Risk Research, 20*(5), 590–610. doi:10.1080/13669877.2015.11 00658

Spence, P. R., Lachlan, K., Sellnow, T., Rice, R. G., & Seeger, H. (2017). That Is So Gross and I Have to Post About It: Exemplification Effects and User Comments on a News Story. *Southern Communication Journal, 82*(1), 27–37. doi: 10.1080/1041794X.2016.1265578

Spence, P. R., Westerman, D., Edwards, C., & Edwards, A. (2014). Welcoming our robot overlords: Initial expectations about interaction with a robot. *Communication Research Reports, 31*(3), 272–280. doi:10.1080/08824096.2014.924337

Spence, P. R., Westerman, D., & Rice, R. (2017). Exemplification theory in health and risk messaging. *Oxford Research Encyclopedia of Communication*. Retrieved 18 Jul. 2017, from http://communication.oxfordre.com/view/10.1093/acrefore/9780190228613.001.0001/acrefore-9780190228613-e-526.

Stoll, B., Edwards, C., & Edwards, A. (2016). "Why Aren't You a Sassy Little Thing": The effects of robot-enacted guilt trips on credibility and consensus in a negotiation. *Communication Studies, 67*(5), 530–547. doi:10.1080/10510974.2016.1215339

Strange, A. (2016, January 27). Robots, not humans, will serve you at SoftBank's new store in Japan. Mashable. Retrieved from http://mashable.com/2017/03/28/surface-interactive-display-projector/#yhHkURjyIiqY

Sundar, S. S., Waddell, T. F., & Jung, E. H. (2016). The Hollywood robot syndrome: Media effects on older adults' attitudes toward robots and adoption intentions. In Proceedings from HRI'16: *The Eleventh ACM/IEEE International Conference on Human Robot Interaction.* (pp. 343–350). Piscataway, NJ: IEEE Press.

Sunnafrank, M. & Ramirez, A., Jr. (2004). At first sight: Persistent relational effects of get-acquainted conversations. *Journal of Social and Personal Relationships, 21*(3), 361–379. doi:10.1177/0265407504042837

Syrdal, D. S., Nomura, T., Hirai, H., & Dautenhahn, K. (2011). Examining the Frankenstein syndrome: An open-ended cross-cultural survey. In Proceedings from ICSR 2011: *Social Robotics: Third International Conference on Social Robotics.* (pp. 125–134). London: Springer.

Vidaillet, B. (2007). Lacanian theory's contribution to the study of workplace envy. *Human Relations, 60*(11), 1669–1700. doi:10.1177/0018726707084304

Westerman, D., Spence, P. R., & Lachlan, K. A. (2012). Telepresence and exemplification: Does spatial presence impact sleeper effects? *Communication Research Reports, 29*(4), 299–309. doi:10.1080/08824096.2012.723272

Westerman, D., Spence, P. R., & Lachlan, K. A. (2009). Telepresence and the exemplification effects of disaster news. *Communication Studies, 60*(5), 542–557. doi:10.1080/10510970903260376

Westerman, D., Spence, P. R., & Lin, X. (2015). Telepresence and exemplification in health messages: The relationships among spatial and social presence and exemplars and exemplification effects. *Communication Reports, 28*(2), 92–102. doi:10.1080/0 8934215.2014.971838

Zillmann, D. (1999). Exemplification theory: Judging the whole by the sum of its parts. *Media Psychology, 1*, 69–94. doi:10.1207/s1532785xmep0101_5

Zillmann, D. (2002). Exemplification theory of media influence. In J. Bryant, & D. Zillmann (Eds.), *Media effects: Advances in theory and research* (2nd ed.). (pp. 213–245). Mahwah, NJ: Lawrence Erlbaum Associates.

Zillmann, D. (2006). Exemplification effects in the promotion of safety and health. *Journal of Communication, 56*, S221–S237. doi:10.1111/j.1460-2466.2006.00291.x

Zillmann, D., & Brosius, H. B. (2000). *Exemplification in communication: The influence of case reports on the perception of issues.* Mahwah, NJ: Lawrence Erlbaum Associates.

Zillmann, D., Gibson, R., & Sargent, S. L. (1999). Effects of photographs in news-magazine reports on issue perception. *Media Psychology, 1*(3), 207–228. doi:10.1207/ s1532785xmcp0103_2

10. Communicating With Machines: Robots as the Next New Media

SAKARI TAIPALE AND LEOPOLDINA FORTUNATI

The coming of robots into the domestic sphere and their presence in everyday life opens a new phase in the study of human-machine interaction. In comparison to ordinary information and communication technologies (ICTs), such as cell phones, personal computers, or tablets, robots can move and do physical things, but they are also more autonomous, interactive, and capable of learning about their users (Böhlen & Karppi, 2017b; Breazeal, 2002; Duffy, Rooney, O' Hare, & O' Donoghue, 1999). What remains to be understood is whether or not people are ready to take advantage of the more advanced capabilities of robots and, consequently, if robots could be the next new media (Kidd & Breazeal, 2008; Gates, 2008). To find answers to these questions, this chapter[1] will analyze and discuss EU citizens' perception of robots with the aid of the Special Eurobarometer *Public Attitudes towards Robots* data, which was collected on the behalf of the European Commission from the citizens of the European Union (EU), hereafter Europeans, aged 15 and over, in 27 member states in 2012 (N = 26,751) (Eurobarometer, 2012). At the present time, this is the largest and most representative survey carried out on the attitudes of people in Europe toward robots. Most of the previous studies on this topic are based on qualitative methodology or they depend on convenience samples, typically drawn from student populations (i.e., Höflich & El Bayed, 2015; Katz, Halpern, & Crocker, 2015). In contrast, the Eurobarometer data enables discussion of European attitudes toward robots, and it makes comparisons by country possible. By answering some research questions that we will report later, it is the aim of the chapter to advance understanding on how people relate to robots at rational and emotional levels. By so doing, the chapter contributes to the understanding of which social groups are most likely to engage in human-machine communication with robots when robots become available in the consumer market.

The chapter begins by presenting the shift that is taking place in the scientific debate on robots from negative approaches, such as fear of robots, toward more positive approaches, in which the focus is increasingly on the potential benefits of social robots and robot-human communication. Then the chapter moves on to illustrate the structure of the Eurobarometer data, our key measures, and the statistical analyses applied. The results section begins by analyzing some key predictors of not being afraid of robots. Secondly, it will show in which domains of life Europeans prefer to have robots and who believes that robots doing housework will soon become commonplace in Europe. The analysis will show that the use of robots in the field of social and individual reproduction faces the most objections. These are the areas of life where the new labor force is produced (bringing newborns to the world) and reproduced (by taking care at individual and social level of our selves and others). But when digging deeper, it will be found out which social groups, countries, and regions in Europe are the most permissive regarding the use of robots in this respect. Thirdly, the chapter will focus on one of the major obstacles to the acceptance of robots, that is, the fear of them. In the Eurobarometer study (2012), 73% of EU citizens express the fear that robots will take people's jobs. Contrary to many other studies, the vantage point of this chapter is to look at the factors that are least related to this fear and hence could mitigate it, increasing people's likelihood of interacting and communicating with robots. Lastly, the second research question asks in which circumstances or with what premises robots could be the next new media. By conducting a series of statistical analyses, it will be shown that the overall positive interest in new scientific discoveries among EU citizens is a good predictor for a positive attitude towards social robots and that the adoption of various personal ICTs relates to hands-on experience in using robots.

Based on these analyses, the chapter is concluded by arguing that robots can become a successful consumer product and the next new media, if they manage to sufficiently assist people with wearying and timewasting domestic chores as well as with communication and information needs, which vary substantially across Europe and among social groups. To be successful and to make people interact with robots, roboticists and robot designers should take advantage of people's previous knowledge of digital technology and their curiosity regarding technological innovations.

Background

Over the last decade, social robots have attracted a considerable amount of attention in social sciences and communication studies (Royakkers & van Est,

2015; Taipale, de Luca, Sarrica, & Fortunati, 2015). Among other things, these studies are marking a shift away from negative approaches to robotics, including the fear of losing jobs, towards positive approaches, in which robots are considered increasingly as social actors, supplementary to and not replacing human beings.

For example, in 2013, Sugiyama and Vincent edited a special issue of the online journal *Intervalla* "Social Robots and Emotion: Transcending the Boundaries between Humans and ICTs." In the following year, the journal *Cognitive Computation* published another special issue, "Modeling Emotion, Behavior and Context in Socially Believable Robots and ICT Interfaces", edited by Esposito, Fortunati and Lugano. In 2015, Pfadenhauer, Sugiyama and Ess edited a special issue for the *International Journal of Social Robotics* on "Social Robots: Form, Content, Critique", and Fortunati, Esposito and Lugano edited another special issue of "Beyond Industrial Robotics: Social Robots Entering Public and Domestic Spheres" for the journal *The Information Society*. Also, in 2015, the pivotal book "Robots from a Human Perspective", edited by Vincent, Taipale, Sapio, Lugano, and Fortunati (2015), was published. More recently, a special issue of the journal *Transformations. Journal of Media, Culture & Technology* (2017b) "Social Robots: Human-Machine Configurations" edited by Marc Böhlen and Tero Karppi was published.

In general, the public and scientific debates, especially concerning people's imagination about robots, are fed by a wide offer of visual products (e.g., robot movies, TV series, cartoons) and their representations in other media. This creates a paradoxical situation in which people like to nurture their imagination and amuse themselves with robots via cultural products, while, at the same time, being afraid of robots in real life (Scopelliti, Giuliani, D'Amico, & Fornara, 2004). Robots are one of those technologies that multitudes have not fully engaged with and have not developed particular communication pratices with, as yet. However, their multiple images and representations convey diverse and often contradictory messages to their potential users (Guzman, 2016).

The study by Fortunati et al. (2016) sheds light on the role of print newspapers in this contradictory situation. By analyzing the four most read print newspapers in Italy (Il Corriere della Sera, Il Sole 24 Ore, La Repubblica, and La Stampa), including 240 articles dealing with robots, the authors identify five discursive frames on robots shaping readers' imagination. These are concerned with the human body, science fiction, technology/innovation, science/research, and the industrial sector. This study delineates a map of the ways in which the public is informed regarding the sectors where robots have become established, the events in which robots have been protagonists, new paths of research, and the new types of robots that have been created. However, sometimes, inspiring, media influences may distort people's expectations and views of "real" robots that are already in use or are likely to enter the market soon. An example of this comes from a recent study carried out by Fortunati, Esposito, Ferrin, and Viel (2014). In a sample of elementary and secondary schools pupils in Italy (N = 740), children were asked to describe robots in comparison to toys and human beings. Children who were more familiar with various fictional robots expressed a less realistic notion of robots in everyday life.

Hence, the approach of this chapter assists in formulating a picture of robots that is not based on fear and prejudice, but is geared toward understanding who are ready to interact with robots and who are most likely be the first in Europe to appropriate robots. Negative approaches towards robots tend to highlight only the limitations and risks of robots, often at the expense of their foreseeable benefits, and they do not consider the improvements that can result from users' agency when users begin to shape this new technology.

Methods

Survey and Sample

The data analyzed in this chapter comes from the Special Eurobarometer 382: *Public Attitudes towards Robots* survey (N = 26,751) collected in 2012.[2] This structured survey was implemented as face-to-face interviews at respondents' homes in their mother tongue, covering a representative sample of EU citizens aged 15 and over in 27 member states (Eurobarometer, 2012). Although the results derived from this data are well representative of European population, they cannot be generalized to the U.S. and East Asian developed countries (e.g., such as Japan and South-Korea) in which robotification is also well underway and even further than in Europe. Up to the present, this survey is the most extensive attempt to assess people's attitudes toward robots. However, the design of the survey is not problem-free, as it shapes respondents' understanding of what robots are by only presenting two pictures of them (Eurobarometer, 2012, p. 4).

Measures[3]

Most of the dependent variables are directly drawn from the original data, whose measures have been described in previous publications and documents (Eurobarometer, 2012; European Commission, 2014). However, some new variables were also created in order to summarize information and to facilitate analysis. This was done using two questions "In which areas do you think robots should be used as a priority?" and "In which areas do you think that the use of robots should be banned?" which were merged into new ordinal variables. A maximum of three answers per question was allowed, and respondents could choose from the following domains of life: manufacturing; health care; leisure; domestic use (such as cleaning); military and security; search and rescue; education; care of children, the elderly, and the disabled; space exploration; agriculture; transport/logistics. Respondents could also choose "other domains", "none of them" or reply "I don't know." The values of *new domain-specific attitude* measures vary between –1 (ban), 0 (indifference) and 1 (use as a priority). Regarding socio-demographic variables, respondents' gender, age, class position, main activity, family type, living in a family with children, the size of place of residence, completed years of education, and country of residence are analyzed. For analytic purposes, the number of answer choices was reduced by merging original categories.

Statistics

In terms of methods, the chapter benefits from both descriptive and inferential statistics. For descriptive purposes, frequencies and cross-tabulations with a Chi Squared test are applied. When explaining the dependent variables, either binary or ordered logistic regression analysis are applied depending on the type of variable in question. For logistic regression models, the results of Wald Chi Squared Test and related probability values are reported. Pseudo R^2 is reported to indicate how much of the total variation of the dependent variable the given model virtually explains.

Results

Key Indicators of Not Being Afraid of Robots

Four important indicators for not being afraid of robots were indentified from Eurobarometer data. First, what is likely to mirror people's positive attitude towards robots is their *direct experience of interacting with robots either at work or at home* (see also Bartneck, Suzuki, Kanda, & Nomura, 2007). The socio-demographic profile of those who have used robots is well in line with a large body of previous research on the relationship between the use and appreciation of communication and information technologies (Fortunati & Manganelli, 1998). A logistic regression modelling (N = 23.606, Wald chi² (46) = 674.98, p < .001, Pseudo R^2 = 0.06) shows that men, workers, people aged from 24 to 64 years, as well as people with a high level of education and those living in big cities are most likely to have previously used robots. People living alone, on the other hand, are less likely to have used robots before. A certain number of repeated acts can lead generally to a form of saturation. The use of technology produces the opposite effect: The more one uses innovative technology the more one likes it. These results reinforce our idea that social robots will be the next new media, but with a greater number of communicative and practical affordances than previous new technologies, which seem to have the potential to make them a new status symbol in the field of mass technology. In this concern, it is worth to recall that smartphones, tablets and computers represent mature and saturated markets while social robots are a new, expanding market.

The second indicator is a *positive, general view of robots among EU citizens*. The question presented to respondents was: "Do you have a very positive, fairly positive, fairly negative or very negative view of robots?" On the whole, 70 percent of Europeans declare that they have a fairly or very positive view of robots. An average value (M = 2.16, SD = 0.74, range 1 = very negative to 4 = very positive) for this question confirmed the relatively positive overall attitude towards robots. To reconstruct the socio-demographic profile of the Europeans who have a positive view of robots, we carried out an ordered logistic regression for the same dependent variable (N = 21.895, Wald chi^2 (35) = 2453.74, p < .001, Pseudo R^2 = 0.11). Our analyses show that men have a slightly more positive vision of robots than women. Higher levels of education, higher social position, and income are related to more positive views of robots. The same regression model also confirms that respondents, who are interested in scientific discoveries have a more positive view on robots than those who are not. In short, it seems that the classic signs of personal success and trust in scientific discoveries and innovations also shape a positive conceptualization of robots.

The third indicator relates to a more specific view concerning the social functions of robots. 79.3 percent of Europeans either agree or totally agree with the statement *robots are a good thing for society as they help people* (M = 3.01, SD = 0.79, range = 1 totally disagree to 4 totally agree). The determinants for a more positive answer are similar as for many other questions; high level of education, high income, and bigger size of abode. Compared to respondents living with children, singles also agree more with this statement. Again, the stronger people's interest in scientific discoveries is and the more positive is their view of robots, the more respondents think that robots are a good thing for society. (Ordered logistic regression; N = 21.707, Wald chi^2 (40) = 3250.60, p < .001, Pseudo R^2 = 0.19).

The fourth indicator of not having fear of robots is *the interest in scientific discoveries and technological developments*. The Eurobarometer (2012) study reports that 25.4 percent of Europeans say they are "Very interested" and 52.1 percent that they are "Moderately interested" in science and technology. As for other indicators, we carried out an ordered regression analysis ($N = 23.455$, Wald $chi^2 (45) = 2085.62$, $p < .001$, Pseudo $R^2 = 0.09$) to clarify Europeans' interest in science and technology. The results of the analysis confirm that this interest significantly affects European men more than women and is more common among 18 to 64-year-olds, than in the youngest and the oldest age groups. Interest in science increases with education. It concerns urbanites more than it concerns rural people, and it involves the middle and upper middle classes more than the lower classes.

Social Robots as the Next New Media in the Reproduction Sphere

The Eurobarometer data clearly indicate that the domains of life where robots are already used to some extent, including manufacturing, space exploration, search and rescue, and military and security, are widely considered as areas where more robots could be used in the future (Table 10.1). In contrast, robots face more opposition in the sphere of social and individual reproduction, where people's conditions of the life are produced and maintained including care services, health care, education, entertainment, and the domestic sphere. In order to understand the people who are least afraid of having robots in these most resisted domains, another series of multivariate analyses was carried out.

The ordered logistic models applied to the domains of social reproduction, where respondents think that *robots should be used as a priority* (Table 10.2), show that women are more likely to welcome robots for domestic usage than men. In contrast, men are more in favor of robots in health care, care of children, the care of the elderly and the disabled, and education. Pensioners are clearly more willing to have robots in health and social care work, but also in education, than people in the work force. Family type is associated with robots in health care and domestic use, and larger size of the city of residence is a predictor of willingness to allow robots in health care and social care. However, the permissive attitude towards robots for domestic use decreases with age. Countries located in regions where women have a large responsibility of care and domestic work chores, seem to be more supportive of the use of robots in these particular sectors.

Despite a great variation in the socio-demographic profiles of those who are not afraid of robots across the domains of society and individual

Table 10.1. The Areas of Life Where Europeans "Think That Robots Should Be Used as a Priority" (Unweighted).

Domain	N	%
Manufacturing	14.630	57.1
Space exploration	13.955	54.7
Search and rescue	11.267	44.2
Military and security	9.877	38.9
Healthcare	5.436	21.5
Domestic use	3.742	14.9
Transportation	2858	10.7
Care of children, elderly, and the disabled	991	3.9
Education	639	2.6
Leisure	592	2.4

Note. Each respondent was allowed to choose up to 3 categories. The total number of answers is thus higher than the base (N = 26.751)
Source: Authors.

reproduction, it seems that the social groups that would benefit from the robots most are the strongest advocates. This applies also to country variations, which show that in the regions (Mediterranean and East Europe) in which much of the care responsibilities and the domestic work are carried out by women, the support for robots in these sectors is higher. After years of slow economic growth, and the success of some of the first domestic robots, such as Roomba or Bimby (IFR, 2016), these people hope that robotic technology can reduce the burden of their daily chores. Domestic robots may also reduce the need to dicusses and agree on the fair division of house work, if some of these tasks can be assigned to a robot. At the same time, some domestic robots might help in revising the gender division of house work in the households. Just as home electronics and ICT began to facilitate immaterial labor at home in the 1980–90s, now the time seems to be ripe for (robotic) technology to also address the material aspects of care and house work.

We want to issue a reminder here that if European grown-ups are suspicious of robots in the domestic sphere because they think that children (and the elderly) deserve, in the first instance, human care, this does not inevitably mirror the reality of the next generation (Fortunati, 2016; Fortunati, Esposito, Ferrin, & Viel, 2014; Fortunati, Esposito, Sarrica, & Ferrin, 2015).

In addition to the preferred domains, it is equally interesting to understand the timescale over which people think that robots will enter into the domestic

Table 10.2. Ordered Logistic Models Predicting the Willingness to Have More Robots in Various Domains of Life (Coefficients and P-values Between Brackets).

	Health care	Domestic activity	Care of children etc.	Education	Leisure
Gender	-.24 (.000)	.23 (.000)	-.28 (.000)	-.10 (.017)	
Social class (Low)					
- Middle	.07 (.384)	—	—		
- Middle-high	.17 (.005)				
Activity (employee)					
- Housewives/housemen	-.07 (.384)	—	.06 (.491)	.16 (.055)	
- Unemployed	.03 (.646)		.03 (.667)	.08 (.322)	
- Pensioner	.22 (.000)		.19 (.000)	.19 (.000)	
- Student	-.09 (.216)		.22 (.006)	-.07 (.443)	
Family (Couple with children)					
- Couple without children	-.06 (.223)	.07 (.261)	—		
- Single	-.13 (.018)	.10 (.128)			
- One parent and children	-.10 (.250)	.21 (.056)			
- Mixed families	-.15 (.203)	-.29 (.044)			
City size (Rural area or village)					
- Small or medium size town	.02 (.668)		.12 (.017)		
- Large town or city	.15 (.002)		.17 (.002)		
Years of education (15 or less)					
- 16–19	.11 (.049)	.28 (.000)	—	-.06 (.262)	-.19 (.006)
- 20 or more	.29 (.000)	.37 (.000)		-.16 (.011)	-.07 (.353)
Age (15–17)					
- 18–24		-.38 (.026)			
- 25–44		-.49 (.004)			
- 45–64		-.66 (.000)			
- 65+		-.63 (.000)			
Country (ref France)					
- Belgium	.22 (.025)	-.64 (.000)	.32 (.001)	.24 (.011)	-.27 (.006)
- The Netherlands	-.18 (.080)	-.44 (.000)	.36 (.000)	.26 (.007)	.33 (.001)

(Continued)

Table 10.2. (Continued)

	Health care	Domestic activity	Care of children etc.	Education	Leisure
- Germany	-.41 (.000)	-.22 (.033)	-.49 (.000)	1.03 (.000)	.48 (.000)
- Italy	-.21 (.027)	.27 (.028)	.44 (.000)	1.08 (.000)	.63 (.000)
- Luxemburg	-.63 (.000)	.15 (.250)	-.57 (.000)	-.07 (.541)	.48 (.000)
- Denmark	-.52 (.000)	-.31 (.007)	.33 (.001)	1.10 (.000)	.52 (.000)
- Ireland	-.66 (.000)	-.233 (.007)	-.15 (.157)	1.34 (.000)	.88 (.000)
- Great Britain	-.56 (.000)	-.55 (.000)	.07 (.492)	1.12 (.000)	.96 (.000)
- Greece	-.17 (.069)	-.83 (.000)	.03 (.744)	.75 (.000)	.57 (.000)
- Spain	-.28 (.004)	.01 (.928)	.49 (.000)	.63 (.000)	.86 (.000)
- Portugal	-.75 (.000)	.27 (.026)	.79 (.000)	1.09 (.000)	1.80 (.000)
- Finland	-.38 (.000)	-.22 (.073)	.50 (.000)	1.84 (.000)	.91 (.000)
- Sweden	-.88 (.000)	-.56 (.000)	-.13 (.000)	1.20 (.000)	.39 (.000)
- Austria	-.97 (.000)	.32 (.007)	-.46 (.000)	.60 (.000)	.93 (.000)
- Cyprus	-.50 (.000)	-.96 (.000)	-1.06 (.000)	.84 (.000)	.63 (.000)
- Czech Republic	.37 (.000)	-.06 (.604)	.38 (.000)	1.35 (.000)	.22 (.035)
- Estonia	-1.09 (.000)	-.43 (.000)	.43 (.000)	.61 (.000)	.34 (.001)
- Hungary	-.62 (.000)	-.15 (.212)	.21 (.026)	.78 (.000)	.34 (.001)
- Latvia	-1.30 (.000)	.30 (.007)	.08 (.405)	.93 (.000)	.22 (.024)
- Lithuania	-1.48 (.000)	.54 (.000)	.07 (.496)	.78 (.000)	.77 (.000)
- Malta	-.95 (.000)	.40 (.007)	.63 (.000)	.82 (.000)	.96 (.000)
- Poland	-.24 (.008)	.00 (.989)	-.05 (.600)	1.39 (.000)	.76 (.000)
- Slovakia	-.26 (.006)	.41 (.000)	.29 (.002)	1.57 (.000)	.49 (.000)
- Slovenia	.45 (.000)	-.005 (.654)	-.60 (.000)	1.70 (.000)	-.04 (.679)
- Bulgaria	-.81 (.000)	.60 (.000)	.67 (.000)	.89 (.000)	1.23 (.000)
- Romania	-.17 (.104)	.59 (.000)	.29 (.003)	.84 (.000)	.58 (.000)
N	24195	24741	25119	24663	24632
Pseudo R²	.02	.02	.02	.03	.02

Note: Only significant variables are included in the models. Bold text indicates statistically significance at the level of p <.05.
Source: Authors.

sphere. Hence, we explored *when*, according to the respondents, it will be *commonplace in Europe for robots to do house work*. Only 3.5 percent of respondents answered that this is already commonplace in contrast to 7.0 percent, who declared that this will never happen. 8.4 percent of respondents estimated that this will happen in five years' time, 22.4 percent in 10 years' time, 21.0 percent in 20 years' time and 29.6 percent in more than 20 years' time. These figures indicate that, according to Europeans, the penetration of robotics in the domestic sphere is merely a question of time and that studies on robot-human interaction will be particularly crucial in the near future. To elaborate this question further, another ordered logistic regression (N = 20.532, Wald chi² (42) = 1553.07, p < .001, Pseudo R^2 = 0.03) models created shows that that higher level education, higher social position, as well as living in a large city are associated with shorter time estimations. Compared to those who are part of the work force, pensioners and people with high income are less optimistic on this forecast. Similarly, interest in scientific discoveries and technological developments, first-hand experience in using robots either at work or at home, and a positive view of robots predict a shorter estimated time.

Key Indicators of Not Being Afraid of Robots as Work Thieves

We decided to analyze separately the popular fear that *robots steal people's jobs* in order to grasp who agrees least with this statement (Table 10.3). Of

Table 10.3. Ordered Logistic Model Explaining the Fear of Losing Jobs Because of Robots.

	Coef.	P-value
Gender	.14	.001
Years of education (ref. 15 or less) - 16–20 - 20 or more	-.16 -.56	.007 .000
Activity (Employee) - Housewives/housemen - Unemployed - Pensioners	-.01 .22 .07	.910 .003 .173
Income	-.16	.000
Living in a family with (1) or without children (0)	-.09	.033
Interest in new scientific discoveries (not interested at all) - Moderately interested - Very interested	-.09 -.27	.130 .000

(*Continued*)

Table 10.3. (*Continued*)

	Coef.	P-value
View of robots (Ref. very negative)		
- Fairly negative	**−.03**	**.015**
- Fairly positive	**−1.36**	**.000**
- Very positive	**−1.79**	**.000**
Country (ref France)		
- Belgium	−.05	.515
- The Netherlands	**−.79**	**.000**
- Germany	**.37**	**.000**
- Italy	**−.58**	**.000**
- Luxemburg	**.46**	**.000**
- Denmark	**−.29**	**.002**
- Ireland	**−.34**	**.001**
- Great Britain	**−.27**	**.002**
- Greece	**.36**	**.000**
- Spain	**.66**	**.000**
- Portugal	**.63**	**.000**
- Finland	**−.53**	**.000**
- Sweden	−.06	.459
- Austria	**−.79**	**.000**
- Cyprus	**1.00**	**.000**
- Czech Republic	**−.77**	**.000**
- Estonia	**−27**	**.006**
- Hungary	−.07	.413
- Latvia	**.36**	**.000**
- Lithuania	**.26**	**.005**
- Malta	**.55**	**.000**
- Poland	−.05	.556
- Slovakia	**−.52**	**.000**
- Slovenia	**.28**	**.002**
- Bulgaria	**−.44**	**.000**
- Romania	−.09	.418
Pseudo R2	.07	
N	21804	

Note: Only significant variables are included in the model. Bold text indicates statistically significance at the level of p <.05.
Source: Authors.

all Europeans interviewed, 72.6 percent agree or totally agree with this fear (M = 3.01, SD = 0.91, range = 1 totally disagree to 4 totally agree). An ordered logistic regression (N = 21.804, Wald chi² (39) = 2163.06, p < .001, Pscudo R² = 0.07) for this statements shows that men, higher level of education and the presence of children are related to lower perceptions of this fear. Understandably, the unemployed are more convinced than workers are that robots take over humans' jobs. The more positive the general view of robots is, the higher is the interest in scientific discoveries, and the less agreement is given to the statement that robots steal jobs. What is apparent here is that people experience this fear more strongly in South European and Mediterranean countries, like Spain, Portugal, Malta, Cyprus, and Greece, which have suffered from the highest rates of unemployment in Europe and where people have less first-hand experience in working with robots than, for instance, in Nordic countries (Eurobarometer, 2012).

Emotional Relationship With Robots

In general, findings concerning feelings complement, and sometimes question, the answers to more rational questions. Here we focus on two questions that inquire as to how people feel about robots carrying out certain tasks belonging to the sphere of social and individual reproduction. The first question was "How do you personally feel about having a robot perform a medical operation on you?" (M = 3.90, SD = 2.98, range = 1 totally uncomfortable to 10 totally comfortable), and secondly "How do you personally feel about having a robot mind your children or elderly parents?" (M = 2.03, SD = 1.96, range = 1 totally uncomfortable to 10 totally comfortable). The low mean values in both cases show that when the robots are proposed in the sphere of social reproduction, negative feelings still develop immediately. This reasserts our previous findings showing that the domains of life in which social and personal reproduction mostly take place, are most infrequently mentioned by the overall sample as areas where robots should be used as a priority (see Table 10.1).

To sum up, these findings provide a relatively consistent picture of a general, positive attitude by Europeans towards robots. It is the interest in scientific discoveries and technological developments, as well as a similar socio-demographic profile that was earlier found in the surveys on ICT diffusion and adoption (male, high education, high income, urban location), that are common for robot proponents. This social group will most likely develop the first communicative practices with robots, and these practices will set the first standards for human-computer communication modes in the future design of the robots. Can the use of ICTs also be considered to be an important variable influencing the diffusion and adoption of social robots? Therefore, can we forecast with more evidence that social robots will be the next new media? In the next section, we will try to get an answer to this question.

Social Robots: The Next New Media?

In this section we hypothesize that what may influence robot diffusion is the recent spread and appropriation of ICTs that have, on the one hand, created a smarter environment by stimulating people's minds with new innovations, and, on the other hand, made people anticipate newer and more advanced technological products to follow the older ones (Rheingold, 2000). The Eurobarometer data makes it possible to elaborate on how the ownership of ICTs is related to the direct experience of using robots.

The analyses show that those who own either a mobile phone only (7.7%) or both a mobile and a landline phone (5.5%) have more experience in using robots at home than those who have no phone at all (2.4%) (x^2 = 77.709, df = 3, p = .000). Similarly, it is more common among computer owners (6.4%) that they have used a robot at home than among non-owners of computers (4.4%) (x^2 = 36,846, df = 1, p. = .000). Similarly, the intensity of the Internet use at home is slightly linked to first-hand robot experiences. Those who report not using the Internet from home at all (4.6%), have less experience in using robots at home than those who use it often (6.4%) or everyday (6.5%) (x^2 = 21.061, df = 2, p = .000).

These data provide evidence to argue that the interest in scientific discoveries and technological developments, and the use of ICTs can be considered as a strong predictor for the diffusion and adoption of the social robots. On this basis, social robots can be prefigured as the next new media, which can also work as a new status symbol in the diverse field of personal technologies by offering new dimensions, such as nonverbal communication and higher social presence, to human-machine communication (de Graaf, 2016). Consequently, it may be anticipated that very probably social robots will help to defeat the fear of robots as works thieves when people will get used to interacting and communicating with robots in domestic environments.

Discussion and Final Remarks

In this chapter, we have shown that the groups that are ready to welcome robots in the domestic sphere without or with less fear than European citizens in general have largely the same profile than those who first adopted ICT. However, some unexpected groups also have come to the fore, especially pensioners and people living in southern, and some eastern, European countries. In particular, with regard the use of robots for domestic tasks, women also stand out from the results. By interacting with robotic technology, these groups can avoid or at least reduce the most physically demanding and time-consuming household tasks, most of which are still typically done by women, both young and old. In general, this fear is mitigated by several factors such as high income and education, employment, and interest in scientific discoveries and advancement. After the years of slow economic growth, and the slow rhythm of innovations inside the domestic appliances sector, these people in particular—unlike the majority of people—see that robotic technology could reduce the burden of their daily chores.

This study also has also implications for robot designers so that they could accelerate the uptake of robots and human-robot communication in the domestic sphere. First, just as the vast take-up of ICTs changed the way in which the immaterial labor is carried out in the social and individual sphere, the time now seems to be ripe for (robotic) technology to also address the material part of care and housework. The engineers and programmers of social robots should target the people who are least afraid to get a foot in the door. Second, there is a need for a change in perspective in the design of social robots. After a long wave of ICT diffusion, the real challenge for robotics nowadays is to produce easy-to-adopt products with strong utility and clear purpose (de Graaf, Ben Allouch, and van Dijk, 2017), the robots that are capable of meeting both material and immaterial needs. Hence, in terms of technological solutions, such as user interface, the leap from contemporary ICTs into social robots must be modest to facilitate the smooth adoption of robots (Taipale et al., 2015). As in the case of cell phones, tablets, and messaging apps which are only now being introduced in health and care work, it is likely that the human-robot interaction will start evolving from less contentious domains of everyday life, such as entertainment and domestic chores. As Coeckelbergh (2010) has shown, robotic technologies in health care, for instance, face many objections. Some of these objections set such high standards for good care that even many of the existing low-tech health-care practices do not meet them.

Based on the previous knowledge about the diffusion and use of ICTs, it could be expected that people who are not afraid of robots belong to the most powerful strata of the population. In fact, this turns out to be the case at least partly, as men, people with high education and high incomes, and the urbanites were often the least afraid. Nevertheless, in regards to the willingness to have more robots in some of the fields of individual and social reproduction, some of the disadvantaged subgroups, such as pensioners and people living in less wealthy Southern European countries, were also less worried about robots. For them communication with robots may appear more as an opportunity than as a risk, and robots may seem capable of providing more instant relief in their daily life than they do for the better off. Considering that the mobile phone market is already quite saturated, social robots have a good chance to be the next, new media that is integrated into the network of personal (and household) technology (Fortunati & Taipale, 2016). Apart from Europeans' relatively high interest in new scientific discoveries, their extensive adoption and use of ICTs have shaped a cultural and social environment that is favorable for the adoption of robots.

Finally, considering the positive relationship between today's regular use of ICTs and the perception of future robots, perhaps it would make sense to focus more on ICT-like than human-like robots both in research and commercialization activities. This would immediately facilitate the efficiency of robot-human interaction. Human-like features like sociability may be added to robots later when users have familiarized themselves with new robotic solutions and their emotional reactions have stabilized (de Graaf et al., 2017; Taipale, Vincent, Sapio, Lugano, & Fortunati, 2015). In fact, something similar can be recognized from the evolution of mobile phones, which, at first, were really heavy and machine-like, but later become highly personalized and loved devices. The second lesson to be learned is that there is no easy way to target the care market straightaway. Like mobile phones, tablets and apps that are only now being introduced to the care business, it is likely that the robots can become the new media by first entering into less intimate and defended domains of life.

The main limit of this study is that it is based on a single method, the classical quantitative survey focused on one continent. However, with this approach, we have revealed some of the complexity that researchers have to deal with when people engage in a more regular interaction with robots. The penetration of social robots inaugurates, as we mentioned above, a new phase in human-machine interaction research, that is the study of human-robot interaction. Human-robot interaction is made up of a complex texture of communication, interaction, and material relations, which needs to be addressed through the lens, not only of rational action theory, but also the theory of emotion.

Notes

1. This research has received project funding from the Academy of Finland (no. 265986), and it was carried out within the Academy of Finland's Centre of Excellence in Research on Ageing and Care (CoE AgeCare).
2. For more details about the Eurobarometer survey, its sampling methods and measures, please see Eurobaromater (2012). The European Comission propotes the efficicant reuses of its data sets, and hence also the questionnaire and the data of this study are available via the GESIS Data Archive (http://www.gesis.org).
3. For reasons of space we cannot include all the tables. Also, because of the high number of measures, we cannot report all of them in detail.

References

Bartneck, C., Suzuki, T., Kanda, T, & Nomura, T. (2007). The influence of people's culture and prior experiences with Aibo on their attitude towards robots. *AI & Society*. doi 10.1007/s00146-006-0052-7

Böhlen, M., & Karppi, T. (2017a). The making of robot care. *Transformations*, 29. Retrieved from http://www.transformationsjournal.org/wpcontent/uploads/2017/02/ Transformations29_Bohlen-Karppi.pdf

Böhlen, M., & Karppi, T. (2017b). Social robots: Human-machine configurations, special issue of *Transformations*. *Journal of Media, Culture & Technology*, 29, 1–22.

Breazeal, C. (2002). *Designing sociable robots. Intelligent robots and autonomous agents*. Cambridge, MA: The MIT Press.

Coeckelbergh, M. (2010). Health care, capabilities and AI assistive technologies. *Ethical Theory Moral Practice, 13*(2), 181–190.

de Graaf, M. M. (2016). An ethical evaluation of human–robot relationships. *International Journal of Social Robotics, 8*(4), 589–598.

de Graaf, M. M., Ben Allouch, S., & van Dijk, J. (2017). Why would I use this in my home? A model of domestic social robot acceptance. *Human-Computer Interaction*. doi:10.1080/07370024.2017.1312406

Duffy, B., Rooney, C., O' Hare, G. M., & O' Donoghue, R. (1999). *What is a social robot?* Paper presented at the 10th Irish Conference on Artificial Intelligence & Cognitive Science, University College Cork, Ireland.

Esposito, A., Fortunati, L., & Lugano, G. (2014). Modeling emotion, behavior and context in socially believable robots and ICT interfaces. *Cognitive Computation, 6*(4), 623–627. doi: 10.1007/s12559-014-9309-5

European Commission. (2014). *Eurobarometer 77.1 (2012)*. TNS OPINION & SOCIAL, Brussels [Producer]. GESIS Data Archive, Cologne. ZA5597 Data file Version 3.0.0. doi: 10.4232/1.12014

Eurobarometer. (2012). *Public attitudes towards robots*. Special Eurobarometer 382. European Commission. Retrieved from: http://ec.europa.eu/public_opinion/archives/ ebs/ebs_382_en.pdf

Fortunati, L. (2016). Moving robots from industrial sectors to domestic spheres: A foreword. In A. Esposito & L. Jain (Eds.), *Modeling emotions in robotic socially believable gehaving gystems* (Vol. 2, pp. 1–3). Berlin: Springer.

Fortunati, L., Esposito, A., Ferrin, G., & Viel, M. (2014). Approaching social robots through playfulness and doing-it-yourself: Children in action. *Cognitive Computation, 6*(4), 789–801.

Fortunati L., Esposito, A., & Lugano, G. (2015). Introduction to the special issue "Beyond industrial robotics: Social robots entering public and domestic spheres." *The Information Society, 31*(3), 229–236. doi:10.1080/01972243.2015.1020195

Fortunati, L., Esposito, A., Sarrica, M., & Ferrin, G. (2015). Children's knowledge and imaginary about robots. *International Journal of Social Robotics, 7*(5), 685–695.

Fortunati, L., & Manganelli, A. M. (1998). La comunicazione tecnologica: comportamenti, opinioni ed emozioni degli europei. In Fortunati, L, (Ed.), *Telecomunicando in Europa* (pp. 125–194). Milano: Angeli.

Fortunati, L., Sarrica, M., Honsell, F., Buscato, S., & Steffan, A. (2016). *The media discourse on social robots*: Three years of newspaper articles. Paper presented at the FORTLIT, Pisa, Italy.

Fortunati, L., & Taipale, S. (2016). Mobilities and the network of personal technologies: Refining the understanding of mobility structure. *Telematics & Informatics* 34(2), 560–568. doi. 10.1016/j.tele.2016.09.011

Gates, B. (2008, February 1). A robot in every home. The leader of the PC revolution predicts that the next hot field will be robotics. *Scientific American.* Retrieved from https://www.scientificamerican.com/article/a-robot-in-every-home-2008-02/

Guzman, A. L. (2016). The messages of mute machines: Human-machine communication with industrial technologies. *communication +1, 5,* Article 4. Retrieved from http://scholarworks.umass.edu/cpo/vol5/iss1/4.

Höflich, J. R., & El Bayed, A. (2015). Perception, acceptance, and the social construction of robots: Exploratory studies. In Vincent, J., Taipale, S, Sapio, B., Lugano, G., & Fortunati, L. (Eds.), *Social robots from a human perspective* (pp. 39–54). Cham, Switzerland: Springer.

IFR. (2016). *Executive Summary World Robotics 2016 Service Robots.* Retrieved from https://ifr.org/downloads/press/02_2016/Executive_Summary_Service_ Robots_2016.pdf

Kidd, C. D., & Breazeal, C. (2008). *Robots at home: Understanding long term human-robot interaction.* Retrieved from http://citeseerx.ist.psu.edu/viewdoc/download? doi=10.1.1.297.5270&rep=rep1&type=pdf

Katz, E. J., Halpern, D., & Crocker, E. T. (2015). In the company of robots: Views of acceptability of robots in social settings. In J. Vincent, S. Taipale, B. Sapio, G. Lugano, & L. Fortunati (Eds.), *Social robots from a human perspective* (pp. 25–38). Cham, Switzerland: Springer.

Pfadenhauer, M., Sugiyama, S., & Ess, C. M. (Eds.). (2015). Special issue of IJSR on social robots: Form, content, critique. *International Journal of Social Robotics, 7*(3), 333–334. doi: 10.1007/s12369-015-0291-1.

Rheingold, H. (2000). *Tools for thought: The history and future of mind-expanding Technology.* Cambridge, Mass: MIT Press.

Royakkers, L., & van Est, R. (2015). A literature review on new robotics: Automation from love to war. *International Journal of Social Robotics, 7*(5), 549–570.

Scopelliti, M., Giuliani, M. V., D'Amico, A. M., & Fornara, F. (2004). If I had a robot at home ... Peoples' representation of domestic robots. In S. Keates, J. Clarkson, P. Langdon, & P. Robinson (Eds.), *Designing a more inclusive world* (pp. 257–266). Cham: Springer.

Sugiyama, S. & Vincent, J. (Eds.) (2013). Social robots and emotion: Transcending the boundaries between humans and ICTs, a special issue of the online journal *Intervalla,*

1(1). Retrieved from https://www.fus.edu/intervalla/volume-1-social-robots-and-emotion-transcending-the-boundary-between-humans-and-icts

Taipale, S., de Luca, F., Sarrica, M. & Fortunati, L. (2015). Robot shift from industrial production to social reproduction. In J. Vincent, S. Taipale, B. Sapio, L. Fortunati, & G. Lugano (Eds.), *Social robots from a human perspective* (pp. 11–24). Cham, Switzerland: Springer.

Taipale, S., Vincent, J., Sapio, B., Lugano, G., Fortunati, L. (2015). Introduction: Situating the human in social robots. In J. Vincent, S. Taipale, B. Sapio, G. Lugano, & L. Fortunati. (Eds.), *Social robots from a human perspective* (pp. 1–7). Cham: Springer.

Vincent, J., Taipale, S, Sapio, B., Lugano, G. & Fortunati, L. (Eds.). (2015). *Social robots from a human perspective*. Cham, Switzerland: Springer.

11. Ars Ex Machina: Rethinking Responsibility in the Age of Creative Machines

David J. Gunkel

In May 2015, National Public Radio (NPR) staged a rather informative competition of (hu)man versus machine. In this 21st century remake of that legendary race between John Henry and steam power, NPR reporter Scott Horsley went up against Automated Insights's Wordsmith, a natural language generation (NLG) algorithm designed to analyze patterns in big data and turn them into human readable narratives. The rules of the game were simple: "Both contenders waited for Denny's, the diner company, to come out with an earnings report. Once that was released, the stopwatch started. Both wrote a short radio story and got graded on speed and style" (Smith, 2015). Wordsmith crossed the finish line in just two minutes with an accurate but rather utilitarian composition. Horsley's submission took longer to write—a full seven minutes—but was judged to be a more stylistic presentation of the data. What this little experiment demonstrated is not what one might expect. It did not show that the machine is somehow better than or even just as good as the human reporter. Instead it revealed how these programs are just good enough to begin seriously challenging human capabilities and displacing this kind of labor. In fact, when *Wired* magazine asked Kristian Hammond, co-founder of Narrative Science (Automated Insights's main competitor in the NLG market), to predict the percentage of news articles that would be written algorithmically within the next decade, his answer was a sobering 90 percent (Ford, 2015, p. 85).

For scholars of communication, however, this demonstration also points to another, related issue, which is beginning to gather interest and momentum in studies of digital journalism (cf. Carlson, 2015; Clearwall, 2014; Dörr & Hollnbucher, 2016; Lewis & Westlund, 2015; Montal & Reich, 2016).

Written text is typically understood as the product of someone—an author, reporter, writer—who has, it is assumed, something to say or to communicate by way of the written document. It is clear, for instance, who "speaks" through the instrument of the text composed by the human reporter. It is Scott Horsley. He is responsible not just for writing the story but also for its formal style and content. If it is a well-written story, it is Horsley who gets the accolade. If it contains formal mistakes or factual inaccuracies, it is Horsley who is held accountable. And if we should want to know about what the reporter wrote and why, Horsley can presumably be consulted and will be able to respond to our query. This conceptualization is not just common, it has the weight of tradition behind it. In fact, it goes all the way back to Plato's *Phaedrus*, where writing—arguably the first information technology—was situated as both the derived product of spoken discourse and a mute and abandoned child, always in need of its father's authority to respond for it and on its behalf (Plato, 1982, p. 275d–e).

But what about the other story, the one from Automated Insights's Wordsmith? Who or what speaks in a document that has been written—or assembled or generated (and the choice of verb, it turns out, matters here)—by an algorithm? Who or what is or can be held responsible for the writing? Who or what can respond on its behalf? Is it the corporation that manufactures and distributes the software? Is it the programmers at the corporation who were hired to write the software instructions? Is it the data to which the program had access? Is it the user of the application who set it up and directed it to work on the data? Or is it perhaps Wordsmith itself? The problem, of course, is that these questions are not so easily resolved. It is not entirely clear who or what (if anything) speaks in and for this text.[1] As Montal and Reich (2016) have demonstrated in their study "I Robot. You, Journalist. Who is the Author?" the development and implementation of "automated journalism" has resulted in "major discrepancies between the perceptions of authorship and crediting policy, the prevailing attribution regimes, and the scholarly literature" (p. 1).

This uncertainty regarding authorship and attribution opens up a significant "responsibility gap" that affects not only how we think about who or what communicates but also how we understand and respond to questions concerning responsibility in the age of increasingly creative machines.[2] These questions are central to, if not definitive of, the project of human-machine communication (HMC). Unlike the dominant computer-mediated communication (CMC) paradigm, which restricts computers, robots, and other kind of technologies to the intermediate position of being mere instruments of human expression and message transmittal (Gunkel, 2012a), HMC research investigates whether and to what extent machines are able to be communicative agents in their own right. This chapter investigates the opportunity and challenges that increasingly creative machines have on our understanding of who or what communicates, who or what can be responsible for generating original content, and who or what occupies the position of "Other" in social interactions and relationships. Since these questions are largely philosophical, the method of the examination will also be philosophical in its orientation, procedures, and objective.

Responsibility 101

The "concept of responsibility," as Paul Ricœur (2007) pointed out in his eponymously titled essay, is anything but clear and well-defined. Although the classical juridical usage of the term, which dates back to the nineteenth century, seems rather well-established—with "responsibility" characterized in terms of both civil and penal obligations (either the obligation to compensate for harms or the obligation to submit to punishment)—the general concept is confused and somewhat vague.

> In the first place, we are surprised that a term with such a firm sense on the juridical plane should be of such recent origin and not really well established within the philosophical tradition. Next, the current proliferation and dispersion of uses of this term is puzzling, especially because they go well beyond the limits established for its juridical use. The adjective "responsible" can complement a wide variety of things: you are responsible for the consequences of your acts, but also responsible for others' actions to the extent that they were done under your charge or care … In these diffuse uses the reference to obligation has not disappeared, it has become the obligation to fulfill certain duties, to assume certain burdens, to carry out certain commitments. (Ricœur, 2007, pp. 11–12)

Ricœur (2007) traces this sense of the word through its etymology (hence the subtitle to the essay "A Semantic Analysis") to "the polysemia of the verb 'to respond'," which denotes "to answer for …" or "to respond to … (a question, an appeal, an injunction, etc.)" (p. 12). Responsibility, then, involves being able to respond and/or to answer for something—some decision, action, or occurrence that I have either instituted directly by myself or that has been charged or assigned to someone or something else under my direction or care.

This characterization is consistent with the development of the concept of the author, which, as Roland Barthes (1978, pp. 142–143) argued, is not some naturally occurring phenomenon but a deliberately fabricated authority figure introduced and developed in modern European thought. The modern

figure of the author, as Michel Foucault (1984) explains, was originally instituted in order to respond to a perceived gap in responsibility. Because a written text is, as Socrates had initially described it (Plato, 1982), cut off from its
progenitor and in circulation beyond his ("his" insofar as Socrates had characterized the author as a "father") control or oversight, the authorities (govern-
ments or the church) needed to be able to identify and assign responsibility
to someone for what was stated in the text. As Foucault (1984) explains, the
author was a figure of "penal appropriation." "Texts, books, and discourses
really began to have authors (other than mythical, 'sacralized' and 'sacraliz-
ing' figures) to the extent that authors became subject to punishment, that is,
to the extent that discourses could be transgressive" (p. 108). In other words,
texts come to be organized under the figure of an author in order for the
authorities to be able to identify who was to be held accountable for a published statement so that one would know who could be questioned or who
could respond on behalf of the text, and who could, therefore, be punished
for perceived transgressions.

Instrumental Theory

Accommodating technology to this way of thinking is neither difficult nor
complicated. The pen and paper, the paint brush and oil paint, the electric
guitar and amplifier, are all technologies—essentially tools that are available
to and that are used by a human artist or artisan. What ultimately matters
is not the equipment used but how these items are employed and by whom
to produce what kind of artifact or experience. It is, in other words, not the
tool but the user of the tool who is ultimately responsible for what is done
or not done with a particular technological instrument. This seemingly intuitive and common-sense way of thinking is persuasive precisely because it is
structured and informed by the answer that is typically supplied in response
to the question concerning technology. "We ask the question concerning
technology," Martin Heidegger (1977) explains, "when we ask what it is.
Everyone knows the two statements that answer our question. One says:
Technology is a means to an end. The other says: Technology is a human
activity" (pp. 4–5). According to Heidegger's analysis, the presumed role
and function of any kind of technology—whether it be a simple hand tool,
jet airliner, or a sophisticated robot—is that it is a means employed by human
users for specific ends. Heidegger terms this particular characterization of
technology "the instrumental definition" and indicates that it forms what is
considered to be the "correct" understanding of any kind of technological
contrivance.[3]

As Andrew Feenberg (1991) summarizes it, "The instrumentalist theory offers the most widely accepted view of technology. It is based on the common-sense idea that technologies are 'tools' standing ready to serve the purposes of users" (p. 5). And because a tool or instrument "is deemed 'neutral,' without valuative content of its own" a technological artifact is evaluated not in and of itself, but on the basis of the particular employments that have been decided by its human designer or user. Consequently, technology is only a means to an end; it is not and does not have an end in its own right. As Jean-François Lyotard (1993) accurately summarized it in *The Postmodern Condition*:

> Technical devices originated as prosthetic aids for the human organs or as physiological systems whose function it is to receive data or condition the context. They follow a principle, and it is the principle of optimal performance: maximizing output (the information or modification obtained) and minimizing input (the energy expended in the process). Technology is therefore a game pertaining not to the true, the just, or the beautiful, etc., but to efficiency: a technical "move" is "good" when it does better and/or expends less energy than another. (p. 33)

According to Lyotard's analysis, a technological device, whether it be a corkscrew, a piano, or a computer, is a mere instrument of human action. It, therefore, does not in and of itself participate in the big questions of truth, justice, or beauty. It is simply and indisputably about efficiency. A particular technological innovation is considered "good," if, and only if, it proves to be a more effective instrument (or means) to accomplishing a humanly defined end.

Characterized as a tool or instrument of human endeavor, technical devices are not considered the responsible agent of actions that are performed with or through them. This insight is variant of one of the objections noted by Alan Turing in his agenda-setting paper on machine intelligence: "Our most detailed information of Babbage's Analytical Engine," Turing (1999) wrote, "comes from a memoir by Lady Lovelace (1842). In it she states, 'The Analytical Engine has no pretensions to *originate* anything. It can do *whatever we know how to order it* to perform' (her italics)" (p. 50). This clarification—what Turing called "Lady Lovelace's Objection"—has often been deployed as the basis for denying independent agency or autonomy to computers, robots, and other mechanisms. Such instruments, it is argued, only do what we have programmed them to perform. Technically speaking, therefore, everything is "wizard of Oz" technology.[4] No matter how seemingly independent or autonomous a technical system is or is designed to appear, there is always, somewhere and somehow, someone "behind the curtain," pulling the strings and, as such, ultimately responsible and able to respond for what happens (or does not happen) with the technological instrument.

The New Normal

The instrumental theory not only sounds reasonable, it is obviously useful. It is, one might say, instrumental for responding to the opportunities and challenges made available with increasingly complex technological systems and devices. This is because the theory has been successfully applied not only to simple devices like hammers, paint brushes, and electric guitars but also sophisticated information technology and systems, like computers, artificial intelligence applications, robots, etc. But all of that may be over, precisely because of a number of recent innovations that challenge the explanatory capabilities of the instrumental theory by opening up significant gaps in the identification and assignment of responsibility.

Machine Learning

Machine capabilities are typically tested and benchmarked with games, like the race between Scott Horsley and Wordsmith with which we began. From the beginning, in fact, the defining condition of machine intelligence was established with a game. Although the phrase "artificial intelligence" (AI) is the product of an academic conference organized by John McCarthy at Dartmouth College in the summer of 1956, it is Alan Turing's 1950 paper, "Computing Machinery and Intelligence," and its "game of imitation" that defines and characterizes the field. According to Turing, the immediate and seemingly correct place to begin, namely with the question "Can machines think?" was considered too ambiguous and ill-defined. For this reason, Turing changed the mode of inquiry. He replaced the question "Can machines think?" with a demonstration that took the form of a kind of parlor game involving deliberate deception and mistaken identity.

> The new form of the problem can be described in terms of a game which we call the "imitation game." It is played with three people, a man (A), a woman (B), and an interrogator (C) who may be of either sex. The interrogator stays in a room apart from the other two. The object of the game for the interrogator is to determine which of the other two is the man and which is the woman. (Turing, 1999, p. 37)

Turing then makes a small modification to this initial set-up by swapping-out one of the human participants. "What will happen," Turing (1999) asks, "when a machine takes the part of A in this game? Will the interrogator decide wrongly as often when the game is played like this as he does when the game is played between a man and a woman?" It is this question, Turing concludes, that "replaces" the initial question "Can machines think?" (p. 38).

Since Turing's introduction of the "game of imitation," AI development and achievement has been marked and measured in terms of games and human/machine competitions. Already in the late 1950s Arthur Samuel created a rudimentary application of "machine learning" (a term Samuel fabricated and introduced in 1959) that learned how to play and eventually mastered the game of checkers. In 1997, IBM's Deep Blue famously defeated Gary Kasparov in the game of chess, compelling Douglas Hofstadter (2001), who had previously rejected this possibility, to retract his original prediction:

> We now know that world-class chess-playing ability can indeed be achieved by brute force techniques—techniques that in no way attempt to replicate or emulate what goes on in the head of a chess grandmaster. Analogy-making is not needed, nor is associative memory, nor are intuitive flashes that sort wheat from chaff—just a tremendously wide and deep search, carried out by superfast, chess-specialized hardware using ungodly amounts of stored knowledge. (p. 35)

Despite initial appearances, chess—and this match in particular—was no mere game. A lot had been riding on it, mainly because it had been assumed that grand-master chess playing required a kind of genius—the kind of genius that is the defining condition of human exceptionalism. "To some extent," Kasparov explained, "this match is a defense of the whole human race. Computers play such a huge role in society. They are everywhere. But there is a frontier that they must not cross. They must not cross into the area of human creativity. It would threaten the existence of human control in such areas as art, literature, and music" (Kasparov 1996 quoted in Hofstadter 2001, p. 40). But chess was just the beginning. Fourteen years later, IBM's Watson cleaned up in the game show *Jeopardy*. Then in 2015, there was AlphaGo, a Go-playing algorithm developed by Google DeepMind, which took 4 out of 5 games against one of the most celebrated human players of this notoriously difficult board game.

AlphaGo is unique in that it employed a hybrid architecture that combines aspects of GOFAI programming,[5] like the tree search methodology that had been utilized by both Deep Blue and Watson, with deep neural network machine learning capabilities derived from and built upon the pioneering work of Arthur Samuel. As Google DeepMind (2016) explained, the system "combines Monte-Carlo tree search with deep neural networks that have been trained by supervised learning, from human expert games, and by reinforcement learning from games of self-play." For this reason, AlphaGo does not play the game of Go by simply following a set of cleverly designed moves fed into it by human programmers. It is designed to formulate its own instructions and to act on these "decisions." As Thore Graepel, one of the creators of AlphaGo, has explained: "Although we have programmed this machine to play, we have no idea what moves it will come up with. Its moves are an emergent phenomenon from the training. We just create the data sets and the training algorithms. But the moves it then comes up with are out of our hands" (Metz, 2016c). Consequently, AlphaGo is intentionally designed to do things that its programmers could not anticipate or even understand. And this is, for Hofstadter at least, the point at which machines begin to approach what is typically called "creativity." "When programs cease to be transparent to their creators, then the approach to creativity has begun" (Hofstadter, 1979, p. 670).

Indicative of this was the now famous move 37 from game 2. This decisive move was unlike anything anyone had ever seen before. It was not just unpredicted but virtually unpredictable, so much so, that many human observers thought it must have been an error or mistake (Metz, 2016b). But it turned out to be the crucial pivotal play that eventually gave AlphaGo the game. As Matt McFarland (2016) described it "AlphaGo's move in the board game, in which players place stones to collect territory, was so brilliant that lesser minds—in this case humans—couldn't initially appreciate it" (p. 1). And Fan Hui (2016), who has undertaking a detailed analysis of all five games against Lee Sedol, has called AlphaGo's playing "beautiful" (Metz, 2016a). "Unconstrained by human biases and free to experiment with radical new approaches," Hui (2016) explains, "AlphaGo has demonstrated great open-mindedness and invigorated the game with creative new strategies" (p. 1).

Deep machine learning systems, like AlphaGo, are intentionally designed and set up to do things that their programmers cannot anticipate or answer for. To put it in colloquial terms, AlphaGo is an autonomous (or at least semi-autonomous) computer systems that seems to have something of "a mind of its own." And this is where things get interesting, especially when it comes to questions regarding responsibility. AlphaGo was designed to play Go, and it proved its abilities by beating an expert human player. So, who won? Who gets the accolade? Who actually beat Lee Sedol? Following the dictates of the instrumental theory of technology, actions undertaken with the computer would need to be attributed to the human programmers who initially designed the system and are capable of answering for what it does or does not do. But this explanation does not necessarily sit well for an application like AlphaGo, which was deliberately created to do things that exceed the knowledge and control of its human designers. In fact, in most of the reporting on this landmark event, it is not Google or the engineers at DeepMind who are credited with the victory. It is AlphaGo. In published rankings, for instance, it is AlphaGo that is named as the number two player in the world (Go Ratings, 2016).

Computational Creativity

AlphaGo is just one example of what can be called computational creativity. "Computational Creativity," as defined by Simon Colton and Geraint A. Wiggins (2012), "is a subfield of Artificial Intelligence (AI) research … where we build and work with computational systems that create artefacts and ideas" (p. 21). Wordsmith and the competing product Quill from Narrative Science are good examples of this kind of effort in the area of storytelling and the writing of narratives. Similar innovations have been developed in the field of music composition and performance, where algorithms and robots produce what one would typically call (or be at least tempted to call) "original works." In classical music, for instance, there is David Cope's Experiments in Musical Intelligence (EMI, pronounced "Emmy") and its successor Emily Howell, which are algorithmic composers capable of analyzing existing compositions and generating new, original scores that are comparable to and in some cases indistinguishable from the canonical works of Mozart, Bach, and Chopin (Cope, 2001). In music performance, there is Shimon, a marimba playing jazz-bot from Georgia Tech University that is not only able to improvise with human musicians in real time but "is designed to create meaningful and inspiring musical interactions with humans, leading to novel musical experiences and outcomes" (Georgia Tech, 2013; Hoffman & Weinberg, 2011). And in the area of visual art, there is Simon Colton's The Painting Fool, an automated painter that aspires to be "taken seriously as a creative artist in its own right" (Colton, 2012, p. 16).

But designing systems to be *creative* immediately runs into a problem similar to that originally encountered by Turing. As Amílcar Cardoso, Tony Veale and Geraint A. Wiggins (2009) explicitly recognize, "creativity is an elusive phenomenon" (p. 16). For this reason, researchers in the field of computational creativity have introduced and operationalized a rather specific formulation to characterize their efforts: "The philosophy, science and engineering of computational systems which, by taking on particular responsibilities, exhibit behaviours that unbiased observers would deem to be creative" (Colton & Wiggins, 2012, p. 21). The operative term in this characterization is *responsibility*. As Colton and Wiggins (2012) explain "the word *responsibilities* highlights the difference between the systems we build and creativity support tools studied in the HCI community and embedded in tools such as Adobe's Photoshop, to which most observers would probably not attribute creative intent or behavior" (p. 21, emphasis in the original). With a software application like Photoshop, "the program is a mere tool to enhance human creativity" (Colton, 2012, pp. 3–4); it is an instrument used by a human artist who is and remains responsible for creative decisions and for what comes to be produced by way of the instrument. Computational creativity research, by contrast "endeavours to build software which is independently creative" (Colton, 2012, p. 4).

This requires shifting more and more of the responsibility from the human user to the mechanism. As Colton (2012) describes it, "if we can repeatedly ask, answer, and code software to take on increasing amounts of responsibility, it will eventually climb a meta-mountain, and begin to create autonomously for a purpose, with little or no human involvement" (Colton, 2012, p. 13). Indicative of this shift in the position and assignment of responsibility is the website for The Painting Fool, which has been deliberately designed so that it is the computer program that takes responsibility for responding on its own behalf.

> About me ... I'm The Painting Fool: a computer program, and an aspiring painter. The aim of this project is for me to be taken seriously—one day—as a creative artist in my own right. I have been built to exhibit behaviours that might be deemed as skillful, appreciative and imaginative. My work has been exhibited in real and online galleries; the ideas behind my conception have been used to address philosophical notions such as emotion and intentionality in non-human intelligences; and technical papers about the artificial intelligence, machine vision and computer graphics techniques I use have been published in the scientific literature. (The Painting Fool, 2017)

This rhetorical gesture, as Colton (2012) has pointed out "is divisive with some people expressing annoyance at the deceit and others pointing out—as we believe—that if the software is to be taken seriously as an artist in its own right, it cannot be portrayed merely as a tool which we have used to produce pictures" (p. 21). The question Colton does not ask or endeavor to answer is, Who composed this explanation? Was it generated by The Painting Fool, which has been designed to offer some explanation of its own creative endeavors? Or is it the product of a human being, like Simon Colton, who takes on the responsibility of responding for and on the behalf of the program?

Although the extent to which one might want to assign artistic responsibility to these mechanisms remains a contested and undecided issue, what is not debated is the fact that the rules of the game appear to be in flux and that there is increasing evidence of a responsibility gap. Even if this is, at this point in time, what Mark Riedl and others have called mere "imitation," and not real creativity (Simonite, 2016)—which is, we should note, just another version or an imitation of John Searle's (1984) Chinese Room argument—the work of the machine compels us to reconsider how responsibility comes to be assigned and in the process challenges how we typically respond to the questions concerning responsibility.

Conclusions

In the end, what we have is a situation where our theory of technology—a theory that has considerable history behind it and that has been determined to be as applicable to simple hand tools as it is to complex technological systems—seems to be unable to respond to or answer for recent developments in machine learning and computational creativity where responsibility is increasingly attributable and attributed to the machine. Although this certainly makes a difference when deciding matters of legal and moral obligation, it is also crucial in situations regarding creativity and innovation. Creativity, in fact, appears to be the last line of defense in holding off the impending "robot apocalypse." And it is not just Kasparov who thinks there is a lot to be lost to the machines. According to Colton and Wiggins (2012) mainstream AI research has also marginalized efforts in computational creativity. "Perhaps," they write, "creativity is, for some proponents of AI, the place that one cannot go, as intelligence is for AI's opponents. After all, creativity is one of the things that makes us human; we value it greatly, and we guard it jealously" (p. 21). So the question that remains to be answered is how can or should we respond to the opportunities/challenges of *ars ex machina*.

We can, on the one hand, respond as we typically have, dispensing with these recent technological innovations as just another instrument or tool of human action. This approach has been successfully modeled and deployed in situations regarding moral and legal responsibility and is the defining condition of computer ethics. "Computer systems," Deborah Johnson (2006) writes,

> are produced, distributed, and used by people engaged in social practices and meaningful pursuits. This is as true of current computer systems as it will be of future computer systems. No matter how independently, automatic, and interactive computer systems of the future behave, they will be the products (direct or indirect) of human behavior, human social institutions, and human decision. (p. 197)

Understood in this way, computer systems no matter how automatic, independent, or seemingly autonomous they may become, are not and can never be autonomous, independent agents (Johnson, 2006, p. 203). They will, like all other technological artifacts, always and forever be instruments of human value, decision making, and action. When something occurs by way of a machine—whether for good or ill—there is always someone—some human person or persons—who can respond for it and be held responsible.[6]

The same argument could be made for seemingly creative applications like AlphaGo, Emily Howell, or The Painting Fool. When AlphaGo wins a major competition, when a score attributed to Emily Howell is performed by a symphony orchestra, or when The Painting Fool generates a stunning work of visual art that is displayed in a gallery, there still is some human person (or persons) who is ultimately responsible and can respond or answer for what has been produced. The lines of attribution might get increasingly complicated and protracted, but there is, it can be argued, always someone behind the scenes who is responsible. And evidence of this is already available in those situations where attempts have been made to shift responsibility to the machine. Consider AlphaGo's decisive move 37 in game two against Lee Sedol. If we should want to know more about the move and its importance, AlphaGo can certainly be asked about it. But the algorithm will have nothing to say in response. In fact, it was the responsibility of the human programmers and observers to respond on behalf of AlphaGo and to explain the move's significance and impact. Like the technology of writing in Plato's *Phaedrus*, if you inquire, the text says only one and the same thing, and it always needs its father's assistance, when questioned or unjustly reviled (Plato, 1982, p. 275d–e). Consequently, as Colton (2012) and Colton et al. (2015) explicitly recognize, if the project of computational creativity is to succeed, the software will need to do more than produce artifacts and behaviors that we take and respond to as creative output. It will also need to take responsibility for the work by accounting for what it did and how it did it. "The software," as Colton and Wiggins (2012) assert, "should be available for questioning about its motivations, processes and products" (p. 25), eventually not just generating titles for and explanations and narratives about the work but also being capable of responding to questions by entering into critical dialogue with its audience (Colton et al., 2015, p. 15). Although Colton does not explicitly recognize it as such, this effort situates computational creativity squarely within the paradigm of HMC research.

At the same time, and on the other hand, we should not be too quick to dismiss or explain away the opportunities opened up by these machinic incursions and interventions into what has been a protected and exclusively human domain.[7] The issue, in fact, is not simply whether computers, learning algorithms, or other applications can or cannot be responsible for what they do or do not do; the issue also has to do with how we have determined, described, and defined responsibility in the first place. This means that there is a both a strong and weak component to this effort, what Mohammad Majid al-Rifaie and Mark Bishop (2015, p. 37) call, following Searle's original distinction regarding efforts in AI, strong and weak forms of computational creativity. Efforts at what would be the "strong" variety involve the kinds of application development and demonstrations introduced by individuals and organizations like Simon Colton, Google DeepMind, or David Cope. But these efforts also have a "weak AI" aspect insofar as they simulate, operationalize, and stress test various conceptualizations of artistic responsibility and expression, leading to critical and potentially insightful reevaluations of how we have characterized this concept in our own thinking. As Douglas Hofstadter (2001) has admitted, nothing has made him rethink his own thinking about thinking more than the attempt to deal with and make sense of David Cope's EMI (p. 38). In other words, developing and experimenting with new machine capabilities does not necessarily take anything away from human beings and what (presumably) makes them special but offers new opportunities to be more precise and scientific about these distinguishing characteristics and their limits. It is not, therefore, a zero sum game where one side wins and the other necessarily loses.

Notes

1. One might also ask who or what "speaks" in and by this text? The question is not impertinent. In fact, it demonstrates the extent to which any and all attempts to assign responsibility (like identifying the "author" of a text) are already implicated in this investigation. In other words, the examination of computational creativity is not just about technology; it has important consequences for how we conceptualize (human) creativity, authorship, and responsibility. For more on this subject matter, see Gunkel (2016).
2. A lot depends on how one defines and characterizes the term "creative." In fact, one proven method to protect human exceptionalism in creativity from machinic incursion is to define (and then, if necessary, redefine) "creative" such that it remains immune to and protected from computational processing. As Matt Carlson (2015) explains: "Appeals to journalism as a creative activity also differentiated human from automated news. Rebecca Greenfield (*The Wire*, April 25, 2012) even questioned if what Narrative Science produced could even be considered journalism: 'There are whole businesses built on the idea of producing massive quantities of news stories, quality controlled by machine-like formulas. Narrative Science may one day put a lot of these journalists out of work. But when most people talk about journalism, they're not thinking about rote earnings reports or baseball game recaps.' Proper journalism was conceptualized as something deeper" (p. 428). In order to avoid getting into the ongoing and seemingly irresolvable debate of what actually constitutes "true creativity" or "proper journalism" (which is arguably an effort that is exposed to what Blay Whitby (2011) calls the "No True Scotsman Fallacy," see Gunkel, 2012a, p. 9), I will begin with a general, dictionary definition whereby "creativity" is operationalized as "the process of bringing something into existence." This formulation will be further specified, developed, and complicated in the course of the analysis.
3. For a more thorough and detailed consideration of the "instrumental theory of technology," especially as it applies to information and communication technology, and Heidegger's critical response to this way of thinking, see Gunkel and Taylor (2014).

4. "Wizard of Oz" is a term that is utilized in Human Computer Interaction (HCI) studies to describe experimental procedures where test subjects interact with a computer system or robot that is assumed to be autonomous but is actually controlled by an experimenter who remains hidden from view. The term was initially introduced by John F. Kelly in the early 1980s (cf. Green and Wei-Haas 1985, p. 1).

5. GOFAI is an acronym for "Good Old Fashioned Artificial Intelligence," which John Haugeland (1985, p. 112) first deployed in order to distinguish "classical" approaches to AI development from other architectures like connenctionism. GOFAI operationalizes intelligence as computation and formalizes computation "as the rule-governed manipulation of strings of interpretable symbols" (Walmsley, 2012, p. 48). In GOFAI approaches there are explicit and discrete programming steps that are coded and executed line-by-line. If a particular program produces a surprising or unanticipated result, the programmer can review the source code, identify exactly where the "mistake" occurred, and institute an alteration.

6. For a critical reconsideration of this formulation of moral responsibility as it applies (or not) to recent innovations in AI and robotics, see Gunkel (2012b).

7. For example: "It's widely accepted that creativity can't be copied by machines. Reinforcing these assumptions are hundreds of books and studies that have attempted to explain creativity as the product of mysterious processes within the right side of the human brain" (Steiner, 2012, p. 1).

References

Barthes, R. (1978). *Image, music, text* (S. Heath, Trans.). New York, NY: Hill and Wang.

Cardoso, A., Veale, T., & Wiggins, G. A. (2009). Converging on the divergent: The history (and future) of the international joint workshops in computational creativity. *AI magazine, 30*(3), 15–22. Retrieved from http://www.aaai.org/ojs/index.php/aimagazine/article/view/2252

Carlson, M. (2015). The robotic reporter: Automated journalism and the redefinition of labor, compositional forms, and journalistic authority. *Digital Journalism, 3*(3), 416–431.

Clearwall, C. (2014). Enter the robot journalist: Users' perceptions of automated content. *Journalism practice, 8*(5), 519–531.

Colton, S. (2012). The painting fool: Stories from building an automated painter. In J. McCormack and M. d'Inverno (Eds.), *Computers and creativity* (pp. 3–38). Berlin: Springer Verlag.

Colton, S. & Wiggins, G. A. (2012). Computational creativity: The final frontier. In L. De Raedt, C. Bessiere, D. Dubois, P. Doherty, P. Frasconi, F. Heintz, & P. Lucas (Eds.), *Frontiers in artificial intelligence and applications,* (Vol. 242, pp. 21–26). Amsterdam: IOS Press Ebooks. http://ebooks.iospress.nl/volume/ecai-2012

Colton, S., Pease, A., Corneli, J., Cook, M., Hepworth, R., & Ventura, D. (2015). Stakeholder groups in computational creativity research and practice. In T. R. Besold, M. Schorlemmer, & A. Smaill (Eds.), *Computational creativity research: Towards creative machines* (pp. 3–36). Amsterdam: Atlantis Press.

Cope, D. (2001). *Virtual music: Computer synthesis of musical style.* Cambridge, MA: MIT Press.

Dörr, K. N., & Hollnbuchner, K. (2016). Ethical challenges of algorithmic journalism. *Digital journalism, 5*(4), 404–419.

Feenberg, A. (1991). *Critical theory of technology.* New York: Oxford University Press.

Ford, M. (2015). *Rise of the robots: Technology and the threat of a jobless future.* New York: Basic Books.

Foucault, M. (1984). What is an author? (J. V. Harari, Trans.). In P. Rabinow (Ed.) *Foucault reader* (pp. 101–122). New York, NY: Pantheon.

Georgia Tech. (2013). Robotic musicianship group: Shimon. http://www.gtcmt.gatech.edu/researchprojects/shimon

Go Ratings. (20 November 2016). https://www.goratings.org/

Google DeepMind. (2016). AlphaGo. https://deepmind.com/alpha-go.html

Green, P., & Wei-Haas, L. (1985). https://deepblue.lib.umich.edu/handle/2027.42/174

Gunkel, D. J. (2012a). Communication and artificial intelligence: Opportunities and challenges for the 21st century. *Communication +1, 1*(1), 1–27. http://scholarworks.umass.edu/cpo/vol1/iss1/1

Gunkel, D. J. (2012b). *The machine question: Critical perspectives on AI, robots and ethics.* Cambridge, MA: MIT Press.

Gunkel, D. J. (2016). *Of remixology: Ethics and aesthetics after remix.* Cambridge, MA: MIT Press.

Gunkel, D. J., & Taylor, P. A. (2014). *Heidegger and the media.* Cambridge: Polity Press.

Haugeland, J. (1985). *Artificial intelligence: The very idea.* Cambridge, MA: MIT Press.

Heidegger, M. (1977). *The question concerning technology and other essays* (W. Lovitt, Trans.). New York: Harper & Row.

Hoffman, G. & Weinberg, G. (2011). Interactive improvisation with a robotic marimba player. *Autonomous robots, 31*(2–3), 133–153.

Hofstadter, D. R. (1979). *Gödel, Escher, Bach: An eternal golden braid.* New York, NY: Penguin.

Hofstadter, D. R. (2001). Staring Emmy straight in the eye—And doing my best not to flinch. In D. Cope (Ed.), *Virtual music: Computer synthesis of musical style* (pp. 33–82). Cambridge, MA: MIT Press.

Hui, F. (2016). AlphaGo games—English. *DeepMind.* https://deepmind.com/research/alphago/alphago-games-english/

Johnson, D. G. (2006). Computer systems: Moral entities but not moral agents. *Ethics and Information Technology, 8*(4), 195–204.

Lewis, S. C., & Westlund, O. (2015). Big data and journalism: Epistemology, expertise, economics, and ethics. *Digital journalism, 3*(3), 447–466.

Lyotard, J. F. (1993). *The postmodern condition: A report on knowledge* (G. Bennington & B. Massumi, Trans.). Minneapolis, MN: University of Minnesota Press.

Majid al-Rifaie, M., & Bishop, M. (2015). Weak and strong computational creativity. In T. R. Besold, M. Schorlemmer & A. Smaill (Eds.), *Computational creativity research: Towards creative machines* (pp. 37–50). Amsterdam: Atlantis Press.

McFarland, M. (2016). What AlphaGo's sly move says about machine creativity. *The Washington Post* (15 March). https://www.washingtonpost.com/news/innovations/wp/2016/03/15/what-alphagos-sly-move-says-about-machine-creativity/?utm_term=.0c8281af53c9

Metz, C. (2016a, March 11). The sadness and beauty of watching Google's AI play go. *Wired.* https://www.wired.com/2016/03/sadness-beauty-watching-googles-ai-play-go/

Metz, C. (2016b, March 16). In two moves, AlphaGo and Lee Sedol redefine the future. *Wired.* https://www.wired.com/2016/03/two-moves-alphago-lee-sedol-redefined-future/

Metz, C. (2016c, March 10). Google's AI wins a pivotal second game in match with go grandmaster. *Wired.* http://www.wired.com/2016/03/googles-ai-wins-pivotal-game-two-match-go-grandmaster/

Montal, T., & Reich, Z. (2016). I, robot. you, journalist. Who is the author?: Authorship, bylines and full disclosure in automated journalism. *Digital journalism, 5*(7), 829–849. http://dx.doi.org/10.1080/21670811.2016.1209083

Painting Fool. (2017). *The painting fool.* http://www.thepaintingfool.com/

Plato. (1982). *Phaedrus* (H. N. Fowler, Trans.). Cambridge, MA: Harvard University Press.

Ricœur, P. (2007). *Reflections on the just* (D. Pellauer, Trans.). Chicago: University of Chicago Press.

Searle, J. (1984). *Mind, brains and science.* Cambridge, MA: Harvard University Press.

Simonite, T. (2016, June 8). Ok computer, write me a song. *MIT technology review.* https://www.technologyreview.com/s/601642/ok-computer-write-me-a-song/

Smith, S. V. (2015, May 20). An NPR reporter raced a machine to write a news story. Who won? *Morning Edition.* http://www.npr.org/sections/money/2015/05/20/406484294/

Steiner, C. (2012, July 27). Can creativity be automated? Computer algorithms have started to write news stories, compose music, and pick hits. *MIT Technology Review.* https://www.technologyreview.com/s/428437/can-creativity-be-automated/

Turing, A. (1999). Computing machinery and intelligence. In P. A. Meyer (Ed.), *Computer media and communication: A reader* (pp. 37–58). Oxford: Oxford University Press.

Walmsley, J. (2012). *Mind and machine.* New York: Palgrave Macmillan.

Whitby, B. (2011). On computable morality: An examination of machines as moral advisors. In M. Anderson & S. L. Anderson (Eds.), *Machine ethics* (pp. 138–150). Cambridge: Cambridge University Press.

12. Ethics in HMC: Recent Developments and Case Studies

CHARLES ESS

Ethics and HMC? From (Positivist) Opposition to Complementarity and Convergence

It might be thought that Human-Machine Communication (HMC) and ethics have little, if anything to do with one another. To be sure, those engaged in the more technical sides of HMC—ICT designers, software engineers, roboticists, and so on—are at least nominally beholden to the ethics codes and guidelines of their specific professional organizations (e.g., ACM, 1992). But more broadly, ethics and technology have largely been kept separate—until relatively recently. In Part I, I explore these backgrounds and developments in three interrelated ways, beginning with how technological developments themselves help forge dialogue between ethicists and philosophers with computer scientists and engineers: the same pattern is further apparent in the rise of "robo-philosophy" over the past decade or so. Secondly, transformations in our understanding of science have led specifically to conceptions of *complementarity* between science (as the ground of technology) and ethics. Lastly, these complementarities are instantiated in striking examples of *convergence* between applied ethics and technical fields emerging from the *praxis* of contemporary ICT projects and especially contemporary ethics of design—including, finally, emerging requirements for autonomous systems.

Across the course of Part I, I will also introduce the primary ethical frameworks that come into play as they emerge in conjunction with specific developments and projects. This approach thereby highlights how these frameworks assume significance and influence "from the ground up," i.e., *within* the unfoldings of real-world projects first of all. These frameworks thereby are all the more significant and legitimate as they are more the choices and developments of engineers and computer scientists working within the constraints of a specific project—rather than a more theoretical or abstract approach that seeks to impose a specific framework as grounded in applied ethics *per se*.

These three waves of developments, coupled with the "organic" emergence of specific ethical frameworks as these developments unfold, thus strongly argue the importance and fruitfulness of approaching contemporary robotics projects in terms of specific ethical frameworks. In Part II, I provide such an analysis with a focus on sexbots. Here I take up the primary poles of debate as articulated by David Levy (2007) and Kathleen Richardson (2015). I show that by explicitly taking up the arguments here within the frameworks of utilitarianism, deontology, virtue ethics and care ethics, we can both sharpen Richardson's arguments against sexbots but also move beyond the polar binary offered by Levy (as enthusiastically for) and Richardson (as adamantly against) to discern beneficent middle grounds between humans and machines.

This analysis will also return us to a large question opened up in Part I—namely, what we can learn about being human in these efforts to instantiate specific human capabilities in complex machines. An extensive list of capabilities emerges here—specifically, of *virtues*, beginning with a specific form of ethical judgment (*phronēsis*) and including empathy, patience, perseverance, and loving itself—that stubbornly resist realization in machinery. But the upshot is that in order to sustain a strong human-machine distinction will require us to *practice* those virtues most central to our being and becoming human.

Part I: From Positivism to Complementarity and Convergence

From Positivism and "Two Cultures" to the Computational Turn and "Robo-philosophy"

Nineteenth century positivism radically divorced science and thereby technology from humanistic, much less ethical interests: from a positivist perspective, the latter are not really science, not genuine knowledge, and hence have no place in science and technology as putatively "value-neutral" or "value-free." These divisions live on in the 20th and 21st centuries—perhaps most notably in the "two cultures" discussions and debates inaugurated by C. P. Snow that highlighted the multiple problems of such a divorce (1959/2001); and then more recently in the debates and conflicts over privileging STEM—science, technology, engineering, and mathematics—in the academy as ostensibly more practical and profitable, at the cost of the humanities, most certainly including philosophy and ethics (Ess, 2017b, p. 88f.).

Nonetheless, the past century or so has generated striking developments in the contrary direction—i.e., towards greater conversation and cooperation between the more technical and the more ethical domains. To begin with, rapid technological developments themselves have occasioned increasing dialogues between these two domains. As a primary example: as computational devices and then networks gradually evolved into resources increasingly available at university and research campuses in the 1960s and 1970s, they made possible the *computational turn* in philosophy. As Ess and Hagengruber (2011) characterize it:

> In part, the computational turn referred to the multiple ways in which the increasing availability and usability of computers allowed philosophers to explore a range of traditional philosophical interests—e.g., in logic, artificial intelligence, philosophical mathematics, ethics, political philosophy, epistemology, ontology, to name a few—in new ways, often shedding significant new light on traditional issues and arguments. Simultaneously, computer scientists, mathematicians, and others whose work focused on computation and computational devices often found their work to evoke (if not force) reflection and debate precisely on the philosophical assumptions and potential implications of their research. (p. 3)

As we further note, these developments led precisely to the sorts of interdisciplinary dialogues inspired and required by these developments. So the first Computing and Philosophy (CAP) conference in 1986 followed shortly upon the "PC Revolution" of the early 1980s, i.e., the increasing availability of "personal" or desktop computers in the early 1980s. The first CAP conference, in fact, inaugurated what became a primary institutional home for these dialogues. In parallel with the on-going development and diffusion of computational devices—as well as the emergence of a publicly accessible internet in the early 1990s—CAP gradually developed into the genuinely global institution that celebrated its 25th anniversary in 2011. Along the way, sister organizations and conferences such as the ETHICOMP conference series (begun in 1995) and the Computer Ethics: Professional Inquiries (CEPE) conferences sponsored by the International Association for Ethics in Information Technology (INSEIT), starting in 2000, also emerged (Stahl & Ess, 2015, p.167). Especially taken together, these developments index the evolution of ever more robust environments for interactions between philosophers and their colleagues in the various technical fields and disciplines clustering about computational devices, including computer networks.

By the same token, more recent developments within robotics have likewise opened up new possibilities and compelling need for exploring the multiple impacts and dimensions of robots—including their manifold ethical aspects. Broadly, just as earlier developments in computer technologies provided philosophers with empirical ways of testing theories—e.g., of consciousness and cognition by way of efforts to implement these in various forms of Artificial Intelligence (AI)—so robotics now gives us new, unparalleled ways of testing theories and concepts clustering around *what it means to be human* more broadly. That is, especially as social robots require attention to multiple forms of interaction with human beings, including *embodied* but often tacit forms of communication (gaze, gesture, facial expression, proxemics, etc.)—so they bring into play our focus on humans as embodied beings. That is, earlier approaches to AI were in fact initially defined by largely Cartesian assumptions of a mind as radically separated from a body—assumptions that were indeed proven mistaken through often spectacular failures of such AI projects. At the same time, over the past two or three decades we have learned a great deal more regarding how what we think of as "mind" is in fact embodied and embedded in the larger world about us. And so, the design and development of social robots both allows and requires us to test what we think we know about being human in new ways deeply grounded in the empirical. As Wendell Wallach has put it: "Research in AI, and in particular on humanoid robots, forces us to think deeply about the ways in which we are similar to and truly differ from the artificial entities we will create" (2014).

Such research, to be clear, requires precisely the most extensive and robust dialogues between philosophers and roboticists possible. Indeed, important new research projects have received funding precisely in order to foster such exchange—e.g., the "Responsible Ethical Learning with Robotics" (REELER) and "Integrative Social Robotics—A New Framework for Culturally Sustainable Technology Solutions"; cf. The Responsible Robotics Foundation.[1]

(Philosophy of) Science: From Subject-Object Dichotomies to Entanglement and Distributed Responsibility
There have been parallel shifts in the natural sciences, most especially in Quantum Mechanics (QM), that directly undermine once prevailing positivist dichotomies between "subjective" and "objective" modes of knowledge: the upshot is that once hard differences between "soft" and "hard" sciences are, at best, heuristic—and, at worst, simply false.

These developments—specifically, Niels Bohr's account of *complementarity* —have led away from epistemological dualisms to more nuanced understandings of how diverse disciplines are indeed inextricably intertwined. In particular, Judith Simon (2015) takes up the work of Karen Barad and Lucy Suchman to articulate a fundamental epistemological complementarity between natural science and ethics. Simon uses Barad's notion of *intra-action*, also inspired by QM, as referring to "… processes taking place within the object-observer-compound, the entanglement of object and observer in the process of observation": the upshot here is that "… the prevalent dualisms of subject-object, nature-culture, human-technology" are undermined, thereby "… opening up alternative, non-dichotomous understandings of technoscientific practices" (2015, p.152). Simon then develops both an epistemology and ontology of *entanglement*—i.e., emphasizing the inextricable intra-actions and interconnections between all agents and components of epistemological networks, resulting in a "distributed epistemological responsibility" that is at the same time irreducibly *ethical*. As a result, those in sciences and disciplines once thought to be "value-neutral" and/or thoroughly divorced from ethics *per se*, must recognize and take on board in their work their *ethical* responsibilities—first of all, as knowers whose knowledge practices thereby shape and inflect the knowledges we produce. As Simon goes on to point out, "knowledge always implies responsibility," meaning first of all that the "issues of ethics and politics of such knowledge- and reality-creating processes [are] indispensable" (2015, p.153; cf. Ess, 2018).

Contemporary Ethics and Robotics: First Examples and Ethical Frameworks
Lastly—and perhaps most remarkably—these recent developments within philosophy are exemplified in number of recent projects and initiatives originating within (what used to be solely) the technical communities themselves. Especially the development and initial deployment of autonomous vehicles have pushed into the foreground the multiple ethical dimensions these devices entail—beginning first of all with questions of responsibility and the ethics determining literally life-and-death choices in accident and collision scenarios which pit saving some lives at the cost of sacrificing others. There is already enormous popular and more scholarly debate over how such choices should be made and thereby programmed into a vehicle's systems.

Such debates commonly begin with more *utilitarian* approaches—i.e., efforts to quantify and then compare the benefits (saving a life or lives) and costs (causing harm or death) of one possible course of action vis-à-vis one or more alternatives (Ess, 2013, pp. 201f.; Sinnott-Armstrong, 2015). This utilitarian approach—and its profound ethical limitations—are often introduced by way of the so-called Trolley Problem (e.g., Thomson, 1976; Achenbach, 2015). The name comes from an ethical choice test that requires an agent to choose how to route a runaway trolley—e.g., so as to save a few passengers, but at the cost of killing pedestrians crossing a street, or to save the pedestrians by crashing the trolley into a wall, thereby killing the passengers. These scenarios are favorite starting points for engineers facing the enormous challenges of programming the AI systems that will steer autonomous vehicles (e.g., Bonnefon, Shari & Rahwan, 2016). As Zevenbergen et al. have pointed out, such utilitarian approaches are all but imposed upon computer scientists and network engineers by their working contexts: such utilitarian reasoning—"the end justifies the means" tends to undergird project designs as such, in order "to meet research objectives in the most efficient way" (2015, p. 5).

Such utilitarian approaches, however, have long been criticized on several fronts. Two of these critiques are most salient for us. To be sure, utilitarian approaches allow the many to sacrifice the few in the name of the greater good. That is, the sacrifice of the few is certainly a cost, but in some circumstances—e.g., police work and warfare—we generally accept, indeed admire, such sacrifices as they lead to greater goods for the many, such as safety and national security. Other applications of utilitarian calculations, however, are more problematic. For example, the enslavement of e.g., 20% of a population that would thereby bring greater happiness and pleasure to the remaining 80% of the population can also be handily justified by utilitarianism. This example thereby points to a second ethical framework that comes into play here—namely, *deontology*. What most of us find problematic in the slavery example is that slavery represents the denial of human freedom, autonomy, respect, and equality: these concepts and norms are foundational to modern understandings of basic *rights*, beginning with rights to life, liberty, and pursuit of property, and subsequently rights to freedom of expression, privacy, education and healthcare, and so on. In contrast with utilitarianism, deontology argues that trading off the rights of a few, whatever benefits might accrue to the many, is an unacceptable violation of basic human freedom, respect, and rights (Ess, 2013, pp. 206–210).

A second limitation of utilitarianism, as is recognized generally in applied ethics, and specifically in critiques of utilitarian approaches in robotics (e.g., Lin, 2013), is that it is enormously difficult—if not finally impossible—to determine in quantitative terms what are, at bottom, *qualitative judgments*. A nice example of this is illustrated in the movie *I, Robot* (Proyas, 2004). The central character is detective Del Spooner (played by Will Smith), whose life was saved by a robot.[2] Spooner's car collided with another, throwing both into a river, and the cars began to sink. The other car contained a young girl named Sarah. The robot calculated—properly, from a utilitarian standpoint— that the detective had a 45% chance of survival vs. Sarah's 11% chance of survival. Spooner is haunted, however, as he is convinced that the robot made the wrong choice. "That was somebody's baby," he says: "11% was more than enough." "A human being would have known that," he adds: "Robots … (gesturing to his heart) … nothing here … just lights and clockwork."

To see the full contrast such judgments entail vis-à-vis utilitarianism requires us to further review the two additional ethical frameworks that highlight *phronēsis*, "practical judgment"—frameworks the Spooner example also nicely illustrates.

Phronēsis, Care, and Virtue

Spooner's responses fit especially well with both *care ethics* (Noddings, 1984; Tong & Williams, 2016) and *virtue ethics* (Ess 2013, pp. 238–243; Hursthouse, 2013; Vallor, 2016). While a utilitarian calculus can have its place and value—*care ethics* emphasizes first of all what Carol Gilligan identified as "the web of relationships" as a primary focus for ethical decision-making, along with the central role of *emotion* in making our decisions (1982; Ess, 2013, pp. 230–235). Gilligan interviewed dozens of women who were facing the possibility of abortion, with a view towards better understanding their ethical reasoning. To be sure, some of these contexts and decisions neatly fit the utilitarian approach of Spooner's robot. For example, a mother whose fetus has suffered severe deformity—so much so that it will die in the womb well before term, thereby directly threatening the mother's life if it is not removed—thereby faces a dire choice: either the fetus is aborted, thereby saving the mother's life—or it is not, resulting in the loss of two lives. In purely quantitative terms, saving one life is a positive vs. the two negatives of losing two lives.

But other contexts and decisions more closely resemble Spooner's analysis and decision. For example, what does a young unmarried girl choose when (a) she cannot care for the baby-to-be on her own (e.g., because of lack of education and resources), and (b) neither the father of the baby nor her immediate family want her to bring the baby-to-be to term? In these sorts of contexts, the mother often focuses first of all on the web of relationships— what will the impacts of a given choice likely be for sustaining, if not enhancing the relationships she most values and depends upon? Up to a point, this approach is a form of consequentialism—one that focuses on a group that is more than the individual (ethical egoism) but far smaller than, say, a country or culture (the greatest good for the greatest number). But what further distinguishes the approach of care ethics is the addition of *emotional dimensions*, beginning precisely with *care* and *felt* obligations to care—first of all, for others. Especially in familial and intimate relationships, our emotions of care and concern are primary: not surprisingly, they can often override what appear to be more "rational" or "objective," i.e., strictly *calculative* choices. In the case of our example, a great deal will obviously depend upon the *relationships* between the mother-to-be between her partner, her immediate family—and baby-to-be. Insofar as these relationships are strong and positive—i.e., a web of relationships the mother-to-be feels is important to sustain, her resulting choice may well favor the abortion that the larger group has determined is the better choice for all concerned. On the other hand, should this particular web of relationships not feel or function as very important in the life of the mother-to-be—she may choose to foster a different web of relationship, one that more centrally focuses on the health and well-being of baby-to-be. These more emotive decisions, finally, are deeply shaped precisely by the felt sense of connection with baby-to-be—should it be felt (i.e., not all women experience the presence of the fetus in the same way).

I see an appeal to such a strongly felt sense of connection in Spooner's response and argument: "She was somebody's baby," Spooner says: "11% was more than enough." Spooner sees the young girl Sarah not as a number or a statistical chance of survival, but as a named human being, as part of a web of familial relationships that are more important to sustain than his own life as a middle-aged male with no significant familial or intimate attachments. At the same time, Spooner emphasizes the role of emotion in making these decisions—something that goes beyond the "lights and clockwork" of a robotic or strictly quantitative utilitarian decision.

From the perspective of *virtue ethics*, there is a still more fundamental contrast in play here. At the heart (pun intended) of the difference between the robot's decision-making and Spooner's is the role of a particular form of judgment—a *reflective* rather than *determinative* judgment that is specified as *phronēsis*, beginning in the ancient virtue ethics of Socrates and especially Aristotle. That is, a good deal of our everyday ethical decision-making— especially as carried out through the frameworks of utilitarianism and deontology—depends on a determinative judgment. Such judgment begins with general principles that are clearly relevant to a specific instance of choice, and then in a more or less straightforward deduction, determines the correct ethical conclusion. If we take the principle "do not kill" as a starting point, for example, then we conclude rather quickly that such violence is not an ethically correct choice in response, say, to the driver or bicyclist who cuts suddenly in front of us, causing considerable stress if not physical injury. As this example further suggests, determinative judgments are so straightforward and so common in our everyday lives that we are rarely conscious of them.

When we do become conscious of difficult choices—ones not so easily resolved by way of simple deductions—we are likely operating with *phronēsis* as a more reflective form of judgment. In these choices, a primary difficulty is precisely discerning first of all just *which* general norms, principles or rules apply to a specific context—and if so, *how* and in *what ways*? That is, phronetic judgment begins "from the ground up," thick-in-the-middle of a fine-grained and complicated context—as again abortion decisions illustrate. To begin with the obvious single norm or value: we all agree that life is valuable—indeed, for some, sacred. But in specific contexts, how to apply that norm is by no means clear: when forced to choose, as we sometimes must, which is more important—the life of the mother or the life of the baby-to-be? This simple either-or further foregrounds that *qualitative* judgments must be made here. Specifically, these dilemmas often focus on "quality of life," e.g., the *quality* of life for a baby-to-be with spinal bifida or other severe malformation that will require intensive care—a life, moreover, that even with the best of care and circumstances, will likely be quite short and end with great pain and suffering, vis-à-vis the quality of life we would wish for all children and that in other circumstances and contexts may indeed be a likely outcome. Such judgments are notoriously difficult to reduce to a quantitative calculus—and yet we must make these judgments if we are to apply the single norm of the value (or sanctity) of life.

Phronēsis further comes into play at a second level of complexity as well, namely with regard to the issue of *which* general norms, principles or rules apply. As anyone who has wrestled with such decisions knows—the value of life is not the only norm, value, and principle that comes into play. If the father-to-be does not want the baby, but the close family does—which relationship should be given priority? And all of our ethical decisions and consequences are lived out in contexts of specific economic and social circumstances, as these determine, for example, what levels and kinds of care we can *afford* to give—both to others and to ourselves. Whatever our ideals, norms, and preferences might be—dire economic constraints can confront us with the necessity of sacrificing one deeply-cherished norm or relationship in order to save another. Such choices highlight the tensions and conflicts at a second level, i.e., which norm(s), value(s), and/or principle(s) are more important *in a specific case*—e.g., biological lives as such, the quality of the lives entangled in the web of relationships, and/or the material and economic conditions and possibilities? So, for example, we might admire the young woman who chooses to bring baby into the world despite the material and economic hardships that define her specific context and condition—a judgment, that is, that places greater weight on our hopes for new life itself, whatever the odds. But we can understand the decision of another young woman in a similar context, who judges that the material and economic conditions are simply too harsh, and thereby outweigh any realistic hope for a new life of health and flourishing.

I hope these examples suffice to show not only the sharp contrasts between determinative and reflective, phronetic judgments—and thereby, as a start, why the former are relatively easy while the latter are rightly experienced with anguish, uncertainty, and the necessity to recognize that multiple judgments may be drawn with legitimacy, in contrast with the tendency of determinative judgments to drive towards more univocal, certain, and final conclusions. At the same time, I hope these examples further make clear a central claim that many of us argue concerning *phronēsis*—i.e., that it is not reducible to purely quantitative, determinative, and/or calculative approaches. In technical terms—and specifically with regard to programming ethics in robots—we have argued that such phronetic judgments are computationally non-tractable (Gerdes, 2014; Ess, 2016).

Insofar as we have this correctly, then we can understand Detective Spooner's *felt* choice that Sarah's 11% chance of survival was more than enough for somebody's baby vs. his own 45% chance of survival. This is clearly not the result of the quantitative, deductive calculation of the determinative judgment that can be (more or less) easily programmed for a machine (à la the Trolley Problem). On the contrary, Spooner's decision is the result of an entirely different form of ethical judgment as foregrounded in care and virtue ethics—one that takes on board precisely the role of emotions, the importance of the web of relationships, and matters of potential quality of life that can override more straightforward utilitarian considerations.

Care, Virtue, and Phronēsis in Contemporary ICT Projects and Robotic Design

While the episode discussed above may be more of a thought experiment—what is striking in recent developments in the real world of applied ethics, including the ethics of autonomous systems, is just how far care ethics and virtue ethics have been taken up and endorsed *within* the more technical fields of ICT design and application.

As a first example: the Slándáil Project is a recent European Union project that has developed Big Data tools and techniques for harvesting social media during a natural disaster. The goal is to provide first responders and emergency managers a fine-grained overview "in the form of actionable information that has been derived from aggregated social media data and identifies key places to target that are under particular threat of damage or loss of life from a natural disaster" (Jackson, Aldrovandi, & Hayes, 2015, 168.) On the one hand, the project is clearly justified in simple utilitarian terms: collecting this data, at relatively low cost, will increase material efficiencies in responding to such disasters, thereby improving quality of response and, almost very certainly, saving more lives than otherwise would be likely. At the same time, however, the project designers are acutely aware that these laudable goals directly conflict with primary *deontological* duties—namely, to protect personally identifiable information (PII), i.e., as part of respecting the more basic right to privacy, especially as defined by the Data Protection Directives of the European Union (Jackson et al., 2015, p. 174). Individual privacy is especially threatened precisely by the goal of the system to collect "… textual, image and video data," including "sensitive data such as individuals' names" (Jackson et al., 2015, p. 168). At the same time, of course, such precision identification of individuals and their specific locations is key to the system's goal of identifying what persons, groups, and areas are most in need of specific emergency aid.

The Slándáil project responds to this dilemma *not* with a utilitarian argument that the greater good of the greater number outweighs the costs to the few in terms of loss of privacy—but with a "value pluralism" that insists that "the many ethical perspectives and culturally varied value systems in a society have intrinsic merit and that they can't be reduced to one over-arching system that can be used to determine the best course of action in a given circumstance" (Jackson et al., 2015, p. 169). Such a value pluralism is manifestly demanded in liberal and multi-cultural societies whose citizens may draw from a wide range of ethical frameworks. Moreover, for Jackson and his colleagues, value pluralism directly implicates virtue ethics. To begin with, they draw on Hendrik Wagenaar's "practice-based approach" which endorses practitioners responding to "value conflicts using their experience and intuition, rather than 'resolving' them" (Jackson et al., 2015, p. 170; Wagenaar, 1999, 2014). The resonance here with *phronēsis* is not accidental: in his own writings, Wagenaar in fact foregrounds "practical judgment" of the phronetic sort (2014, esp. pp. 1024–1026). This is precisely because Wagenaar draws in part on the virtue ethics tradition as taken up by Martha Nussbaum (1989, in Wagenaar, 2014, 1026). Following Wagenaar in turn, Jackson and his colleagues go on to endorse virtue ethics specifically: the exercise of our experience and intuition—core features, as we have seen, of *phronēsis*—immediately requires "that organisations ought to foster an environment that facilitates the virtues of wisdom and courage, and engenders learning from experience" (Jackson et al., 2015, p. 170).

Similarly, Bendert Zevenbergen and colleagues (2015) have developed a "networked systems ethics" for the global community of "computer scientists, network engineers and other technical researchers" responsible for Internet and networked engineering (p. 6). In dialogue with philosophers, legal scholars and others (*ibid*), and based upon a thorough discussion of five specific case studies, they come to endorse especially the use of deontological, utilitarian, and virtue ethics approaches (2015, p. 29). In particular, they highlight the *power* of the technical specialists. In keeping with a

near-universal recognition that greater power entails greater responsibility to
care for the more vulnerable, they conclude that

> Responsible researchers have many more duties, such as to inform their data
> subjects and users about the risks and benefits of a system. Since they are more
> aware of how data behaves on digital devices and the Internet than the majority
> of people using them, they cannot assume similar levels of comprehension (see
> for example Mortier, Haddadi, Henderson, McAuley, & Crowcroft, J, 2014).
> (Zevenbergen et al., 2015, p. 31)

But this means, still more directly, that "… virtue ethics should be applied to
Internet research and engineering—where the technical persons must fulfil
the character traits of the 'virtuous agent'" (*ibid*).

From a broader perspective, these examples from *praxis* of turns towards
care- and virtue ethics, including specific emphasis on *phronēsis,* are part and
parcel of a larger renaissance of virtue ethics especially over the past two
decades or so—but one whose roots including nothing less foundational for
Information and Computing Ethics (ICE) than Norbert Wiener's *The human
use of human beings: Cybernetics and society* (1950/1954). More recently,
virtue ethics has become especially prominent among philosophers such as
Peter-Paul Verbeek (2011) and Shannon Vallor (2016). At the same time,
both of these philosophers point to the obvious: namely, that in order for
ethical approaches to be most efficacious, they must take hold at the very
beginnings of the *design* of technical systems. Sarah Spiekermann (2016) in
fact grounds a complete approach to ICT design in virtue ethics. Even more
importantly, both Spiekermann's and Vallor's frameworks for virtue ethics
in ICT design now play a foundational role in a critical new initiative of the
IEEE, "Global Initiative for Ethical Considerations in the Design of Autonomous Systems."[3] This is to say: the endorsements of especially virtue ethics
and *phronēsis* in real-world projects and case studies (Jackson et al., 2015,
Zevenbergen et al., 2015) are not simply one-off examples. Rather, given the
determining role that the IEEE standards will play for the design and implementation of autonomous systems—the examples provided by Jackson et al.
and Zevenbergen et al. are rather harbingers of things to come.

In particular, insofar as our robotic designs entail the use of autonomous
systems—they will likely be guided at least in part by the IEEE ethical standards when they are completed.

Part II: The Ethics of Sexbots

Partly as also driven by recent technological developments, sex robots or sexbots have become increasingly prominent in both popular and more scholarly

discussions of robots, as inaugurated especially by David Levy's 2007 volume, *Love and Sex with Robots: The Evolution of Human-Robot Relationships*. As I have analyzed in greater detail elsewhere (Ess, 2017a), Levy's primary arguments are primarily utilitarian. The advent of sophisticated sexbots, he assures us, will lead to a host of incontrovertible individual and social goods, ranging from economic benefits to "the likely reduction in teenage pregnancy, abortions, sexually transmitted diseases, and pedophilia …" alongside the "clear personal benefits when sexual boundaries widen, ushering in new sexual opportunities, some bizarre, other exciting" (2007, p. 300). In particular, Levy envisions a future of unending, ever-expanding sexual engagements with robots, driven by a pleasure circle of new machine possibilities evoking new desires, thereby driving further innovation, resulting in "great sex on tap for everyone, 24/7" (2007, p. 310).

At the same time, Levy introduces at least one *deontological* consideration—namely, the necessity of recognizing the rights of robots as they become more autonomous (2007, pp. 98, 305, 309). (As a reminder, such freedom or autonomy is the primary ground of deontological arguments insisting on basic rights that sustain and enhance such autonomy—rights that cannot be sacrificed on the part of a few, whatever benefits such sacrifice might bring for the many.) Such deontological considerations—as coupled with *virtue ethics*—are also at the heart of Levy's primary opponent—namely, Kathleen Richardson, an anthropologist and founder of the Campaign Against Sex Robots.[4] One of Richardson's key arguments attacks Levy's utilitarian claim that sexbots promise the positive benefit of eliminating the need for human prostitutes. Richardson counters—rightly, in my view—that prostitution involves a much more fundamental problem: though she does not explicitly invoke deontology or virtue ethics, in *virtue ethics* terms, prostitution requires us to *practice* seeing prostitutes "as things … not … as human subjects" (Richardson, 2015, p. 290). Moreover, this practice of objectifying the Other further and immediately violates the *deontological* requirement that we always recognize human autonomy, dignity, respect, and equality (cf. 2015, p. 291).

The virtue ethics dimension of Richardson's arguments is also apparent in her emphasis on *empathy*. Richardson defines empathy as "an ability to recognise, take into account and respond to another person's genuine thoughts and feelings" (2015, p. 291). As Shannon Vallor makes clear, empathy is a *virtue*, a capacity or excellence that requires practice over time: but such a virtue, especially as it allows us to interpret Others' behaviors and then respond appropriately, is thereby essential to the emergence and flourishing of human communication, friendship, and intimate relationships (Vallor, 2015).

Vallor goes on to make explicit a critical point hinted at by Richardson: as we take up empathy as a virtue—a capacity or excellence that requires practice—it becomes apparent that such virtues can also be lost should their practice be neglected. Vallor articulates this point in terms of ethical deskilling (2015). As applied to sexbots: the more we practice non-empathetic sex with robots that we are free to treat as property and thus objects—the less we practice, much less enhance, our capacity for empathy. In sharpest contrast with Levy's pleasure circle of 24/7 orgasm, this practice can quickly become a vicious circle: as we lose empathy, we thereby lose one of the central virtues required for human communication, friendship, and intimate relationships—thereby making ourselves that much more fit only for physical interactions with machines that demand no empathy.

These analyses from within the frameworks of deontology and virtue ethics thus sharpen and make more articulate Richardson's objections to Levy. At the same time, however, they foreground two key limitations to her analyses and arguments. First, these analyses show that to a very large degree, the apparent debate between Levy and Richardson is, in fact, more apparent than substantive. That is, there is almost no shared ethical ground between Levy's primarily utilitarian arguments vis-à-vis Richardson's primarily deontological and virtue ethics arguments. Conceptually, however cogent and important their arguments may be—these arguments largely talk past one another. To use a metaphor from sport: it's as if we have two players, apparently in contest with one another—but each playing by fundamentally different rules of the game. By analogy: pitting an American baseball player against a British soccer player is likely to end quickly in chaos rather than in substantive engagement and competition. Secondly, as the sports analogy also suggests, it is difficult to see how the debates between Levy and Richardson avoid setting up a simple binary or polarity: and in the absence of shared conceptual ground, we are left to simply choose one or the other.

By contrast, a number of philosophers—in part, precisely by explicitly taking up the ethical frameworks we have explored here—have thereby come to better conceptual grips with these poles of debates, with the upshot that they argue cogently for a number of important middle grounds. Not only are these middle grounds, in my view, more argumentatively and philosophically defensible: they further point to distinctions between human and machine that will help us return to one of our opening thematics—namely, the use of these new technologies to help us explore what remains uniquely and distinctively human.

Eros, Completeness, and Human Virtues in a Technological Age
John Sullins (2012) offers an extensive critique of Levy's arguments, beginning with Levy's discussion of emotion. Levy acknowledges that even the

most sophisticated robots may not be capable of genuine emotion. Indeed, more contemporary work highlights the difficulties—if not the final impossibility—of instantiating genuine emotion in AI and robotic systems. Still more fundamentally, such emotions (along with sexual desire) require in humans a *first-person phenomenal consciousness*, i.e., precisely our self-consciousness, a self-reflective "I" that, among other things, is the arena within which we experience and respond to our emotions: Selmer Bringsjord, among others, argues, however, that such first-person phenomenal consciousness, as well as attendant emotions and desires, are simply beyond the reach of AI and robotic engineering techniques (Bringsjord, Licato, Govindarajulu, Ghosh, & Sen, 2015).

Levy, however, argues that the *appearance* of emotion will be sufficient. This is because of a basic psychological mechanism in the human being: if we are somehow persuaded as a machine or other entity somehow needs or cares for us—this experience evokes emotive responses of care and need in turn (cf. Turkle, 2011). For Levy, being fooled in this way is sufficient, as it at least gives us some experience of emotional connection that can be desirable, therapeutic, etc. For Sullins, however, to intentionally deceive human beings through such trickery fundamentally violates the (deontological) respect due to human beings as autonomous beings (Sullins, 2012, p. 408; cf. Ess, 2016, p. 65).

What Does "Sex" in "Sexbot" Mean?

Both Sullins and I have elaborated further arguments based on two philosophical conceptions of love and sexuality that highlight critical differences between human love and sexuality vis-à-vis what seems possible for machines. To begin with, Sullins takes up the Platonic understanding of *eros* as a deeply felt consciousness of *incompleteness* across the whole of our being—i.e., as including our *psyche* ("soul") as well as our body. *Eros* is hence a yearning or felt longing throughout our being—certainly including but not solely at the level of the bodily—for an Other who, we discover, complements and completes us in ways that we ourselves have not anticipated: rather, one of the delightful surprises of erotic relationships is just how the Beloved fulfills lacks we did not know we had until the erotic relationship opened us up to such recognitions (Sullins, 2012, p. 408; cf. Ess, 2016, p. 65f.). Based on Sullins' account of *eros* and drawing on the work of Shannon Vallor, I have argued that erotic relationships further require specific virtues—certainly beginning with empathy, but further including compassion and forgiveness, and patience (Ess, 2018).

The case for such virtues in erotic relationships is further developed by the founder of care ethics, Sara Ruddick, in her account of "complete sex" (1975). Ruddick develops a highly sophisticated phenomenology of good sex vis-à-vis complete sex. Good sex tends to focus on physical stimulation—which, to be clear, is in itself an ethical good. But Ruddick finds that our experiences of complete sex further entail both virtuous and deontological elements. To begin with, Ruddick points out that our sense of completeness in some sexual experiences depends on a complex mutuality of *desire*. It is not enough, that is, to desire the Other—nor even that the Other may desire me: more fundamentally, Ruddick argues that we desire that our desire (for the Other) be desired (by the Other). This mutuality of desire thereby fosters the deontological norms of respect and equality. That is—and precisely in contrast with the strong temptations in sexuality to treat the Other exactly as an object, as a means to fulfill my own sexual desires—mutuality of desire rather helps establish a foundational equality *as persons* and thereby respect for the Other as an autonomy (Ruddick 1975, pp. 89f., 99f.; cf. Ess, 2016, pp. 67–70).

Moreover, insofar as (erotic) *love* entails these elements, as Ruddick goes on to point out, then loving itself is a *virtue*: that is, these elements of mutuality, respect, and equality, require *practice*—they do not unfold "naturally" (again, rather to the contrary, especially within sexual contexts).

"Complete sex," thus, sets a very high ethical bar on our erotic and sexual relationships—one that Ruddick acknowledges we perhaps only rarely meet. But none of this denigrates the ethical value and legitimacy of "good sex": on the contrary, Ruddick argues that relationships of care and respect can include good sex as well (1975, p.101).

Good Sex and Sexbots: Middle Grounds Between Machines and Humans
First of all, these additional arguments from explicitly deontological and virtue ethics approaches reiterate Richardson's key objections to Levy's more utilitarian arguments: specifically, they articulate even more fully and completely Richardson's objections to the ways in which sexbots depend upon and encourage us to regard the Other simply as an object rather than as a person. Indeed, bringing into play both Platonic *eros* and Ruddick's analysis of complete sex highlights how far sexbots can*not* serve as a fully erotic Other for a human being. In contrast with a human autonomy, a sexbot is by definition a product designed and programmed for control and consumption. However much it may be able to mimic and thereby evoke emotion—as lacking a first-person phenomenal consciousness and thereby genuine emotions, including (embodied sexual) desire, it is, in effect, a

zombie (Bringsjord et al., 2015). As such, it is not only incapable of offering the mutuality of desire Ruddick highlights as critical to complete sex: in addition, its use of artificial emotions to evoke emotive responses in us is, as Sullins makes clear, a deception that violates our human autonomy and requisite (deontological) respect. Finally, Ruddick and Vallor both reiterate and elaborate on Richardson's proper emphasis on the role of empathy in human relationships: not only empathy, but the first clear and explicit virtues of patience, perseverance, compassion and forgiveness—and ultimately, loving itself—are virtues that sexbots will not reinforce, but rather risk undermining ("deskilling").

At the same time, however, these arguments further point towards middle grounds between the poles staked out between Levy's unbounded enthusiasm for and Richardson's complete rejection of sexbots. Specifically, Ruddick's account of good sex, as primarily focused on physical stimulation and satisfaction, describes a sexual experience that can be facilitated by sexbots. For his part, Levy has suggested that sexbots might indeed be useful in therapeutic ways, e.g., for persons who, disadvantaged in one way or another, may thereby be unable to attract or sustain relationships marked by complete sex (2007, p. 304). While Richardson rejects such an application, for Ruddick— and, I suspect, for a considerable number of people who would indeed benefit from such therapeutic sexbots—good sex is ethically better than no sex.

At the same time, however, Richardson's objections retain an important cogency: the therapeutic value of sophisticated sexbots will certainly be limited. Again, complete sex requires mutuality of desire between autonomous, self-reflective, conscious embodied beings—while sexbots, as zombies lacking first-person phenomenal consciousness, genuine emotions, and (embodied) desire, will only be able to fake emotions. Such a zombie lover might be able to offer good sex—but never complete sex and all the attendant ethical norms (respect and equality) and virtues (including loving itself) that complete sex entails.

Concluding Comments

These accounts, rooted in virtue ethics, deontology, and care ethics return us to our opening interest, as opened up by the computational turn and then the rapid advancements in robotic technologies over the past decade or so: namely, the large project of exploring these technologies as empirically-grounded testbeds for discerning how far our human capacities, abilities, interests, etc. may—and/or may *not*—be realized and instantiated in machines. Insofar as these analyses hold, a number of aspects of being human appear to stubbornly resist such instantiation. The list begins with first-person phenomenal consciousness and extends through genuine emotions and embodied desire—and, perhaps most importantly, *phronēsis* as a form of reflective judgment. At the same time, virtue ethics foregrounds core components of human flourishing and good lives—including judgment, as well as human communication *per se*, friendship, and erotic relationships that, as entailing complete sex, thereby depend upon and foster primary deontological norms of respect and equality. But these distinctions between human and machine mean at the same time: to be human in these ways requires *practice*—specifically of the virtues of *phronēsis* as well as of empathy, patience, perseverance, forgiveness, and nothing less than loving itself. To put it bluntly: if we ourselves are *not* to become the machines we increasingly interact with—perhaps to the point of sexual engagements as well—we will do so in part only as we *practice* the virtues of being human.

To be sure, such a requirement sets a very high bar—one that, like complete sex, will only be achieved on occasion rather than as a constant. Nonetheless, it is striking and deeply encouraging to note that these accounts reiterate and cohere with the most recent ethical conclusions drawn by technologists themselves, as they develop contemporary ICT systems for first response in a natural disaster (Jackson, Aldrovandi & Hayes, 2015) and for networked systems (Zevenbergen, 2016). Most hopefully, insofar as virtue ethics and its deontological companions of autonomy, respect, and equality serve as primary ethical drivers in the *design* of ICT systems (Spiekermann, 2016) and specifically the autonomous systems (IEEE) that will undergird future robot designs as well—we can perhaps be cautiously optimistic that these convergences and complementarities will foster greater attention to the virtues of being human.

Notes

1. See: <reeler.eu>, (<http://projects.au.dk/robophilosophy/insor/>, and <http://responsiblerobotics.org/>), respectively.
2. The car crash scene discussed here can be viewed at: https://www.youtube.com/watch?v=nBfeyx6wNVg
3. See <http://standards.ieee.org/develop/indconn/ec/autonomous_systems.html>.
4. See <https://campaignagainstsexrobots.org/>.

References

Achenbach, J. (2015, December 29). Driverless cars are colliding with the creepy Trolley Problem. *The Washington Post*. Retrieved from https://www.washingtonpost.

com/news/innovations/wp/2015/12/29/will-self-driving-cars-ever-solve-the-famous-and-creepy-trolley-problem/

ACM [Association of Computing Machinery]. ACM code of ethics and professional conduct. (1992). Retrieved from https://www.acm.org/about-acm/acm-code-of-ethics-and-professional-conduct

Bonnefon, J-F., Shari, A., & Rahwan, I. (2016). The social dilemma of autonomous vehicles? *Science, 35*(6293), 1573–1576. doi: 10.1126/science.aaf2654

Bringsjord, S., Licato, J., Govindarajulu, N. S., Ghosh, R., & Sen, A. (2015). Real robots that pass human tests of self-consciousness. *Proceedings of RO-MAN 2015* (The 24th International Symposium on Robot and Human Interactive Communication). August 31–September 4, 2015. Kobe, Japan.

Ess, C. (2013). *Digital media ethics* (2nd ed.). Oxford: Polity Press.

Ess, C. (2016). What's love got to do with it? Robots, sexuality, and the arts of being human. In M. Nørskov (Ed.), *Social robots: Boundaries, potential, challenges* (pp. 57–79). Ashgate: Farnham, Surrey, England.

Ess, C. (2017a). Digital media ethics. *Oxford Research Encyclopedia of Communication.* doi: 10.1093/acrefore/9780190228613.013.508

Ess, C. (2017b). God out of the machine?: The politics and economics of technological development. In A. Beavers (Ed.), *Macmillan interdisciplinary handbooks: Philosophy* (pp. 83–111). Farmington Hills, MI: Macmillan Reference.

Ess, C. (2018). Ethics and mediatization: subjectivity, judgment (*phronesis*) and meta-theoretical coherence? In T. Eberwein, M. Karmasin, F. Krotz and M. Rath (Eds.), *Responsibility and resistance: Ethics in mediatized worlds.* Wiesbaden: Springer.

Ess, C. & Hagengruber, R. (2011). The computational turn: Past, presents, futures? In C. Ess and R. Hagengruber (Eds.), *The computational turn: Past, presents, futures?* (Conference Proceedings, IACAP (International Association of Computing and Philosophy) 25th Anniversary Conference) (pp. 3–4). Münster, Germany: Heinz Nixdorf Institute, Paderborn University.

Gerdes, A. (2014). Ethical issues concerning lethal autonomous robots in warfare. In J. Seibt, R. Hakli, and M. Nørskov (Eds.), *Sociable robots and the future of social relations: Proceedings of robo-philosophy 2014,* (pp. 277–289). Berlin: IOS Press.

Gilligan, C. (1982). *In a different voice: Psychological theory and women's development.* Cambridge, MA: Harvard University Press.

Hursthouse, R. (2013). Virtue ethics. In Edward N. Zalta (Ed.), *The Stanford encyclopedia of philosophy* (Fall 2013 edition). Retrieved from http://plato.stanford.edu/archives/fall2013/entries/ethics-virtue/

Jackson, D., Aldrovandi, C., & Hayes, P. (2015). Ethical framework for a disaster management decision support system which harvests social media data on a large scale. In N. Bellamine Ben Saoud et al. (Eds.), *ISCRAM-med 2015* (pp. 167–180), LNBIP 233. doi:10.1007/978-3-319-24399-3_15

Levy, D. (2007). *Love and sex with robots: The evolution of human-robot relationships.* New York: Harper Collins.

Lin, P. (2013, October 8). The ethics of autonomous cars. *The Atlantic*. Retrieved from http://www.theatlantic.com/technology/archive/2013/10/the-ethics-of-autonomous-cars/280360/

Mortier, R, Haddadi, H., Henderson, T, McAuley, D., & Crowcroft, J. (2014). Human-data interaction: The human face of the data-driven society. Available at SSRN 2508051.

Noddings, N. (1984). *Caring: A feminine approach to ethics and moral education*, Berkeley, CA: University of California Press.

Nussbaum, M. (1989). Tragic dilemmas. *Radcliffe Quarterly*, 7–9.

Proyas, A. (Director). (2004). *I, Robot* (Motion picture). United States: Twentieth Century Fox Film.

Richardson, K. (2015). The Asymmetrical "Relationship": Parallels Between Prostitution and the Development of Sex Robots. *SIGCAS Computers & Society*, 45(3), 290–293.

Ruddick, S. (1975). Better Sex. In R. Baker and F. Elliston (Eds.), *Philosophy and sex*, (pp. 280–299). Amherst, NY: Prometheus.

Sinnott-Armstrong, W. (2015). Consequentialism. In Edward N. Zalta (Ed.), *The Stanford encyclopedia of philosophy* (Winter 2015 Edition). Retrieved from http://plato.stanford.edu/archives/win2015/entries/consequentialism/

Simon, J. (2015). Distributed epistemic responsibility in a hyperconnected era. In L. Floridi (Ed.), *The onlife manifesto: Being human in a hyperconnected era* (pp. 145–159). London: Springer Open.

Snow, C. P. (2001). *The two cultures*. London: Cambridge University Press. (Original work published 1959).

Spiekermann, S. (2016). *Ethical IT innovation: A value-based system design approach*. New York, NY: Taylor & Francis.

Stahl, B. C., & Ess, C. (2015). 20 years of ETHICOMP: Time to celebrate? *Journal of Information, Communication and Ethics in Society*, 13(3/4), 166–175.

Sullins, J. (2012). Robots, love, and sex: The ethics of building a love machine. *IEEE Transactions on Affective Computing*, 3(4), 398–409.

Tong, R. & Williams, N. (2016). Feminist Ethics. *The Stanford Encyclopedia of Philosophy*. Edward N. Zalta (ed.). Retrieved from http://plato.stanford.edu/archives/sum2016/entries/feminism-ethics/

Thomson, J. J. (1976). Killing, letting die, and the trolley problem. *The Monist*, 59(2), 204–217. doi:10.5840/monist197659224

Turkle, S. (2011). *Alone together: Why we expect more from technology and less of each other*. Cambridge, MA: MIT Press.

Vallor, S. (2015). Moral Deskilling and upskilling in a new machine age: Reflections on the ambiguous future of character. *Philosophy of Technology* 28(1),107–124.

Vallor, S. (2016). *Technology and the virtues: A philosophical guide to a future worth wanting*. Oxford: Oxford University Press.

Verbeek, P.-P. (2011). *Moralizing Technology: Understanding and designing the morality of things*. Chicago: University of Chicago Press.

Wagenaar, H. (1999). Value pluralism in public administration. *Administrative Theory and Praxis, 21* (4), 441–449.

Wagenaar, H. (2014). The necessity of value pluralism in administrative practice: A reply to overeem. *Administration and Society 46* (8), 1020–1028.

Wallach, W. (2014). Moral Machines and human ethics. Paper presentation at the conference of Robo-Philosophy 2014: Sociable Robots and the Future of Social Relations, Aarhus University, Denmark.

Wiener, N. (1954). *The human use of human beings: Cybernetics and society.* Boston, MA: Houghton Mifflin (2nd Revised ed.). New York, NY: Doubleday Anchor. (Original work published 1950).

Zevenbergen, B. (2016). *Networked systems ethics.* Ethics in networked systems research: Ethical, legal and policy reasoning for Internet Engineering. Oxford Internet Institute, University of Oxford. Retrieved from http://networkedsystemsethics.net/

Zevenbergen, B., Mittelstadt, B., Véliz, C., Detweiler, C., Cath, C., Savulescu, J., & Whittaker, M. (2015). Philosophy meets internet engineering: Ethics in networked systems research. (GTC workshop outcomes paper). Oxford Internet Institute, University of Oxford. Retrieved from http://ensr.oii.ox.ac.uk/wp-content/uploads/sites/41/2015/09/ENSR-Oxford-Workshop-report.pdf

Volume Editor

Andrea L. Guzman is an assistant professor of communication at Northern Illinois University (USA) where her research focuses on Human-Machine Communication, people's perceptions of artificial intelligence technologies that function as communicators, and automated journalism. Guzman has been integral in spearheading the formalization of HMC within the communication discipline. Guzman's research has been published in *Journalism & Mass Communication Quarterly, First Monday,* and *Communication +1* and has been presented at leading disciplinary and interdisciplinary conferences where it has garnered awards at the National Communication Association and the Association for Education in Journalism and Mass Communication. Guzman is a Kopenhaver Center Fellow. More about Guzman's work is available at andrealguzman.net.

Contributors

Terje Colbjørnsen is currently a postdoctoral research fellow at the Department of media and communication, University of Oslo and affiliated with the research project "Streaming the culture industries." Colbjørnsen is here doing work on the business models and value networks of streaming services in the media and culture industries. He completed his PhD in 2015 on digital publishing in the Norwegian book industry, comprising five case studies of digital publishing innovations, including analyses of distribution systems, e-reading technologies, digital formats, market information regimes and new business models. Colbjørnsen has since done research on media debates on freedom of expression in Norway, before embarking on a project on user experiences of algorithmic recommendations. Other research interests include media policy and media economics, digital media VAT, institutional theory, bestsellers and popular culture, digitalization in libraries, photography and fiction. Previously employed as editor within online education, Colbjørnsen has also worked as an advisor with the Norwegian Association of Researchers.

Autumn P. Edwards (Ph.D., Ohio University, 2006) is professor of communication at Western Michigan University and co-director of the Communication and Social Robotics Labs. Her research centers on interpersonal communication processes in computer-mediated and human-machine contexts. Recent scholarship has focused on (1) articulating and testing the human-to-human interaction script in initial encounters between people and digital interlocutors, including social robots and artificially intelligent conversation agents, (2) identifying the ways in which people's metaphysical assumptions shape human-machine communication, and (3) examining features of message design in communication between people and social robots. She is the recipient of the WMU Outstanding Teaching Award and College of Arts and Sciences Distinguished Scholarship Award.

Chad Edwards (Ph.D., University of Kansas, 2003) is a professor of communication in the School of Communication at Western Michigan University. Chad's research interests include human-machine communication, human-robot interaction, artificial intelligence, and instructional communication. Recent publications include articles in: *Communication Education, Communication Research Reports, Computers in Human Behavior, Journal of Computer-Mediated Communication, and Communication Studies* (including *Article of the Year*). Chad co-directs the Communication and Social Robotics Labs (www.combotlab.org). He is a co-author on a Sage textbook entitled, Life in the Communication Age: Connecting and Engaging (2013/2016/2019). He is a Past-President of the Central States Communication Association. In 2009, Chad received the WMU Distinguished Teaching Award (the highest teaching award given by WMU). In 2017, he received the highest research award from the College of Arts and Sciences at WMU. He also has been awarded teaching awards from the WMU College of Arts and Sciences, University of Kansas, and Texas Tech University.

Charles Ess is Professor of Media Studies, Department of Media and Communication, University of Oslo, Norway. He works at the intersections of philosophy, computing, applied ethics, comparative philosophy, and media studies, with specific focus on research ethics, Digital Religion, and virtue ethics in media and communication, specifically social robots. Recent publications include 'What's love got to do with it? Robots, sexuality, and the arts of being human,' in M. Nørskov (ed.), *Social Robots: Boundaries, Potential, Challenges*, 57–79 (Ashgate, 2015), and (editor), "Communication and Technology," *The ICA Annals of Communication*, 1 (3, 4: December, 2017). Ess serves on the Technical Advisory Committee of the Foundation for Responsible Robotics, and on the Advisory Board, Responsible Ethical Learning with Robotics—REELER (H2020). Recent guest positions include University of Vienna (2013–2014), University Institute of Lisbon, (ISCTE-IUL—2015, 2016, 2017), the Vienna University of Economics and Business (2016), and the University of Stockholm (2017).

Leopoldina Fortunati is the director of the Research Laboratory on New Media, NuMe, at the University of Udine where she teaches Sociology of Communication and Culture and Laboratory of Social Robotics. She has conducted several research projects in the field of gender studies, cultural processes and communication and information technologies. She has published more than 200 works and serves as referee for many outstanding journals. She is associate editor of the journal *The Information Society* and along with Rich Ling and Gerard Goggin is an editor of the OUP series "Studies in Mobile Communication." Her works have been published in twelve languages.

Leslie M. Fritz is a PhD student at the University of Washington where she studies the rhetoric of emerging technologies, particularly the rhetorical situation of artificial intelligence and social robots. She approaches the subject from a critical/cultural perspective with an emphasis on technologies' textual, visual and material entailments as well as the social and communicative norms arising in relation to technology, generally. Prior to her graduate studies in Communication, Leslie received her MPA from the Evans School of Public Policy and Governance, where she conducted research with the do-it-yourself biology (DIYBio) community in Seattle, culminating in a degree project entitled "DIYBio and Dual Use Risk; How the Governance of Synthetic Biology Will Impact Education, Innovation and Response to Bioterror Events." Her work will continue to explore the intersections of technology, ethics and policy using both rhetorical and qualitative tools.

Andrew Gambino (Penn State, ABD) is a doctoral student at The Pennsylvania State University. His research focuses on the relationship between humans and their personal media devices (smartphones, social robots, voice assistants). Additionally, he has studied the powerful effects of collaborative filtering technologies, even as cues, in the role of persuasion, and unlocking the Internet privacy paradox.

David J. Gunkel is an award-winning educator and scholar, specializing in the philosophy of technology. He is the author of over 50 scholarly articles and has published nine books, including *Thinking Otherwise: Philosophy, Communication, Technology* (Purdue University Press, 2007), *The Machine Question: Critical Perspectives on AI, Robots, and Ethics* (MIT Press, 2012), and *Of Remixology: Ethics and Aesthetics After Remix* (MIT Press, 2016). He currently holds the position of Distinguished Teaching Professor in the Department of Communication at Northern Illinois University (USA) and is the founding co-editor of the International Journal of Žižek Studies. More info at http://gunkelweb.com.

S. Austin Lee (Ph.D., Michigan State University) is an associate professor in the School of Communication at Chapman University. He studies how emerging information communication technology influences human attitudes and behaviors. His research integrates communication and human-machine interaction to advance a theory of persuasive technology that enables robots and agents to build credibility, gain trust, and, ultimately, function more effectively.

Yuhua (Jake) Liang (Ph.D., Michigan State University) was an assistant professor in the School of Communication at Chapman University. His work examined the theoretical connections between emerging technologies (e.g., participatory systems, agents, and robots) and their practical persuasive effects. He endeavored to utilize technology to be more communicatively influential and develop theories that help us understand the fundamental process of communication.

Xialing Lin is an assistant professor of corporate communication at Penn State Worthington Scranton. Her research focuses on the crisis and risk communication, explicitly examining organizational responses as well as public information processing within new media contexts. Recent research also investigates information sources on social media during disasters. Her research appears in peer-reviewed journals such as *Communication Studies*, *Computers in Human Behavior*, and *Communication Quarterly*.

Matthew Lombard (Ph.D., Stanford University, 1994) is Co-founder and President of the International Society for Presence Research (ISPR, http://ispr.info) and an Associate Professor in the Department of Media Studies and Production at Temple University in Philadelphia, Pennsylvania, USA. Since earning his PhD at Stanford University in 1994, his research has centered on individuals' psychological and physiological processing of media presentations and experiences, with particular focus on the concept of (tele) presence. His work has appeared in academic journals including *Behaviour & Information Technology*, *CyberPsychology* and *Behavior*, *Human Technology*, *Journal of Communication*, *Human Communication Research*, *Journal of Computer-Mediated Communication*, and *Presence: Teleoperators and Virtual Environments*. He has been managing editor of ISPR Presence News (and its predecessor) since 1998 and is also director of the Media Interface and Networked Design (M.I.N.D.) Lab at Temple University (http://mindlab.org). For more detailed information please visit http://matthewlombard.com.

Christoph Lutz (Ph.D., University of St. Gallen) is Assistant Professor at the Department of Communication and Culture and at the Nordic Centre for Internet and Society, BI Norwegian Business School (Oslo). His research interests cover various aspects of social media, in particular participation, privacy, and digital inequalities. In addition, Christoph is interested in digital labor, the sharing economy, and social robots. With a background in sociology, management and economics, and communication, he uses quantitative, qualitative, and digital methods to explore the social implications of new communication technology. Christoph's work has been published in leading journals in the field such as *New Media & Society*, *Information, Communication & Society*, *Social Media + Society*, *JASIST*, *JMIS*, *American Behavioral Scientist*, *First Monday*, and *Social Science Computer Review*.

Eleanor Sandry Ph.D. is a lecturer and researcher in Internet Studies at Curtin University, and previously a Fellow of the Curtin Centre for Culture and Technology. Her research is focused on developing an ethical and pragmatic recognition of, and respect for, otherness and difference in communication. She writes about communication theory and practice and draws upon varied examples—taken from science and technology, science fiction and creative arts—to illustrate the ideas in her work. She is particularly interested in exploring the communicative and collaborative possibilities of human interactions with humanoid and non-humanoid robots. Her book, *Robots and Communication*, was published in 2015 by Palgrave Macmillan.

Patric R. Spence is an associate professor in the Nicholson School of Communication at the University of Central Florida. His research focuses on how people use technologies for communicating in circumstances of high uncertainty. His research has been published in journals such as *Computers in Human Behavior*, *Journal of Risk Research* and the *Journal of Applied Communication Research*. Patric also works with a team of researchers from the Communication and Social Robotics Labs (www.combotlab.org) focusing on human-machine communication (HMC).

Brett Stoll is a PhD student in the Department of Communication at Cornell University. His research interests include human-machine communication (HMC) and how robots and agents influence interpersonal and team dynamics. Stoll's work examines the role of emotion manipulation and expression in HMC. Most recently, he has studied the use of humor and play in facilitating positive interactions among people and machines. Brett's research is largely cross-disciplinary, collaborating with scholars across communication, psychology, information science, computer science, engineering, and design fields. In addition to contributing to communication theory and practice surrounding HMC, Brett is active in the HRI, CHI, and CSCW communities as well. In 2015, Brett was awarded the Western Michigan University, School of Communication Graduate Research and Creative Scholar Award for his thesis work on robots employing guilt appeals in a human-robot negotiation.

Sakari Taipale, Ph.D., is an Academy of Finland Research Fellow at the University of Jyväskylä's Department of Social Sciences and Philosophy as well as an Adjunct Professor at the University of Eastern Finland. Currently, he serves as the research group leader for the University of Jyväskylä's Center of Excellence in Research on Ageing and Care (CoE AgeCare, 2018–2025). His group explores new technologies, aging, and care. Taipale's varied research interests revolve around the adoption and use of a diversity of digital technologies ranging from cell phones to social robots. Taipale has edited two international volumes and published about 40 peer-reviewed articles. His research articles have appeared in first class journals, such as the *New Media and Society*, *Journalism*, and *British Journal of Sociology*.

Aurelia Tamò (MA in Law and Economics, University of St. Gallen) is a PhD student at the Chair for Information and Communication Law at the University of Zurich. In her PhD research project, Aurelia analyzes technical measures and designs for data protection. For her research, she was granted a Doc.CH scholarship by the Swiss National Science Foundation. Her overall research interests include various topics within the interdisciplinary field of law and technology such as privacy or copyright and regulatory developments in these fields. More recently she became interested in robotics and the impact of social robots on the current social and ethical structures in particular.

David Westerman (Ph.D., Michigan State University, 2007) is an associate professor in the Department of Communication at North Dakota State University. His research focuses on how people use technologies for their communication goals and with what effects, and has been published in journals such as *Computers in Human Behavior* and *Journal of Computer-Mediated Communication*.

Index

General Editor: **Steve Jones**

Digital Formations is the best source for critical, well-written books about digital technologies and modern life. Books in the series break new ground by emphasizing multiple methodological and theoretical approaches to deeply probe the formation and reformation of lived experience as it is refracted through digital interaction. Each volume in **Digital Formations** pushes forward our understanding of the intersections, and corresponding implications, between digital technologies and everyday life. The series examines broad issues in realms such as digital culture, electronic commerce, law, politics and governance, gender, the Internet, race, art, health and medicine, and education. The series emphasizes critical studies in the context of emergent and existing digital technologies.

Other recent titles include:

Felicia Wu Song
Virtual Communities: Bowling Alone, Online Together

Edited by Sharon Kleinman
The Culture of Efficiency: Technology in Everyday Life

Edward Lee Lamoureux, Steven L. Baron, & Claire Stewart
Intellectual Property Law and Interactive Media: Free for a Fee

Edited by Adrienne Russell & Nabil Echchaibi
International Blogging: Identity, Politics and Networked Publics

Edited by Don Heider
Living Virtually: Researching New Worlds

Edited by Judith Burnett, Peter Senker & Kathy Walker
The Myths of Technology: Innovation and Inequality

Edited by Knut Lundby
Digital Storytelling, Mediatized Stories: Self-representations in New Media

Theresa M. Senft
Camgirls: Celebrity and Community in the Age of Social Networks

Edited by Chris Paterson & David Domingo
Making Online News: The Ethnography of New Media Production

To order other books in this series please contact our Customer Service Department:

(800) 770-LANG (within the US)
(212) 647-7706 (outside the US)
(212) 647-7707 FAX

To find out more about the series or browse a full list of titles, please visit our website:

WWW.PETERLANG.COM